The Book

An Actor's Guide to Chicago

Kevin Heckman
Editor

Published by PerformInk Books, Ltd.

PerformInk Books, Ltd.
3223 N. Sheffield
Chicago, IL 60657

Carrie L. Kaufman, Publisher
ISBN: 1-892296-02-0

Cover and page design by Marty McNulty
Illustrations by Zak Brown
Associate Editor Katie Ayoub

Successor to "Acting, Modeling and Dance," Founding Editors: Allyson Rice-Taylor, Emily Gerson-Saines

Editor's Notes

It's the year 2000 and we're all still alive. Amazing. As we enter a new century (or approach one depending on how you measure things), Chicago seems poised to emerge as the first city of theatre in this country.

If you haven't worked in other cities, it's hard to appreciate the energy, daring and sheer, breathless depth of Chicago theatre. Nowhere else in the U.S. are there so many theatres producing such exciting art.

Each edition that we've produced has acted as an expansion on the previous one. The 1st edition was the foundation, the 2nd gave us walls and a roof and with the 3rd we've got a nice little ranch style duplex. I hope that our next edition can go even further as the Chicago actor's best map for navigating theatre in this city.

While our names are under the title, this book would have been quite nasty to publish had it not been for the wonderful staff at PerformInk. Thanks to our proofreader Claire Kaplan and PerformInk office manager Julie Daley. They both went above and beyond their job descriptions in getting all this information together. We also want to thank the people who contributed their expertise in the form of articles, most notably Adrianne Duncan, Robert Ayres, Greg Mermel, Jason Chin, Tab Baker, Michael Halberstam, Doug Long, Julie Franz, Joan Gunzberg, Lucia Mauro and Nicole Bernardi-Reis. Finally, special thanks to Christine Gatto for coming back from Pennsylvania to help with listings and pursue some research.

Hopefully this book will make your life easier and help get you where you want to go. It's my goal to provide one resource for working actors to turn to in order to answer all their questions. This may be an unattainable goal in the end, but I hope we came a little closer this edition.

Break a leg!

Kevin Heckman

Table of Contents

TOC

Coming to Chicago

Defiant's "Burning Desires" – pictured (clockwise from top left): Kati Brazda, Cynthia Cervini, Katharine Martin, Cherise Silvestri – photo: Geoffrey Fingerhut

What's great about Chicago Theatre...

"There's so much of it."

— Over 200 theatre companies produce in Chicago each year.

"It's everywhere you go."

— There's theatre downtown, uptown, in the suburbs, in the city. If there's a vacant space, a theatre will bloom in it.

"Anyone can put on a show."

— Many actors participate in Chicago's most prevalent sport: starting their own theatre company. Anyone can do it and it's not hard to get started.

"You can wear what you want."

— Not only is theatre prevalent, theatregoers are too – they come from all classes, races and backgrounds.

"It's affordable."

— Most small theatres have ticket prices under $15, many under $10. Actors can often get in for even less on designated industry nights.

"Whatever you like to do, you can do it here."

— Musicals, Shakespeare, improv, multi-media, whatever style you can think of, someone's doing it in Chicago.

Car Considerations!

Owning a car in Chicago can be both helpful and aggravating. There's a lot of things to keep in mind. Check it out.

The Pros

Ever try to carry your groceries on the eL?

Suburban theatres.

The eL's inconsistent scheduling.

Wider choice of neighborhoods to live in.

Less accessible neighborhoods are usually cheaper neighborhoods. In this case, owning a car can actually save you money.

Flexibility.

The Cons

High insurance rates.

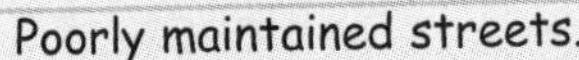

Poorly maintained streets.

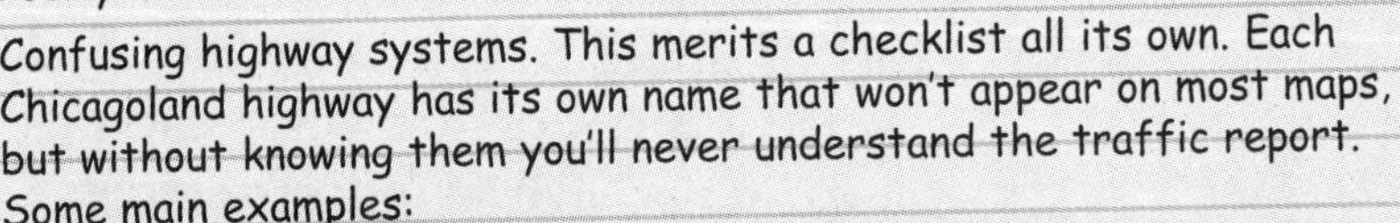

Confusing highway systems. This merits a checklist all its own. Each Chicagoland highway has its own name that won't appear on most maps, but without knowing them you'll never understand the traffic report. Some main examples:

- The Kennedy refers to I90 north of the Loop including the portion where I90 and I94 merge.
- The Eisenhower is actually I290.
- The Edens means I94 north of the I90/I94 merge.
- The Dan Ryan actually means I94 south of the Loop.
- The Stevenson is I55.
- The Tri-State refers to I294.
- The Skyway is actually I90 south of the Loop after I90 and I94 separate.
- Why is it this way? Who knows. Chicago works in mysterious ways.

Tollways.

High gas prices.

Other Chicago drivers.

Difficult parking.

Street cleaning (watch for the orange signs).

The Procedure

If you're still planning on driving in Chicago (and many people, including this author, do), there are some steps you're going to need to take.

Visit the Secretary of State

Within 90 days of your arrival in Chicago, you're supposed to switch over your license and registration. To get an Illinois license, you'll need to have your old license, a social security card, proof of your current address (a piece of mail addressed to you will suffice) and you'll need to take a written test. Additionally, you'll need $10. To transfer your registration, you'll need an Illinois license, $13 to transfer your title and $48 for plates. If you've owned your car "for a while"(vague terms courtesy of the Secretary of State's office), you shouldn't have to pay tax on the updated registration. Call 312/793-1010 for more information.

ILLINOIS
BRKALEG

Visit the City of Chicago Department of Revenue

Every Chicago resident who drives has to pay a "wheel tax" of $60 called a city sticker. The cost is actually going up soon, so be sure to call and confirm the costs. If you don't get it right away, they'll penalize you, and if you don't get one, you can be ticketed. Your city at work. Additionally, some neighborhoods require that you have a residential parking pass, which is a completely different animal from your city sticker. For that you'll need a city sticker, proof of residence and $10. You may be able to take care of both these things at your local currency exchange. Check one out before you bother with the trip downtown. For more information, call 312/744-7409.

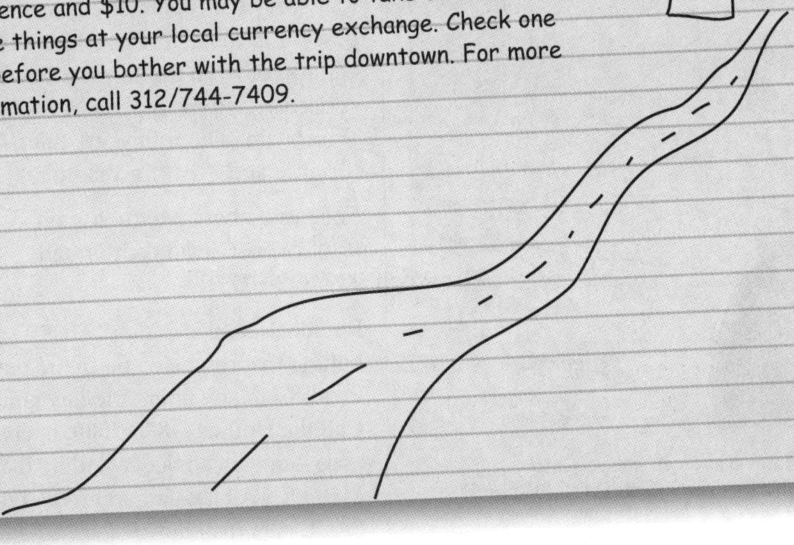

Chicago Transit

In the city, the eL, the bus, and your feet get you where you're going. Mastering the eL is quite fun and adventurous. CTA fares are $1.50 per ride. If taken within two hours, the first transfer is 30 cents, the second is free. Take an eL, then transfer to a bus and get to your destination on $1.80. The CTA doesn't use coins. All riders — bus and eL — use fare cards. Machines are set up in eL stations to purchase cards or add money onto existing ones. To get information about the CTA, check out their website at **www.transitchicago.com** or call **1-888-968-7282.**

What the "eL"?

The eL is a network of frequently-stopping trains that run on *elevated* platforms one-story above street level.

The color-coded eL lines culminate in the heart of the city and "loop" around downtown. Two exceptions, the Red and Blue Lines, descend into subways downtown and tunnel under the Loop.

See page 286 for a detailed map of all Chicago CTA eL stops.

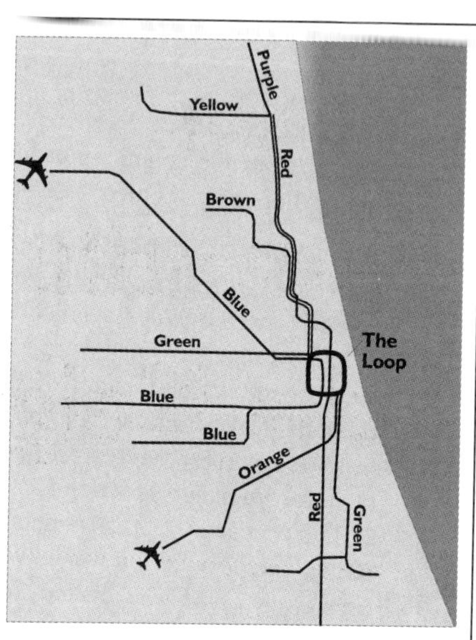

Metra: Training in from the suburbs

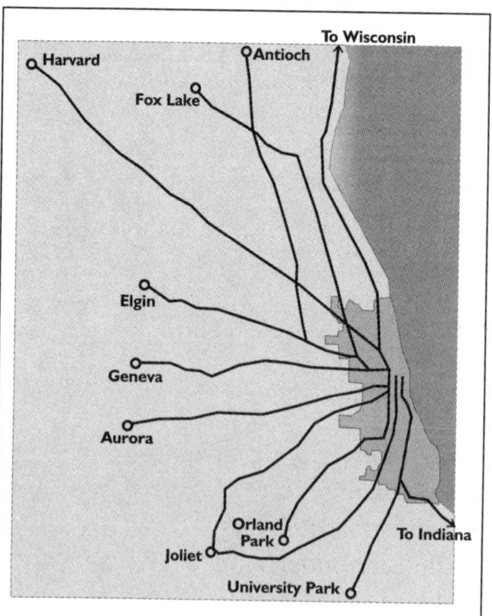

Metra trains can get you into Chicago from all corners of suburbia.

Metra is the train that runs from almost all the Chicago suburbs to the city. Metra riders swear by it and seem to feel sorry for folks dealing with congestion in the city. For under $10, you can travel from the farthest reaches of suburbia, and even parts of Indiana and Wisconsin. The trains are quiet, comfortable and great for reading.

For more about Metra, log on to **www.metrarail.com** or call **312/322-6777.**

Regional Transit Authority has a special hotline that can help you figure out how to get from any point A to any point B. Call the Hotline—**836-7000,** in any area code– and get advice regarding the use of Metra, CTA buses, eL trains, and the PACE suburban bus system.

It's a Beautiful Day In the Neighborhood

Briefly, I dwell
by the Capital.

Chicago is a very simple city. It's laid out on a grid, with the exception of a few conveniently placed diagonal streets. All highways lead downtown, as do all train routes. A new arrival to the city will find it surprisingly easy to make one's way, whether driving or on foot.

Chicago is a very confusing city. All of the highways have names in addition to route numbers that everyone uses, but the names don't appear on most maps. If you ask Chicagoans where they live, they won't say Chicago, and they won't give the street. They'll say they live in Bucktown or Logan Square or Rogers Park. Public transportation, though conveniently color-coded, is referred to instead by its final stops. It's not the Red Line, it's the Howard-Dan Ryan.

Both of these paragraphs are true. Chicago is a simple city that seems to be full of strange codes to a newcomer. No one really knows where particular neighborhoods begin or end, or why it is that I94 West actually heads north. It may take a new arrival months to understand all of the names of the interstates and be able to make sense of a traffic report. What's a newcomer to do?

These streets do have names .... and numbers!

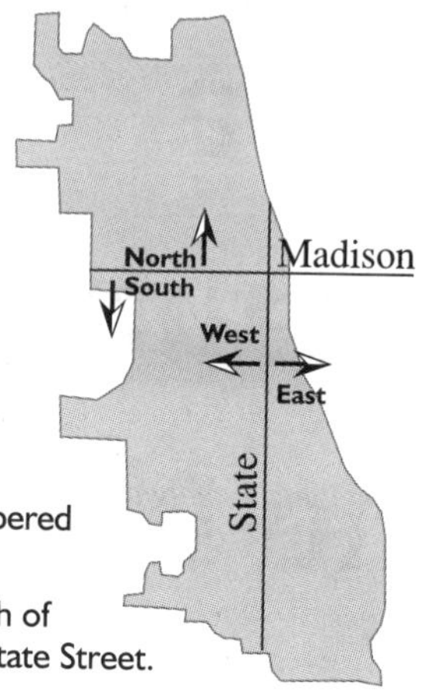

The streets of Chicago form a grid that is conveniently numbered for your navigational sanity. Mastering this system will greatly assist you in getting to know the neighborhoods and help you get around town.

Madison and State Street are the starting lines for this system. The major streets that form the grid increase in number by hundreds. Streets are numbered and tagged with an N, S, E, or W.

Examples: Fullerton is 2400 N., or 24 blocks north of Madison. Halsted is 800 W., or 8 blocks west of State Street.

When it comes to neighborhoods, we can help. Neighborhood names are particularly useful when apartment hunting, as most papers and realtors separate listings this way. Below is a breakdown of information on a selection of Chicago neighborhoods. Included are the boundaries (roughly), average rents for studios, one bedrooms, and two bedrooms, crime ratings and comments from PERFORMINK readers and staffers familiar with the area.

Neighborhood Breakdowns

These descriptions come from the experience of PERFORMINK staffers and subscribers. Please remember these are the compiled thoughts of 2-7 people a neighborhood. The comments are completely unscientific and should be taken as such. The best way to get a feel for a neighborhood is to go there and walk around.

Rent averages are based on those quoted on the CHICAGO READER's Spacefinder at www.chireader.com. Crime ratings are based on stats found on the Chicago Police website for January-September of 1999. Each neighborhood gets two grades, one for violent crime and one for total crime. Each neighborhood has been measured relative to the others listed. Crime rates are given by letter grades. A, of course, is safest. F is least safe, relative to the neighborhoods listed.

Neighborhood Map Key:

[M] –*Metra Train Stop*
[L] – *eL Train Stop*
++++++++++++ –*Train Tracks*
Street name –*Streets*

Andersonville

Comments: *Residents cite the easy parking, affordable rents and great international restaurants in recommending Andersonville. It is home to many artists. Theatres in the neighborhood include The Neo-Futurists and Griffin. There are also a number of actor hangouts: Simon's Tavern (where you can pick up a* **PERFORMINK**), *the Hop Leaf and Kopi, "a traveler's cafe." It also boasts the original Ann Sathers, which is the place for Sunday brunch and cinnamon rolls. The neighborhood is quite multi-cultural, with Scandinavian, Latino and Asian populations — and eateries. It also has a very big lesbian population. Women and Children First — a well-known feminist bookstore — has many special events with authors from around the country.*

Bryn Mawr
Ravenswood
Ashland
Clark
Glenwood
Foster

Bounded by: Glenwood (1400 W.), Ravenswood (1800 W.), Foster (5200 N.) and Bryn Mawr (5600 N.)

Rent: Studio: $460
1 Bedroom: $705 2 Bedroom: $995

Violent Crime: A **Total Crime:** A

Bucktown

Comments: *Right off the expressway, this is a less accessible area by public transportation. A lot of small restaurants and bars are scattered throughout this area. It is quickly being gentrified and is often referred to in conjunction with its neighbor to the south, Wicker Park. There are a lot of filmmakers in Bucktown, many of whom can be found at a local tavern called The Charleston. It is both yuppie and artsy and is quickly rising in price. Trap Door Theatre is in Bucktown.*

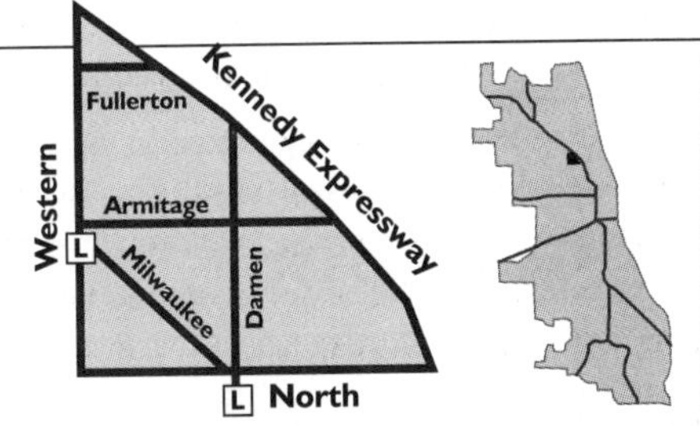

Bounded by: Kennedy Expressway, Western (2400 W.), North (1600 N.) and Fullerton (2400 N.)

Rent: Studio: $595
1Bedroom: $775 2 Bedroom: $1095

Violent Crime: D **Total Crime:** C

Buena Park

Comments: *This quiet neighborhood is "homey for being urban," says one resident. Buena Park is conveniently close to most things — the lake, Lake Shore Drive, Lakeview and public transportation. It is within easy walking distance of an eL, and many major bus routes run through the area, including express buses during the week down to the Loop. Parking is do-able if not always easily found. The neighborhood is praised by the many actors who live here.*

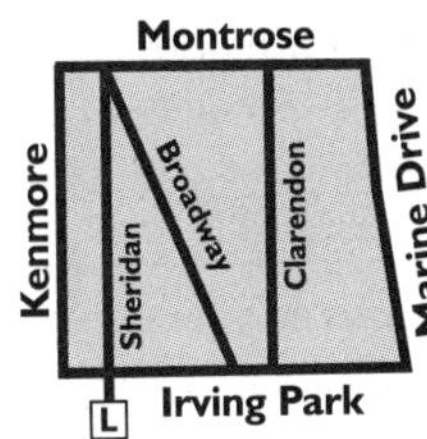

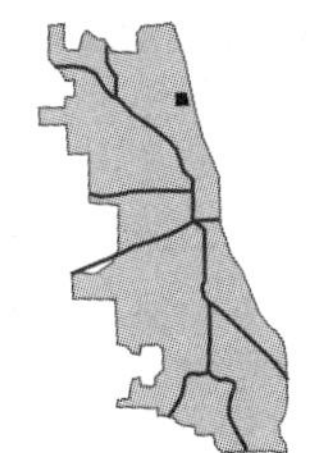

Bounded by: Marine Drive, Kenmore, Irving Park (4000 N.) and Montrose (4400 N.)

Rent: Studio: $555
1Bedroom: $775 2 Bedroom: $1095

Violent Crime: A **Total Crime:** A

Edgewater

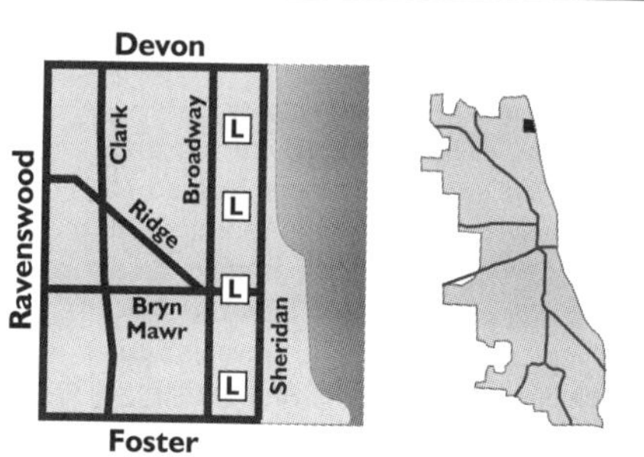

Bounded by: Lake Michigan, Ravenswood (1800 W.), Foster (5200 N.) and Devon (6400 N.)

Rent: Studio: $490
1Bedroom: $760 2 Bedroom: $865

Violent Crime: A **Total Crime:** A

Comments: *Originally settled by German, Swedish, and Irish immigrants, this community was originally designed as a posh residential subdivision for some of Chicago's more prosperous families. But, like many Chicago neighborhoods, Edgewater fell the way of urban decay after the Depression. Due to the combined efforts of the Edgewater Community Council and community volunteers, however, areas of Edgewater have been reclaimed and revitalized by identifying and removing absentee slumlords and renovating these historic properties. Cheaper rents have attracted many actors and artist types. The "Artists in Residence" building — a residence which solely houses artists of all persuasions — is located here. Parking accessibility isn't always top notch depending on where you're located.*

Gold Coast

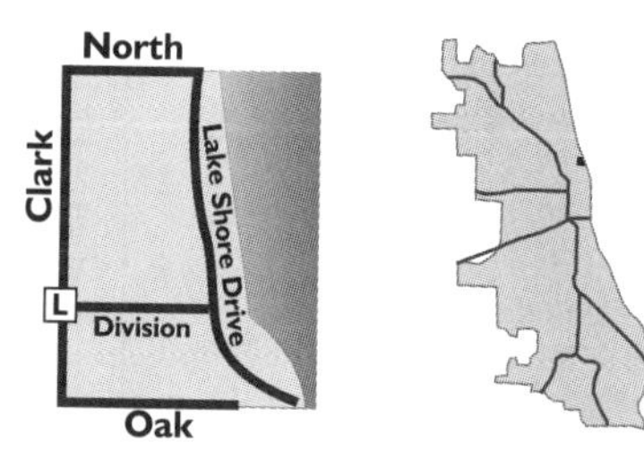

Bounded by: Lake Michigan, Clark, Oak (1000 N.) and North (1600 N.)

Rent: Studio: $730
1Bedroom: $1080 2 Bedroom: $1705

Violent Crime: B **Total Crime:** D

Comments: *This is a "great place to live" if you can afford it. Close to the lake with a lot of (very expensive) shops, "There's always a lot going on in the neighborhood." Again, many of the residents here own rather than rent, and the price for ownership runs in the millions, or at least the high six figures. This is the place, incidentally, where you can find Chicago's Magnificent Mile. It also boasts Mr. J's — one of the best hot dog stands in Chicago. It is very accessible to public transportation and within healthy walking distance of most agents' offices.*

Humboldt Park

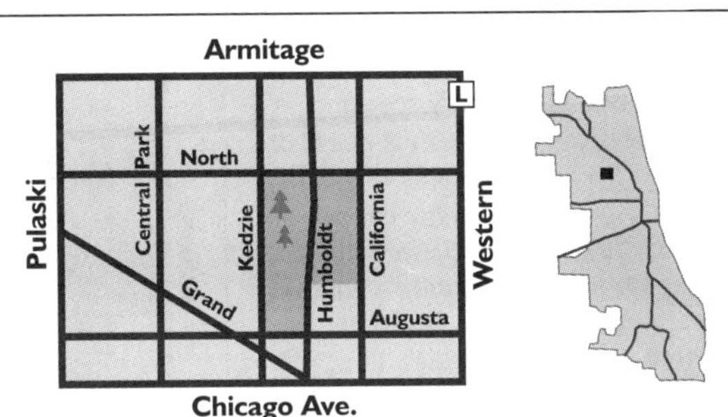

Bounded by: Western (2400 W.), Pulaski (4000 W.) Chicago (800 N.) and Armitage (2000 N.)

Rent: Studio: $500
1Bedroom: $575 2 Bedroom: $770

Violent Crime: D **Total Crime:** C

Comments: *"There's a strong sense of community, lots of artists and lots of gangs," says one resident. The park itself (part of the vast boulevard system designed to link all of Chicago's parks from the north to the south side) is quite beautiful. Gentrification has begun here, but long-time residents — most of whom are Latino — are determined that they will not be priced out by development.*

Hyde Park

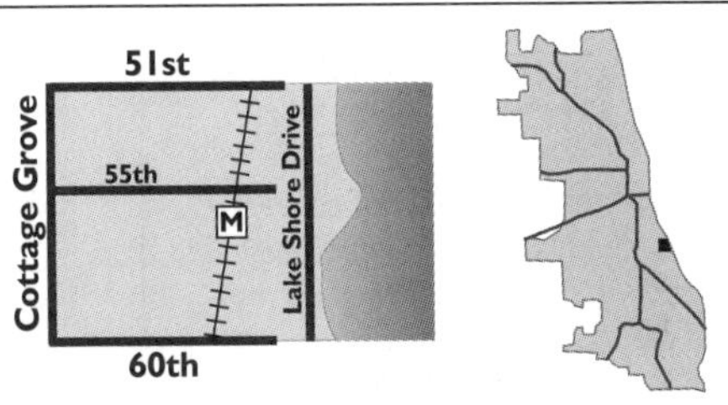

Bounded by: Lake Michigan, Cottage Grove, 60th (6000 S.) and 51st (5100 S.)

Rent: Studio: $520
1Bedroom: $615 2 Bedroom: $900

Violent Crime: C **Total Crime:** B

Comments: *Centered around the University of Chicago, this is a college neighborhood tucked in the South Side. It's a very diverse area with a lot of bookstores, and it has the highest percentage of Nobel prize winners living in the city. Some great old buildings can be found there. If you're an architecture buff, it's definitely the place to be. The neighborhoods surrounding Hyde Park are not the best, so a car is definitely recommended. The Metra station, for instance, is on the boundary and is not quite as safe as the rest of the neighborhood. Court Theatre is in Hyde Park. The South Shore Cultural Center is also close by.*

Neighborhood Map Key:

M *–Metra Train Stop*
L *– eL Train Stop*
++++++++++++ *–Train Tracks*
Street name *–Streets*

Lakeview

Comments: *Statistically speaking, Lakeview is one of the safest neighborhoods in the city. Parking is very difficult — especially at night. The only other complaint is that, while this is largely regarded as a great neighborhood, yuppification has begun in earnest. Frame houses have been torn down to make room for large brick and stone condos.* **PERFORMINK'S** *offices are in Lakeview, as are many theatres, including the Theatre Building, Bailiwick Repertory, Ivanhoe, Briar Street, Stage Left, ComedySportz, ImprovOlympic and About Face. Actor hangouts include the L&L Tavern, Melrose Diner, and Bar San Miguel. It's a very young, post-college crowd with not too many families. Part of Lakeview is also known among the gay community as "Boys' Town."*

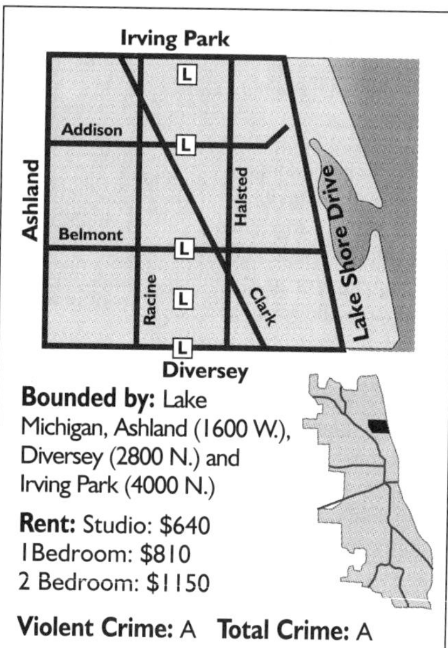

Bounded by: Lake Michigan, Ashland (1600 W.), Diversey (2800 N.) and Irving Park (4000 N.)

Rent: Studio: $640
1Bedroom: $810
2 Bedroom: $1150

Violent Crime: A **Total Crime:** A

Lincoln Park

Comments: *Just south of Lakeview, this is clearly an upper-class neighborhood. Its residents enjoy a great deal of safety and convenience, although parking is, again, very difficult. Lincoln Park was the up and coming neighborhood a decade ago and still boasts a lot of theatres. In fact, the Off-Loop theatre scene pretty much started in Lincoln Park (with a nod to Lakeview just to its north) in the 70's. Victory Gardens is located here in a building that once also housed the famed Body Politic Theatre. Steppenwolf and the Royal George are across the street from each other on Halsted. DePaul University is in Lincoln Park, which makes for an interesting mix of theatre folk, yuppies and frat boys. John Barleycorn is one notable actor hangout, as is Sterch's. The Biograph (where John Herbert Dillinger was shot) is in this neighborhood, along with the Three Penny movie theatre. Most importantly, Act I Bookstore is on Lincoln, next to the Apollo Theatre.*

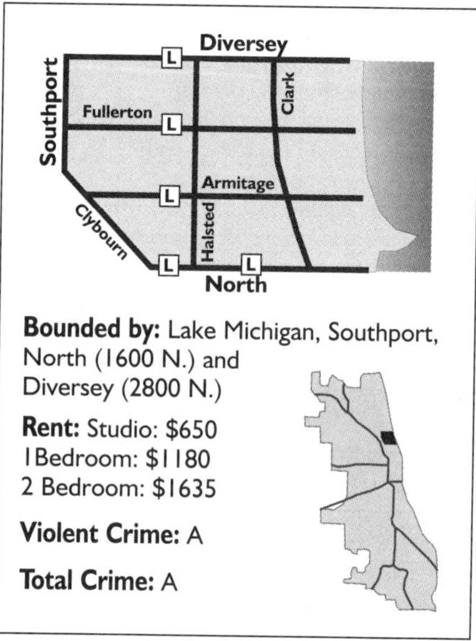

Bounded by: Lake Michigan, Southport, North (1600 N.) and Diversey (2800 N.)

Rent: Studio: $650
1Bedroom: $1180
2 Bedroom: $1635

Violent Crime: A

Total Crime: A

Lincoln Square

Comments: *This neighborhood gets raves from its residents for the people and the community. It's less congested than the lakeside neighborhoods. A car is advantageous, but the eL does have a stop on Western and Lincoln, and there's a bus depot on Western. The buildings have a very German feel, though the population is more a mix of White, Latino and Asian. Great Thai restaurants can be found in the area. There are also wonderful German bakeries. A number of theatres have opened in this area recently, including TinFish, Cornservatory and Phoenix Ascending.*

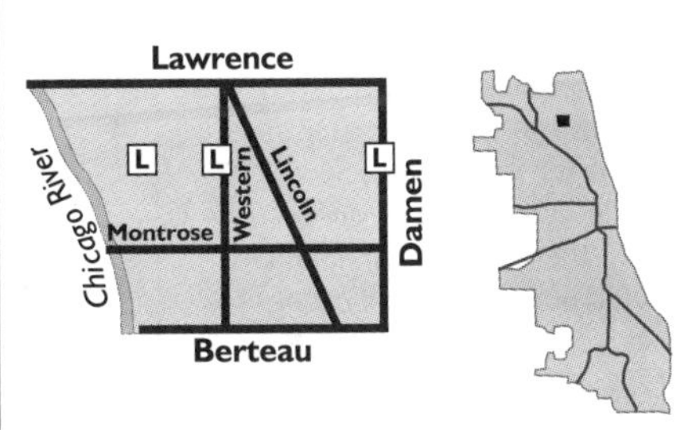

Boundaries: Damen (2000 W.), the Chicago River, Berteau (4200 N.) and Lawrence (4800 N.)

Rent: Studio: $540
1Bedroom: $640 2 Bedroom: $990

Violent Crime: A **Total Crime:** B

Logan/Palmer Square

Comments: *Logan Square is one of the top areas for artists. In fact, artists moving into the neighborhood in the mid-80's helped to start the gentrification that has rapidly spread west and south. It's very community based and multi-everything — race, culture, class. It is marked by large graystones and red brick mostly two and three flats, in a very German/Swedish style of architecture. There are also some mansions that are still single family homes, especially in the Palmer Square area. Logan Square is the beginning of the Boulevard system still in existence. Redmoon Theatre Company is located in the Logan Square area.*

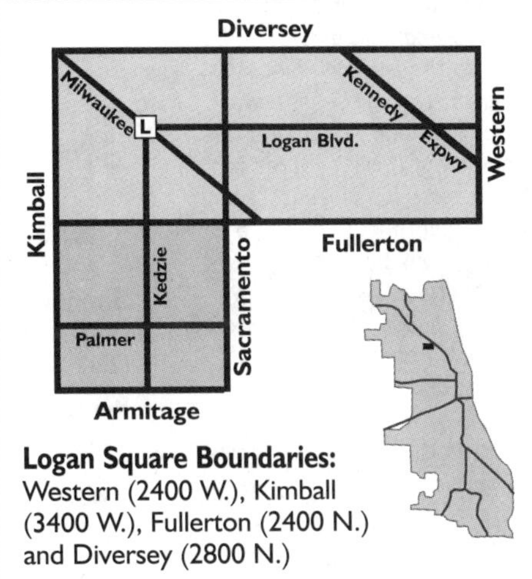

Logan Square Boundaries: Western (2400 W.), Kimball (3400 W.), Fullerton (2400 N.) and Diversey (2800 N.)

Palmer Square Boundaries: Sacramento (3000 W.), Kimball (3400 W.), Armitage (2000 N.) and Fullerton (2400 N.)

Rent: Studio: $480
1Bedroom: $860 2 Bedroom: $1010

Violent Crime: D **Total Crime:** C

Old Town

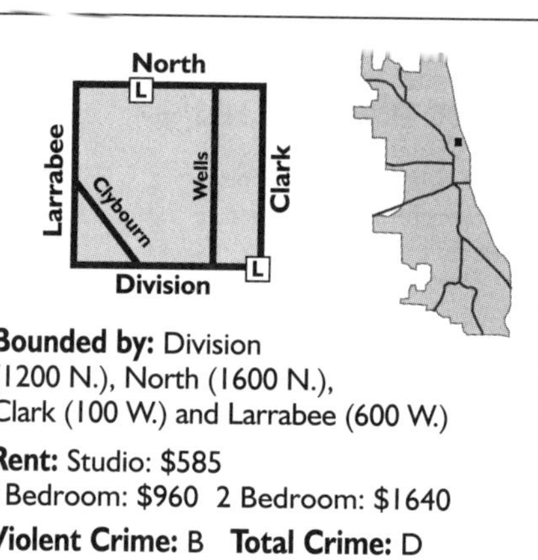

Bounded by: Division (1200 N.), North (1600 N.), Clark (100 W.) and Larrabee (600 W.)

Rent: Studio: $585
1Bedroom: $960 2 Bedroom: $1640

Violent Crime: B **Total Crime:** D

Comments: *"The area's great! It's eclectic, has theatres, bars, restaurants and it's convenient." This sums up the opinions of the residents we spoke with. Second City is in Old Town and, consequently, there are lots of actors' bars and hangouts. The Last Act is across from Second City on Wells. Old Town Ale House is across from Second City on North. A Red Orchid Theatre is also in Old Town, as is Zanies comedy club. Pipers Alley movie theatre is on the corner of North and Wells in the same building that houses Second City. Parking is quite horrendous, unless you pay for it. Old Town butts up against the Gold Coast and Lincoln Park, so it can be kind of pricey.*

Pilsen

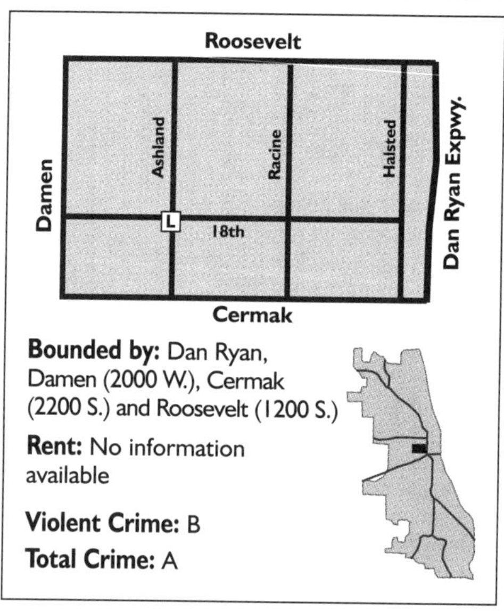

Bounded by: Dan Ryan, Damen (2000 W.), Cermak (2200 S.) and Roosevelt (1200 S.)

Rent: No information available

Violent Crime: B

Total Crime: A

Comments: *Pilsen boasts a very large Mexican population and is home to the Mexican Fine Arts Museum. Decades ago, it was mostly Irish and Polish, and the remnants of those cultures can still be seen. It's currently going through gentrification, which is causing many political problems with longtime, mostly Spanish-speaking residents. There are lots of schools in the area — both Catholic and public. There are also lots of warehouses, which attract both theatre companies and developers. There is a very large artistic population due to the low rents and large spaces. Duncan YMCA Chernin Center for the Arts resides in this area and is the home to several small companies. The University of Illinois at Chicago (UIC) anchors the area to the north.*

Neighborhood Map Key:

M –*Metra Train Stop*
L – *eL Train Stop*
++++++++++ –*Train Tracks*
Street name –*Streets*

Printer's Row/South Loop

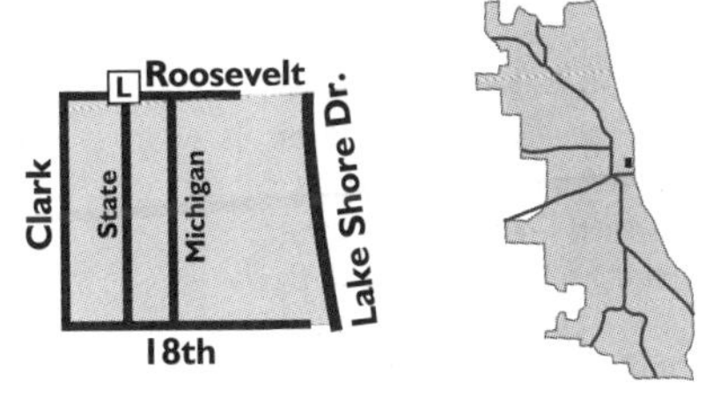

Bounded by: the Lakefront, Clark (100 W.), 18th (1800 S.) and Roosevelt (1200 S.)

Rent: Studio: $730
1Bedroom: $1200 2 Bedroom: $1615

Violent Crime: A **Total Crime:** C

Comments: *This area was a vast wasteland at the beginning of the 90's, but rapid gentrification has made it one of the highest priced neighborhoods in Chicago. New construction overlooks the abandoned freight yards, which only seems to add a quaintness to the area. It helps that Mayor Daley moved from his boyhood neighborhood of Bridgeport (in the shadow of Comiskey Park) to this trendy area a few years ago, leaving traditionalists aghast. Transportation is accessible, with the eL running from the Loop just a mile or so to the north. Buses also are always on time. Parking isn't wonderful — unless you have a garage with your home or apartment, as many do. There are some nice restaurants in Printer's Row, but other than that it's very residential.*

Ravenswood

Bounded by: Clark, Damen (2000 W.), Montrose (4400 N.) and Foster (5200 N.)

Rent: Studio: $565
1Bedroom: $740 2 Bedroom: $945

Violent Crime: A **Total Crime:** B

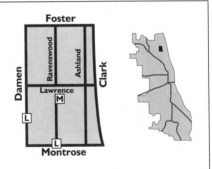

Comments: *"Move here before the rents go up," says one resident. This affordable area is diverse and pretty blue collar, with lots of single family homes. This is a neighborhood in which you will see kids playing in the yard or riding their bikes down the street. It's becoming yuppie, and there is a growing gay population as Andersonville to the northeast becomes too expensive. Pauline's is a great breakfast restaurant that is always crowded. The Zephyr, for ice cream and diner food, is very popular too. Otherwise, there aren't too many hangouts in this residential area. The Ravenswood eL (or the Brown Line) goes through Ravenswood and the Clark bus is always available.*

River West

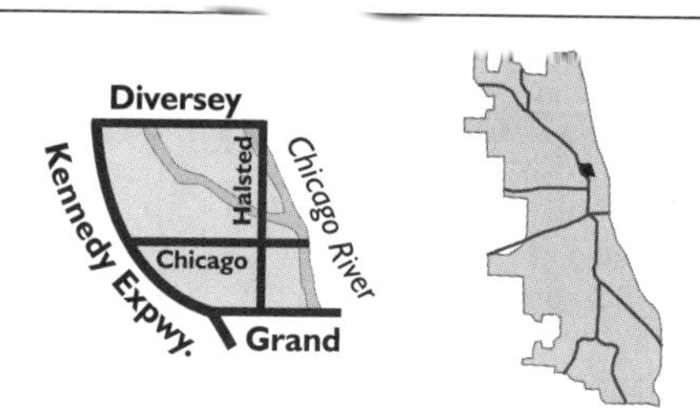

Bounded by: the Chicago River, the Kennedy Expressway, Grand (500 N.) and Division (1200 N.)

Rent: Studio: $725
1Bedroom: $1000 2 Bedroom: $1300

Violent Crime: D **Total Crime:** C

Comments: *Large warehouses and loft spaces make up River West, which made it a prime target for revitalization in the late 80's and early 90's. After a fizzle in the area a few years ago, it is starting to live up to its potential. Chicago Dramatists Workshop is in River West, as is The Chicago Academy for the Arts — Chicago's answer to "Fame." Lots of good restaurants are popping up every day. There are a lot of filmmakers and companies in River West, more so than theatre artists. You definitely need a car in this area. The closest grocery store, for instance, is across the river in the Gold Coast.*

Rogers Park

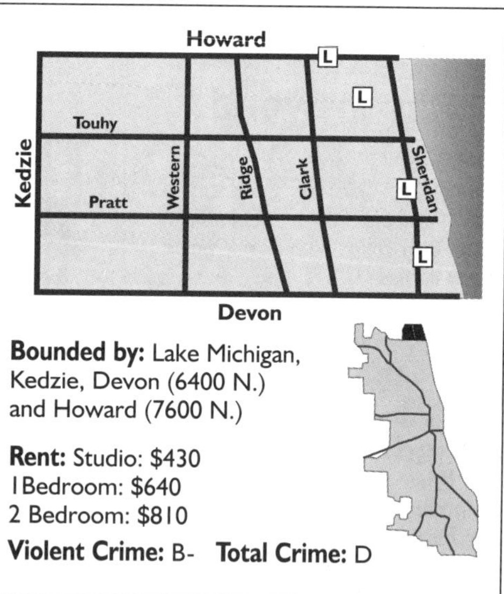

Bounded by: Lake Michigan, Kedzie, Devon (6400 N.) and Howard (7600 N.)

Rent: Studio: $430
1Bedroom: $640
2 Bedroom: $810

Violent Crime: B- **Total Crime:** D

Comments: *This is a huge neighborhood that forms Chicago's northern border. There's a large diverse community — probably the most diverse of all the neighborhoods in Chicago — including orthodox Jewish, Indian and Middle Eastern populations. Gay men moved up to the condos in West Rogers Park in the early 90's. "It's a melting pot," says one resident. Diverse can describe the income ranges, too. Some areas are quite affluent, while others are very poor. Loyola University is in Rogers Park. Raven, Center, Boxer Rebellion and Lifeline are some of the theaters in this area. Don't take safety for granted. In some areas it's fine. In others — like on Howard street bordering Evanston — it's quite unsafe day or night.*

Roscoe Village

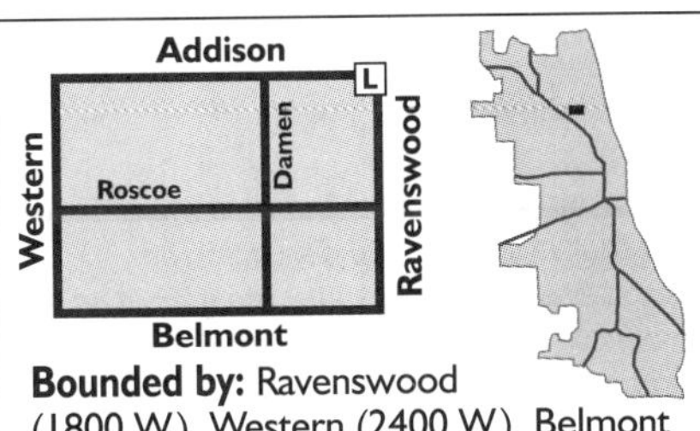

Comments: *This is a close neighborhood, but residents will need to go elsewhere for their entertainment. It's definitely a place where "you can know your neighbors." The Village Tap is an actors' bar. Of particular note is the Four Moon Tavern, a new bar owned and managed by four actors. Higher Ground coffee shop also is quite popular. Many small boutiques and restaurants are just starting to open in this neighborhood. Also, many Chicago filmmakers call this neighborhood home. It borders Lakeview to the east, and rents are rising as people are priced out of Lakeview.*

Bounded by: Ravenswood (1800 W.), Western (2400 W.), Belmont (3200 N.) and Addison (3600 N.)

Rent: Studio: $550
1Bedroom: $770 2 Bedroom: $1000

Violent Crime: A **Total Crime:** B-

Saint Ben's

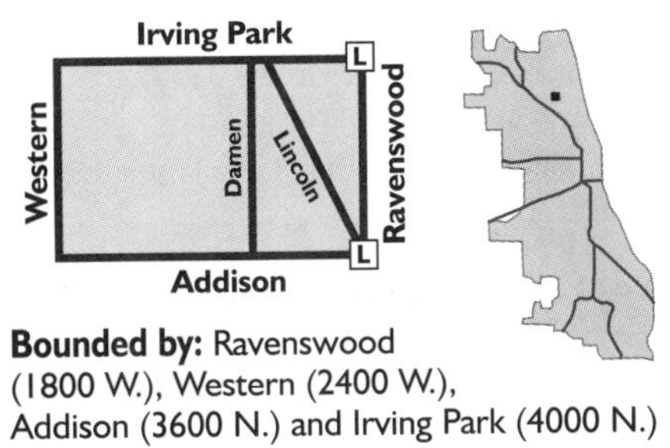

Comments: *This is a working class neighborhood that most residents feel is a "great place to live." One resident complained of the noise, but others praised the quiet feel, so it probably depends on where you are. It's between Roscoe Village and Ravenswood and is going through the same kind of gentrification. American Theater Company (formerly American Blues Theater) and Breadline Theatre Group are located in this neighborhood.*

Bounded by: Ravenswood (1800 W.), Western (2400 W.), Addison (3600 N.) and Irving Park (4000 N.)

Rent: Studio: $550
1Bedroom: $695 2 Bedroom: $1200

Violent Crime: A **Total Crime:** B

Ukrainian Village

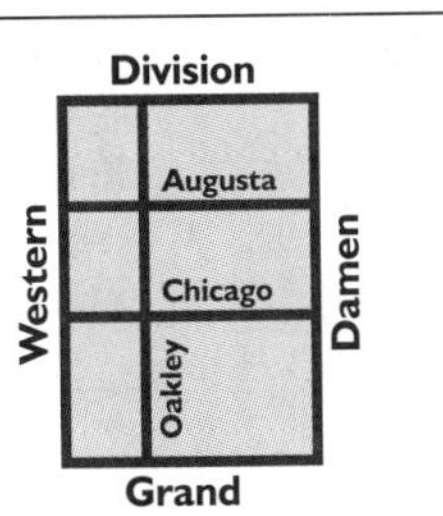

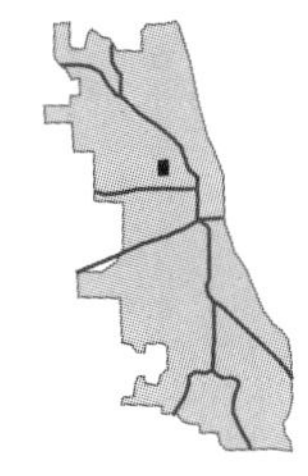

Comments: *This neighborhood lives up to its name and is not as diverse as many Chicago neighborhoods. The large Ukrainian population is augmented by artists who have flocked to the housing, which used to be affordable. It's a very close-knit community. People watch out for one another. The Western Avenue border can be a bit dicey on the safety side, but it's generally pretty well-liked by the people there. Public transportation is not easy.*

Bounded by: Damen (2000 W.), Western (2400 W.), Grand (500 N.) and Division (1200 N.)

Rent: Studio: $370
1Bedroom: $785 2 Bedroom: $850

Violent Crime: B **Total Crime:** A

Uptown

Comments: *Uptown is the once majestic area that has fallen into disrepair. The Aragon Ballroom still stands, though not as grandly as it did in the 20's and 30's. American filmmaking started in Uptown. Charlie Chaplin had a studio there before he went west. The famous Green Mill Lounge — home of the Uptown Poetry Slam — is in this area. Housing is still fairly cheap — and for good reason. Despite its spiffy ratings, safety is still a major concern in some areas. Because it runs along the lake, people have been talking about this neighborhood coming up for some time, but it doesn't seem to be happening. Pegasus Players is in the area, as part of Truman College. The theatre is safe and quite nice, but people often complain about walking from their cars.*

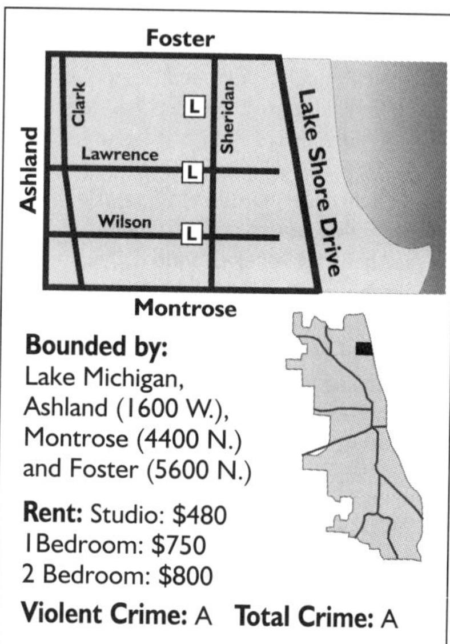

Bounded by:
Lake Michigan,
Ashland (1600 W.),
Montrose (4400 N.)
and Foster (5600 N.)

Rent: Studio: $480
1Bedroom: $750
2 Bedroom: $800

Violent Crime: A **Total Crime:** A

Wicker Park

Comments: *Wicker Park is the neighborhood for any trendy artist in Chicago. If you want to be "in," you want to be in Wicker Park. Architecturally, it is defined by large Victorian mansions that were once grand and graceful and now have been cut up into apartments. There has also been a lot of rehab in the area over the past few years, resulting, sometimes, in a strange mix of brand new brick and stone next door to an old Victorian. This is the area where Nelson Algren lived and wrote, and the neighborhood is as tough and beautiful as an Algren book. Accessibility is somewhat of an issue, but not bad. The eL is the O'Hare line, which runs diagonally across the city to the airport. If you want to get up to Lakeview, where many theatres are, you have to go downtown first, then switch trains and head north. But buses do run regularly down major streets. Latino Chicago Theatre Company is in Wicker Park.*

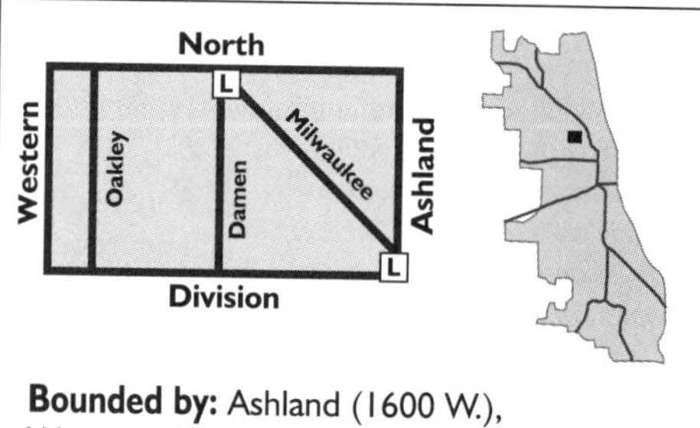

Bounded by: Ashland (1600 W.), Western (2400 W.), Division (1200 N.) and North (1600 N.)

Rent: Studio: $435
1Bedroom: $790 2 Bedroom: $1250

Violent Crime: D **Total Crime:** C

Wrigleyville

Comments: *The home of the Cubs receives high praise from its residents, though parking can be difficult, particularly during baseball season. "I love it. I would recommend it to first-time Chicagoans. Easy access to bars and theatres," says one resident. Wrigleyville is home to many young families, as well as artists. Wrigleyville is technically in Lakeview, but they are proud of their separate identity.*

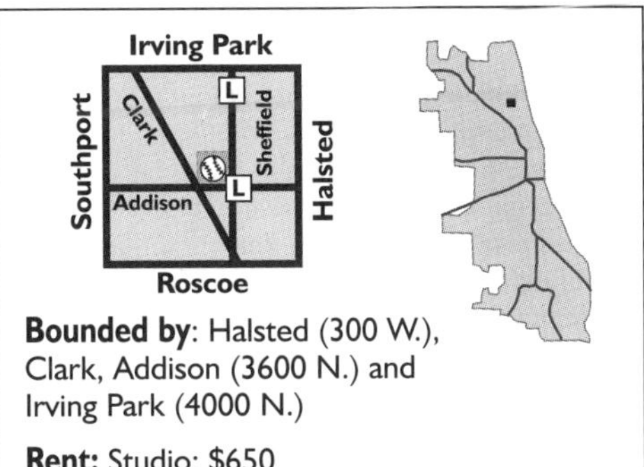

Bounded by: Halsted (300 W.), Clark, Addison (3600 N.) and Irving Park (4000 N.)

Rent: Studio: $650
1Bedroom: $850 2 Bedroom: $1350

Violent Crime: A **Total Crime:** A

Suburbs

Evanston

Comments: *The first of our selected suburbs, Evanston lies just to the north of the city along the lake. Home to Northwestern University, this is a "down to earth, well-rounded community," says one resident. "The neighbors are great because they look out for each other. It's convenient without being crowded," says another. Evanston is mostly made up of houses and mansions. It can be quite exclusive, yet it can also be affordable around the university or west of the Ridge Street dividing line. Even so, living in Evanston is more expensive than living in Chicago. Taxes alone, if you're in the buying mood, can be more than your mortgage payment. Public transportation in Evanston is pretty much limited to buses, but the Evanston Express eL line runs all the way down the lake to the Loop. Residents can go door to door from their apartment in Evanston to the Theatre Building in Lakeview in 20-30 minutes. Fleetwood Jourdain is an African American theatre that has been there for years. The famed Piven Theatre Workshop and Next Theatre are also in Evanston. And the city is expanding its commitment to the arts by building a new cultural center.*

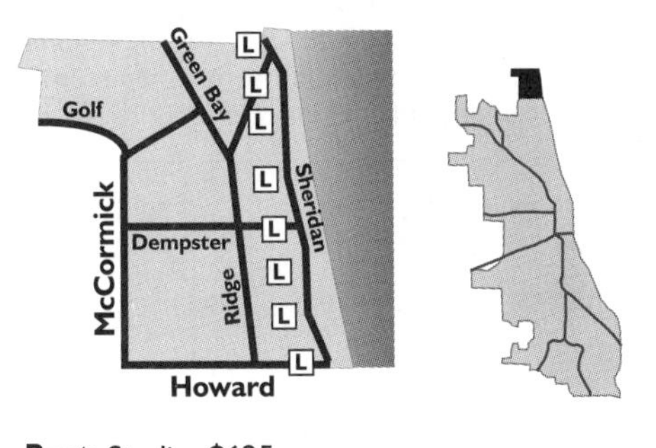

Rent: Studio: $625
1Bedroom: $800 2 Bedroom: $1060

Oak Park

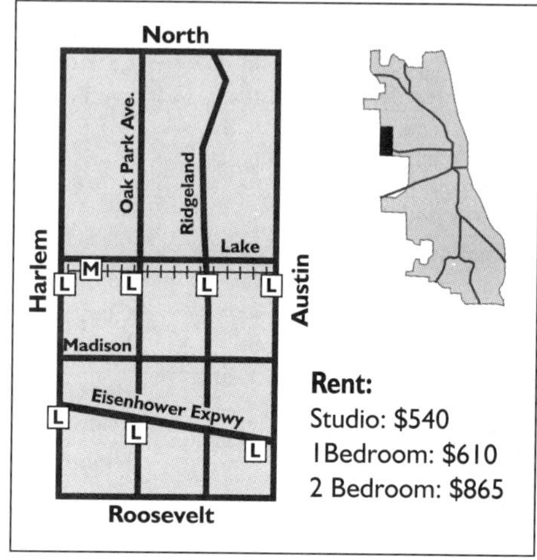

Comments: *This suburb lies just west of Chicago along the Eisenhower Expressway. "It's a diverse community, and we have a lot of cultural things. Oak Park has a lot of actors. You'll always run into someone who's in the business," says a resident. Residents also cite the great schools and the supportive neighborhoods in recommending this suburb. Oak Park is a village and feels like one. You can walk almost anywhere. Some apartments are more affordable than others, but it can be pretty pricey in some areas. Taxes are also a consideration here — the price for those wonderful schools and clean streets. There is also a considerable gay population in Oak Park. In fact, this progressive city is one of the few in the country who give domestic partnership benefits to gay spouses of city employees. Circle Theatre is in Oak Park, as is Oak Park Village Players. And the Oak Park Shakespeare Festival is a staple for actors and theatregoers every summer. You can live in Oak Park without a car. The eL Green Line goes to Oak Park, but it passes through some very poor neighborhoods on Chicago's west side first. More importantly, Metra runs directly from Oak Park to the city.*

Skokie

Rent: Studio: $500
1Bedroom: $675 2 Bedroom: $925

Comments: *Skokie is more diverse and less expensive than its neighborhood to the east, Evanston. While the suburb is largely thought of as the Jewish center of the North Shore, the area has opened up to include many Asians and Latinos. Schools have a solid reputation, and there is an active park district. Convenient bus routes make it easy to reach the Howard eL stop in Evanston and many of the area's shopping and entertainment complexes. You can also take the "Skokie Swift," the one-stop extension of the eL that deposits riders at the Greyhound bus terminal. With the opening of The Northshore Center for the Performing Arts last year, Skokie is a big-time player on the theatre scene. Northlight Theatre is in the Northshore Center, along with the presenting company Centre East. Many companies also rent space in the North Shore Center.*

Finding an Apartment

Your living arrangement can make or break your Chicago experience. As you search for the perfect place to live, keep the following items in mind:

Rooms

How many rooms do you need? Where do you spend your time? How's the layout for sound? For privacy?

Water Pressure

How's the water pressure in the kitchen and bathroom? Can you get hot water from both sinks simultaneously? Check the shower too.

Parking

If you own a car, how tough is parking going to be? Do you need a sticker? Check the neighborhood during both the day and night.

Storage

Do you need places for stuff? Are there enough of such places?

Laundry

Are there facilities on-site? If not, where's the nearest laundromat?

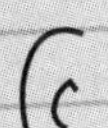

Sound

How much sound is there from the street? Is the eL nearby?

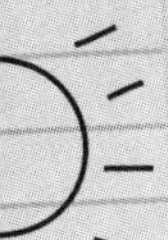

Natural Light

When and from what direction will the apartment get sunlight? Is the light going to wake you in the morning? Will your plants flourish?

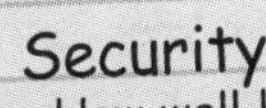

Security

How well lit are the entrances to the building? Are there good locks on the doors? If the apartment is on the first floor, are there grills on the windows? Be sure to check the neighborhood at night as well.

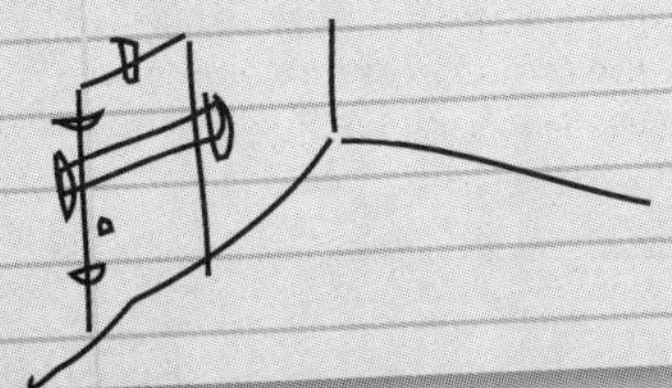

Over

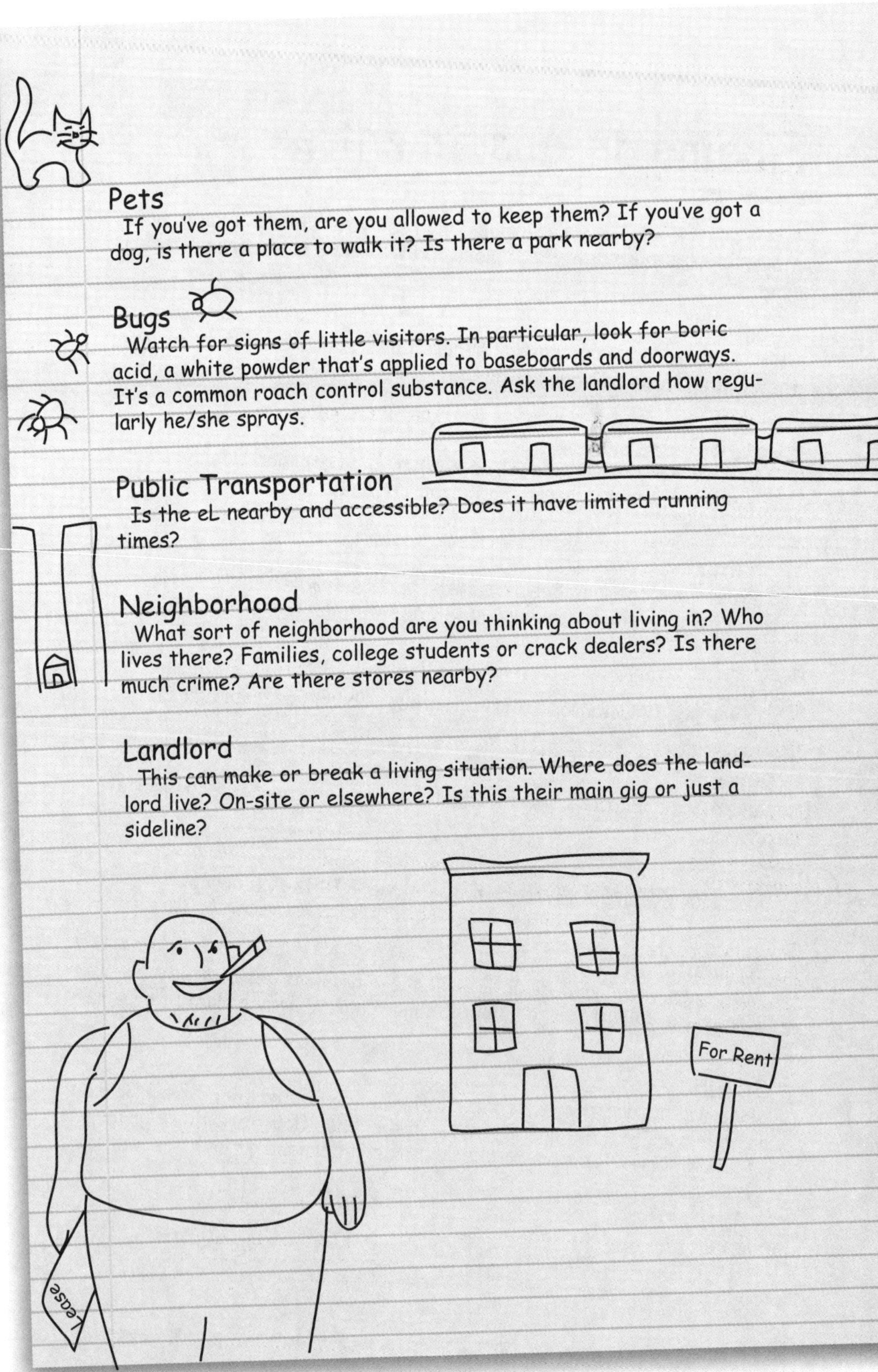

Pets

If you've got them, are you allowed to keep them? If you've got a dog, is there a place to walk it? Is there a park nearby?

Bugs

Watch for signs of little visitors. In particular, look for boric acid, a white powder that's applied to baseboards and doorways. It's a common roach control substance. Ask the landlord how regularly he/she sprays.

Public Transportation

Is the eL nearby and accessible? Does it have limited running times?

Neighborhood

What sort of neighborhood are you thinking about living in? Who lives there? Families, college students or crack dealers? Is there much crime? Are there stores nearby?

Landlord

This can make or break a living situation. Where does the landlord live? On-site or elsewhere? Is this their main gig or just a sideline?

Apartment Services

Apartment Connection
1000 W. Diversey
Chicago, IL 60614
773/525-3888 • 773/525-0210 - fax

The Apartment People
3121 N. Broadway
Chicago, IL 60657
773/248-8800 • 773/248-1007 - fax
www.apartmentpeople.com
Chicago's largest FREE apartment finding service with locations in both Lakeview at 3121 N. Broadway and Evanston at 1718 Sherman. Featuring studios, 1, 2 and 3 bedrooms in all property types, from the S. Loop through Evanston. Call 800/447-3684 to set an appointment. Open everyday!

Apartment Source
2638 N. Halsted
Chicago, IL 60614
773/404-9900 • 773/404-0669 - fax

Cagan Management
3856 W. Oakton St.
Skokie, IL 60076
847/679-5512 • 847/679-5516 - fax

Century 21 - Amquest
2843 N. Halsted
Chicago, IL 60657
773/404-2100 • 773/404-6034 - fax
www.cyber.home.com

City Living Apartment Rentals
1300 W. Belmont
Chicago, IL 60657
773/525-6161

Oak Park Regional Housing Center
1041 South Blvd.
Oak Park, IL 60302
708/848-7150
members.aol.com/RENTinOP/oprhc.html

Realty & Mortgage
928 W. Diversey
Chicago, IL 60614
773/549-8300
www.aptrentals.com

Relcon Apartment Finders
21 W. Elm - 2nd floor
Chicago, IL 60610
312/255-9920 • 312/255-9928 - fax
www.relconapartments.com

Urban Equities R.E.C.
6240 N. Clark
Chicago, IL 60660
773/743-4141 • 773/465-4672 - fax

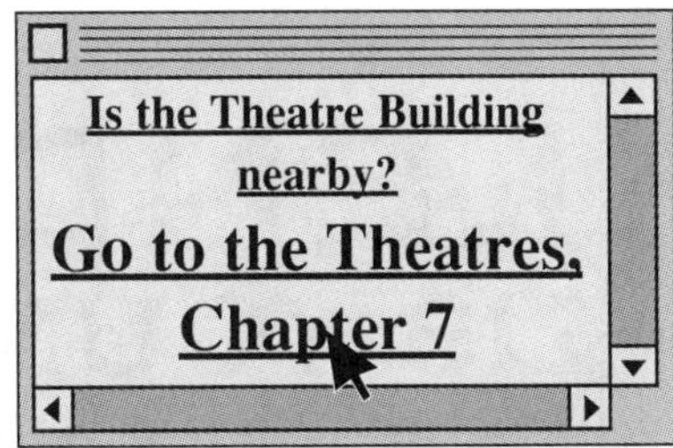

Is the Theatre Building nearby?
Go to the Theatres, Chapter 7

Housing Spots

Artist in Residence
6165 and 6161 N. Winthrop
Chicago, IL 60660
800/LIVE-ART
773/743-8900
773/743-8259 - fax
www.artistsinresidence.com
Artist in Residence has been a home to artists since 1979. We rent solely to people active in fine or applied arts. We have facilities available for use by our residents, including rehearsal spaces, painter's and sculptor's workshops and darkroom. For more information and an appointment, call 773/743-8900 or 1-800-LIVE-ART.

Eleanor Residence
Women Only
1550 N. Dearborn
Chicago, IL 60610
312/664-8245 • 312/664-0888 - fax
eleanorresidence.com

Sovereign Apartments
1040 W. Granville
Chicago, IL 60660
773/274-8000 • 773/274-1321 - fax

Three Arts Club (for women)
(men - June, July, August only)
1300 N. Dearborn
Chicago, IL 60610
312/944-6250 • 312/944-6284 - fax
www.threearts.org

Under the Ginkgo Tree (Bed & Breakfast)
Gloria Onischuk
300 N. Kenilworth
Oak Park, IL 60302
708/524-2327 • 708/524-2729 - fax
Under the Ginkgo Tree Bed and Breakfast Home: The Bed and Breakfast home in the historic district of Oak Park.

Roommate Services

Roommate Connection
160 E. Illinois #303
Chicago, IL 60611
312/755-1887

Utilities

Chicago-based utilities Ameritech, ComEd and People's Gas are vilified by residents frequently and with great imagination. Poor service, uninformed representatives and order errors are all too common. The secret to a good (or tolerable anyway) relationship with these fine institutions is to call. Then call to confirm. You may want to follow up to confirm the confirmation.

Ameritech
800/244-4444

AT&T
800/222-0300

Commonwealth Edison
800/334-7661

MCI
800/950-5555

Peoples Gas Light & Coke Co.
401 S. State
Chicago, IL
312/240-4000

Sprint
800/877-7746

Temp Agencies

A Personnel Commitment
(See our ad on page 290)
208 S. LaSalle #189
Chicago, IL 60604-1003
312/251-5151 • 312/251-5154 - fax

AccuStaff, Inc.
542A W. Dundee Rd.
Wheeling, IL 60090
847/541-6220 • 847/541-6235 - fax
www.accustaff.com

Active Temporary Services
(See our ad on page 27)
25 E. Washington #1717
Chicago, IL 60602
312/726-5771 • 312/726-3273 - fax

Active Temporary Services
3145 N. Lincoln - Main Level
Chicago, IL 60657
773/404-5700 • 773/404-9635 - fax

Adecco Personnel Services
200 W. Madison #520
Chicago, IL 60606
312/372-6783 • 312/372-9732 - fax

Advanced Personnel
(See our ad on page 33)
1020 Milwaukee Ave. #105
Deerfield, IL 60015
847/520-9111 • 847/520-9489 - fax
www.advancedresources.com
Advanced Personnel is a staffing firm supplying office support employees to major financial, healthcare and Fortune 1000 corporations in Chicagoland. Our flexible scheduling helps match actors with temporary and full-time positions. Corporate positions, executive assistants, customer service professionals, production specialists, desktop publishers and administrative assistants. Contact us at 312/422-9333.

Appropriate Temporaries
(See our ad on the back cover)
79 W. Monroe #819
Chicago, IL 60603
312/782-7215 • 312/704-4195 - fax

ASI Staffing Service, Inc.
333 N. Michigan #2106
Chicago, IL 60601
312/782-4690 • 312/782-4697 - fax

BPS Staffing
200 N. LaSalle #1750
Chicago, IL 60601
312/920-6710 • 312/920-6744 - fax

The Choice for Staffing
100 N. LaSalle #1900
Chicago, IL 60602
312/372-4500 • 312/853-4068 - fax
www.choicestaff.com

City Staffing
(See our ad on page 30)
2 N. LaSalle #630
Chicago, IL 60602
312/346-3400 • 312/346-5200 - fax

Dunhill Staffing Systems
211 W. Wacker #1150
Chicago, IL 60606
312/346-0933 • 312/346-0837 - fax
www.dunhillstaff.com

Interim Office Professionals
11 S. LaSalle #2155
Chicago, IL 60603
312/781-7220
www.interim.com

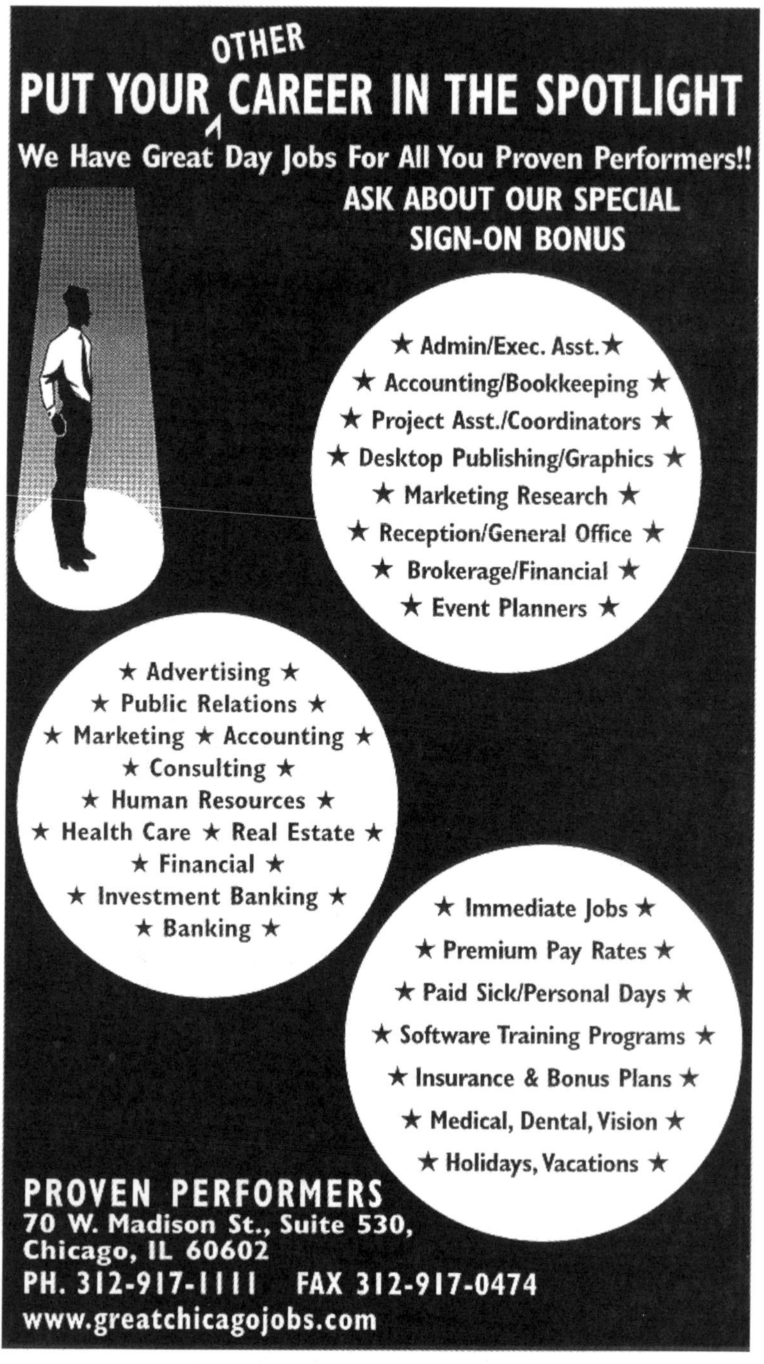
OTHER
PUT YOUR CAREER IN THE SPOTLIGHT
We Have Great Day Jobs For All You Proven Performers!!
ASK ABOUT OUR SPECIAL
SIGN-ON BONUS
★ Admin/Exec. Asst.★
★ Accounting/Bookkeeping ★
★ Project Asst./Coordinators ★
★ Desktop Publishing/Graphics ★
★ Marketing Research ★
★ Reception/General Office ★
★ Brokerage/Financial ★
★ Event Planners ★
★ Advertising ★
★ Public Relations ★
★ Marketing ★ Accounting ★
★ Consulting ★
★ Human Resources ★
★ Health Care ★ Real Estate ★
★ Financial ★
★ Investment Banking ★
★ Banking ★
★ Immediate Jobs ★
★ Premium Pay Rates ★
★ Paid Sick/Personal Days ★
★ Software Training Programs ★
★ Insurance & Bonus Plans ★
★ Medical, Dental, Vision ★
★ Holidays, Vacations ★
PROVEN PERFORMERS
70 W. Madison St., Suite 530,
Chicago, IL 60602
PH. 312-917-1111 FAX 312-917-0474
www.greatchicagojobs.com

Kelly Services
949C N. Plum Grove Rd.
Schaumburg, IL 60173
847/995-9350 • 847/995-9366 - fax
www.kellyservices.com

Larko Group
(See our ad inside the front cover)
11 S. LaSalle #1720
Chicago, IL 60603
312/857-2300 • 312/857-2355 - fax
www.@thelarkogroup.com

Loftus & O'Meara
(See our ad on page 32)
166 E. Superior #410
Chicago, IL 60611
312/944-2102 • 312/944-7009 - fax

Mack & Associates Personnel, Ltd.
Attn: Boula Proutsos
100 N. LaSalle #2110
Chicago, IL 60602
312/368-0677 • 312/368-1868 - fax
www.mackltd.com

Manpower Temporary Services
(See our ad on page 162)
500 W. Madison #2950
Chicago, IL 60661
312/648-4555 • 312/648-0472 - fax
www.manpowerchicago.com
Manpower works as a partner with you in meeting your job needs. We've designed a systematic process that helps us gather essential information about your specific skills and requirements. Our innovative training program helps us perfect that partnership. Let us match your skills with the perfect position for you.

Olstens of Chicago, Inc.
123 W. Madison #500
Chicago, IL 60602
312/944-3880

Paige Temporary, Inc.
5215 Old Orchard Rd.
Skokie, IL 60077
847/966-0111 • 847/966-8479 - fax
www.paigepersonnel.com

Pro Staff Personnel Services
10 S. Wacker #2250
Chicago, IL 60606
312/575-2120 • 312/641-0224 - fax
www.prostaff.com

Profile Temporary Service
222 N. LaSalle #450
Chicago, IL 60601
312/541-4141 • 312/641-1762 - fax

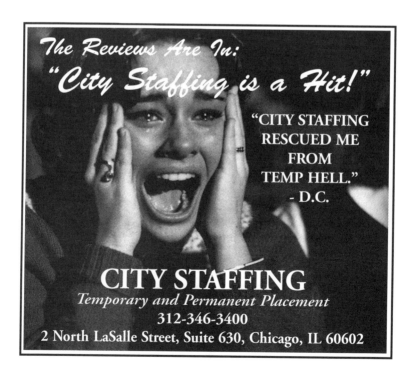

Proven Performers
(See our ad on page 28)
70 W. Madison #530
Chicago, IL 60602
312/917-1111 • 312/917-0474 - fax
www.greatchicagojobs.com

Right Employment Center
25 Tri-State International #145
Lincolnshire, IL 60069
847/914-0229
312/427-3136
www.rightservices.com

Select Staffing
208 S. LaSalle #1244
Chicago, IL 60604
312/849-2229 • 312/849-2234 - fax

Seville Temporary Services
(See our ad on page 26)
180 N. Michigan #1510
Chicago, IL 60601
312/368-1272 • 312/368-0207 - fax
members.aol.com/sevilleinc

Smart Staffing
(See our ad on page 24)
29 S. LaSalle #635
Chicago, IL 60603
312/696-5306 • 312/696-0317 - fax
www.smartstaffing.com

Today's Office Staffing
1701 E. Woodfield Rd. #903
Schaumburg, IL 60173
847/240-5300 • 847/240-5310 - fax

TeleStaff Solutions
6133 N. River Rd. #720
Rosemont, IL 60018
847/318-8600 • 847/318-8508 - fax
www.networkstaff.com

Temporary Opportunities
(See our ad on the inside back cover)
53 W. Jackson #215
Chicago, IL 60604
312/922-5400 • 312/347-1206 - fax
www.opgroup.com

Temporary Professionals
625 N. Michigan #600
Chicago, IL 60611
773/622-1202 • 773/622-1303 - fax

Unique Office Services
203 N. Wabash #608
Chicago, IL 60601
312/332-4183 • 312/332-2688 - fax

Watson Dwyer Staffing
25 E. Washington
Chicago, IL 60602
312/899-8030 • 312/899-8036 - fax
www.watsondwyer.com

Wordspeed
221 N. LaSalle #2463
Chicago, IL 60601
312/201-1171 • 312/201-1279 - fax

Actor-Friendly Jobs

A supportive job that allows you to pursue your career while still paying the bills is a rare and precious thing. These employers offer work that is particularly suited for the actor's schedule.

Chicago Housesitting & Pet Care
1341 W. Fullerton #177
Chicago, IL 60614
773/477-0136 • 773/477-0896 - fax
www.chicagopetcare.com

Chicago Trolley Co.
1709 S. Prairie
Chicago, IL 60616
312/663-0260

Movie Facts, Inc.
1870 Busse Highway #200
Des Plaines, IL 60016
847/299-9700 • 847/299-2321 - fax

Museum of Science & Industry
57th and Lake Shore
Chicago, IL
773/684-9844 • 773/684-0019 - fax
www.msichicago.org

The Princeton Review
Attn. Robb Rabito
2847 N. Sheffield
Chicago, IL 60657
773/868-4400
800/2REVIEW
www.review.com

Spirit of Chicago
Ed Carrella
312/836-7888

SST Communications
1840 S. Halsted
Chicago, IL 60608
312/563-1644
www.sstcommunications.com

Steppenwolf Theatre Telemarketing
Chuck Winans
312/932-2462

A Taste of California
2211 N. Elston
Chicago, IL 60614
773/235-9463 • 773/235-2633 - fax

Those Funny Little People Enterprises
8128 S. Madison
Burr Ridge, IL 60521
630/325-3320 • 630/325-8489 - fax
www.thosefunnylittlepeople.com

Training

Lookingglass' "Baron in the Trees" – pictured: Adrian Danzig, Heidi Stillman – photo: Liz Lauren

Learning the Art of Acting

Let it appear so; make your vaunting true,

And it shall please me well. For mine own part,

I shall be glad to learn of noble men.

By Doug Long

If anyone thinks acting is a fair profession, especially financially, they're not an actor. Many actors make less money acting in a given year than the couple thousand they may spend on a voice-over tape, the several hundred they may invest in headshots, or the money they could spend on additional training.

You need headshots or you can't even audition. But training? Unlike other professions, acting doesn't require a specific degree, and there is no one prescriptive series of courses that will assure you work.

But without it, what kind of actor are you? Acting involves skills and disciplines that can be learned in academic, studio and/or theatre settings; raw talent simply isn't enough.

"While an actor's instinct is the wellspring of their creativity in an explorative rehearsal process, without a secure scaffolding of technique this intuitive work is often unrepeatable or unmodifiable," says director Abigail Deser. "I look to work with actors who understand how to read a text, who are able to access both the emotional and physical aspects of their instrument, whose bodies and voices are free to support their action choices and tools for artistic discovery. I believe that theatre training is very important, whether it be in a formal, academic setting or through practical experience and mentorship."

According to Deser, good actors keep developing, although not always in the areas that need the most attention.

"Physical work is, from my perspective, the aspect of an actor's work that sometimes gets rusty—the willingness to improvise physically and vocally that sometimes gets left by the wayside as actors become older in their careers and farther away from their more formal training," Deser says. "Any work that will keep the actors surprising themselves would be my answer: voice workshops, work with techniques that they are unfamiliar with, work that keeps them curious and daring."

Training and the audition

Unlike directors, designers and stage managers—actors aren't usually already "invited to the party" of putting on a play—they must audition. Any training must come to the fore so an actor can give his or her best.

Goodman Theatre casting director Tara Lonzo stresses that actors should not think of auditions as training environments. She hesitated to give advice on actor training, since she said there is no magic combination of classes that would assure an actor a role at the Goodman.

"It's important to remember the simple fact that I am not your coach, I am not your teacher, I'm not going to give you feedback," Lonzo says. "I'm not here for you, although I really want you to be good."

She said she has high expectations for any actor auditioning for The Goodman. This includes knowing some of the basics of audition etiquette: Honor the time limit and have plenty of memorized monologues ready at all times.

Occasionally a director will make special requests: "Mary Zimmerman wants people who can do very physical work," Lonzo says.

She did share one piece of advice, though: Start by working at the many non-Equity theatres in town.

"You're not going to get a lead at the Goodman if you haven't done much else, no matter how good you are," she says. "You can work in this city. Someone's gonna put you in their play. And it's likely I'll know someone involved with that company. That's a great way to get in."

She also recommends that actors who are making their living acting in shows at night should use their daytime accumulating more skills.

"You could take a foreign language class, a fencing class, a Shakespeare class. Read plays," Lonzo says. "Get in shape, especially if you want to compete with L.A. actors. You will be more flexible. It gives you more opportunities."

Lonzo says actors who can speak another language fluently have a definite advantage for certain roles. The same goes for dialects, although if it's on your resume, casting directors will expect you to be able to do it well now. In addition, actors who can play a musical instrument, sing or dance well will be qualified for many roles over actors who can't. It's never too late to start or brush up any of these skills.

Training in Chicago

There are several undergraduate and graduate acting programs at universities and colleges in the Chicago area which offer extensive courses. Actors who have already received such training can take individual courses with the many studios and private teachers in town. Areas of specialty include vocal work, dance, Meisner acting, improvisation and auditioning. Many teachers are listed in **The Book** and in issues of PERFORMINK.

According to many acting coaches, which classes to choose depends on two things: what training you've already had and where you want your career to go. Some actors only plan on a stage career. Some see Chicago as a "stepping stone" to a film or TV career in L.A. or New York. Some want to support themselves in voice-overs and industrials. Most actors consult other actors when looking for the best classes, but another place to start is with the training centers themselves.

Many of the local training programs start with an interview; some programs don't let everyone in. Most accommodate the trained, working actor and the beginner.

One aspect that guides previously trained actors when choosing classes is finding something that complements what they've learned already. Training for commercials and industrials, for example, is not usually included in a university program. As a result, many non-academic acting programs in Chicago offer topics such as voice-over, acting for the camera and ear prompter.

When shopping for classes, many actors take into consideration the reputation and/or name value of the teacher. Finding a teacher that is the right "match" for an actor can mean many things: What skills can that person teach me? Just because this worked for another actor, will it work for me? Will I get individual attention and will my training be tailored to my strengths and weaknesses?

No matter what training an actor chooses during a career, the key is to create your professional goals, select the training to get you there, and exploit those opportunities to their fullest.

"Having an opportunity to train is such a gift," Deser says. "Take it seriously and make it the focus of your world.

"Some of the best advice I ever heard was from a teacher I had in New York who said the training of an actor is not only constituted by the scene study, character, voice, movement and improvisation training you do in the classroom, but by the books you read, the art you look at, the music you listen to. And, I would add, the dreams you dream," Deser says. "It is all fodder for your imagination. Keep that most important of your instruments fed, watered and stimulated with the widest possible range of nutrients."

Acting Training Checklist

Training should be an ongoing process in an actor's life. There are skills to be acquired and maintained. However, you're most likely to get the most for your money if you ask yourself a few questions first.

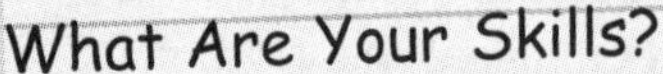

What Are Your Skills?

This is the first question you have to ask yourself. What are you already good at? What have you done? What do you list under special skills?

What Are Your Weaknesses?

What are you bad at? What skills do you need to acquire to make yourself more marketable?

What Are Your Goals?

Anyone can take a class, but if you've got a plan you're more likely to get the best out of the money you spend on training. Most training goals fall into one of two categories:

1. Maintenance

What skills have you acquired but haven't used recently? These are the skills you may need to maintain through a class.

2. Acquisition

What skills would you like to acquire? What skills do you need in order to get work?

Choosing a Class

There are a lot of aspects to a positive class experience. Some you can control, some you can't. Instructors are the most important aspect of the class. If possible, sit in on a class they teach. They may have a fabulous reputation, but does their style mesh with yours?

Coaches

Getting a coach is quite different from taking a class. They're especially useful for prepping audition pieces or getting help with a particularly difficult role. As with a class, carefully interview a potential coach. They're expensive, so be picky.

Summer Programs

A summer program can provide a period of intensive training. Unfortunately, they're also expensive and time-consuming. This is a major investment, and one you should research before enrolling.

Graduate Programs

The ultimate amount of training, of course, is going back to school for your MFA or MA. An MFA is considered, by many institutions, to be a terminal degree, which means that once you've acquired the degree you can teach. Such a program can also hook you up with a peer group of serious artists that can lead to opportunities later.

Acting Classes

Act One Studios, Inc.

(See our ad on page 34)

640 N. LaSalle #535
Chicago, IL 60610
312/787-9384 • 312/787-3234 - fax
www.actone.com

Commercial Technique I - Get "camera-ready" for all types of commercial auditions.

Industrial Film & Ear Prompter - Learn to analyze and perform technical scripts and use an ear prompter.

TV & Film I, II & Workshop - Learn the "ins and outs" of the film and television world.

Fundamentals I, II and Scene & Monologue Workshop - Learn to make efffective choices from the script.

Acting Instinctively - Flexibility, creativity, and imaginative freedom are explored.

Meisner Technique I, II & Workshop - Leads to a very truthful moment-to-moment style of acting.

Monologue Workshop - Prepare two to four monologues for auditions.

Audition Technique I & II - Learn the art of cold reading theatre auditions.

Shakespeare Beg. & Adv. - Approaches based on the work of Shakespeare & Co.

Masters Class - An ongoing scene study class taught by Steve Scott.

Voice-Over I & II - Learn what it takes to be successful in the voice-over market.

Movement Scene Study - Learn to bring a physical life to your character.

Actors' Center

Kay Martinovich
3047 N. Lincoln #390
Chicago, IL 60657
773/549-3303 • 773/549-0749 - fax

Technique (based on Meisner)
Monologues • Scene Study
Physical Character Work
Technique on Camera • TV/Film on Camera
Beginning Scene Study
Auditioning Technique
Acting in Chicago: Where Do I Start?

The Actors Gymnasium

Circus & Performing Arts School
Noyes Cultural Arts Center - 927 Noyes St.
Evanston, IL 60201
847/328-2795 • 847/328-3495 - fax
www.enteract.com/~actorgym

Circus Arts • Stage Combat
Physical Comedy • Scene Study
Capoeira • Drum Performance
Adaptation for the Stage • Commedia

Your body is an instrument--we'll teach you to play it. A variety of physical performance skills, from trapeze to tap dance, juggling to mime. Professional-level classes, run jointly with the Lookingglass Theatre Company. Convenient Chicago and Evanston locations. SAFD stage combat certification workshops. Master classes with renowned performers.

Actors Workshop

(See our ad on page 44)

Michael Colucci
1350 N. Wells #F521
Chicago, IL 60610
312/337-6602 • 312/337-6604 - fax
888/COLUCCI
www.actorsworkshop.org

Beginning Acting-On Camera

Advanced Acting-On Camera

Private Coaching: Ear Prompter, Monologue, Cold Reading, Commercial

Actors Workshop offers weekly ongoing classes for all levels. Each class starts with vocal warm-up, then commercials & scenes on-camera, which you can add to your demo reel. Call 1-888-COLUCCI to arrange a free visit and consultation with director Michael Colucci, author of ***Vocal Workout Booklet****.*

The Artistic Home

Cornelia Arts Building
1800 W. Cornelia
Chicago, IL 60618
773/395-5168 • 708/387-7286

Technique 1, 2, 3

Advanced Repetition

Scene Study

Audition Intensive

Acting for Film 1 & 2

Voice for the Actor

Beginning Playwrighting

The Artistic Home's curriculum is a Meisner-based technique for actors, augmented by L.A. and Chicago working experience, that emphasizes living moment to moment, making strong choices and developing emotional freedom. Playwrights and young directors are offered hands-on experience in scene study, showcases, on-camera and workshops of new scripts.

Instructors: Kathy Scambiattera, John Mossman, Robert Mello, Monica Payne, Penelope Milford, Patrick Thornton, Gillian Kelly

The Audition Studio

(See our ad on page 44)

20 W. Hubbard #2E
Chicago, IL 60610
312/527-4566 • 312/527-9085 - fax

Beginning Acting • Cold Reading II
On-Camera

Scene Study (Beginning and Advanced)

Monologue • Voice Technique

Voice-over (Beginning and Advanced)

Shakespeare Workshop

Ongoing Workshop Series: Voice-Over, Getting Started in the Business, Commericial On-Camera

Beginning Acting - Part 1 & 2: Weekly scene work, improvisation and script analysis help you build a strong foundation.

Cold Reading II - The twelve guideposts are taught through weekly cold reading situations.

On Camera - Strengthen your on-camera auditions. These courses cover all aspects of the commercial, industrial and film audition.

Scene Study (Beginning and Advanced) - In-depth scene work, this class focuses on performance and the rehearsal process.

Monologue - Prepare audition pieces for theatres and agents. Actors will be assigned three pieces from classical to contemporary.

Voice Technique - Based on Kristin Linklater's vocal progression.

Voice-Over (Beginning and Advanced) - Get an inside look into the world of voice-Over. Explore various techniques for breaking down copy. Includes three sessions in a professional recording studio.

Shakespeare Workshop - Combining technical and visceral approaches to the text, this class will provide the actor with the vocal, physical, and emotional equipment necessary for the playing of the classics.

Ongoing Workshop Series - Voice-over, Directing, Getting Started in the Business, Commercial On-Camera

List of Instructors: Kurt Naebig, Rachael Patterson, Lee Roy Rogers, Peter Forster, Phyllis Schuringa, Jack Bronis, Linda Gillum, Chris Stolte, Jim Johnson, Pat Van Oss, Lawrence Grimm

Black Ensemble Theatre
4520 N. Beacon
Chicago, IL 60640
773/769-4451 • 773/769-4533 - fax
Jackie Taylor Workshop - Designed to upgrade performance skills by incorporating acting, dance and music.
Teaching Artists to be Teachers in the Classroom

Center Theater's Training Program for Actors, Directors, Playwrights, and Singers
(See our ad above)
1346 W. Devon
Chicago, IL 60660
773/508-0200 • 773/508-9584 - fax
Professional Classes for beginning to advanced levels:
Technique
Scene Study
Monologues
Camera Technique
Playwrighting
Directing
Advanced Characterization
Audition Intensive
Shakespeare
Singing
Chicago's most complete professional training medium for actors, directors, playwrights and singers, built on the philosophy that professional theater training is essential to establish the theater artist to prosper in the field. Our staff consists exclusively of professionals that augment personal experience to broaden the knowledge of the training artist.

Chicago Actors Studio
1567 N. Milwaukee
Chicago, IL 60622
773/645-0222 • 773/645-0040 - fax
www.actors-studio.net
Acting as a Craft (Master Class)
Voice & Diction • Creating a Character
Scene Study • Shakespeare
Auditioning & Marketing
The Ear Prompter
Film, Commercial & Industrial Techniques
Making it in Trade Shows

CTM Productions
228 State St.
Madison, WI 53703
608/255-2080
www.theatreforall.com
Acting for Adults

Dell Arte School of Physical Theatre
P.O. Box 816
Blue Lake, CA 95525
707/668-5663
707/668-5665 - fax
www.dellarte.com
One year full-time physical theatre performance program and summer workshops.

Eileen Boevers Performing Arts Workshop
595 Elm Pl. #210
Highland Park, IL 60035
847/432-8223 • 847/432-5214 - fax
www.appletreetheatre.com

ETA Creative Arts
7558 S. South Chicago
Chicago, IL 60619
773/752-3955 • 773/752-8727 - fax
Adult Acting - Beginning and Advanced
Sound • Lighting • Stage Management
How to Audition for Commercials

Training

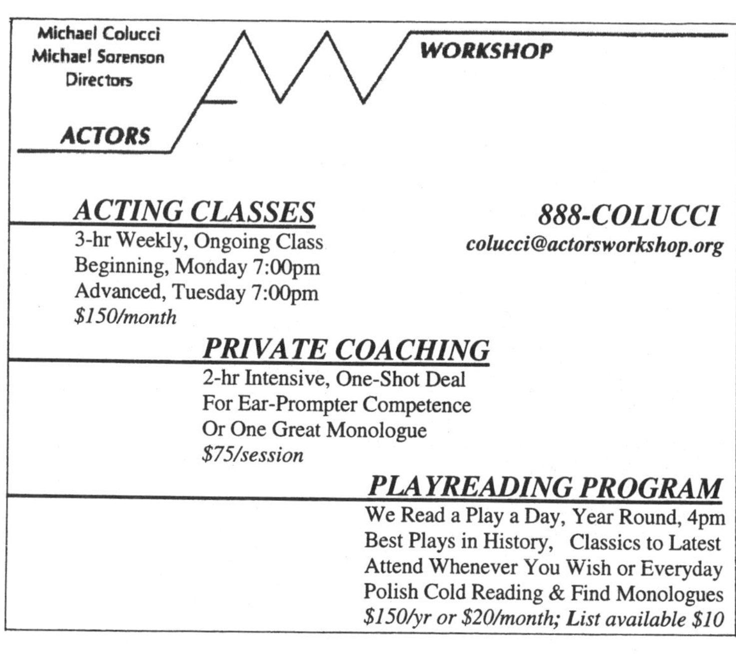
Michael Colucci
Michael Sorenson
Directors
ACTORS
WORKSHOP
ACTING CLASSES
3-hr Weekly, Ongoing Class
Beginning, Monday 7:00pm
Advanced, Tuesday 7:00pm
$150/month
888-COLUCCI
colucci@actorsworkshop.org
PRIVATE COACHING
2-hr Intensive, One-Shot Deal
For Ear-Prompter Competence
Or One Great Monologue
$75/session
PLAYREADING PROGRAM
We Read a Play a Day, Year Round, 4pm
Best Plays in History, Classics to Latest
Attend Whenever You Wish or Everyday
Polish Cold Reading & Find Monologues
$150/yr or $20/month; List available $10

MYSTERY & SECRET ■ RELATIONSHIP ■ DISCOVERIES
IMPORTANCE ■ EVENTS ■ PLACE ■ OPPOSITES
You're Brilliant.
Are your auditions?
Get the training that helps you get the job.
THE
Audition
STUDIO
312.527.4566
Observe a class for free. Then decide.

Fleetwood-Jourdain Theatre
2010 Dewey Ave.
Evanston, IL, 60201
847/328-5740 • 847/328-9093 - fax

GATE
(See our ad below)
Gregory Abels Training Ensemble
28 W. 27th St.
New York, NY 10001
212/689-9371
888/277-GATE
www.GATEacting.com
Study at the highest level with Master Teacher Gregory Abels and faculty.
Explore New York City as your base.
One intense, disciplined year of thirteen conservatory courses and workshops.
Ensemble of only 12 student actors ensures careful attention to craft.
Two productions performed for the public.
Scholarships available.
Not for absolute beginners.
Auditions held in Chicago.
Separate two-week Summer Workshop.

The Green Room
P.O. Box 6242
Chicago, IL 60680-6242
312/458-0883
Scene Study
Ongoing Scene Study
Directing
Actorcize

Illinois Theatre Center
P.O. Box 397
Park Forest, IL 60466
708/481-3510 • 708/481-3693 - fax
Acting Workshop (by invitation only)
Advanced Acting Ensemble (permission of instructor only)
Beginning Acting for Adults

It's Only A Stage
1847B W. Jefferson Ave.
Naperville, IL 60540
630/416-7974
www.onlyastage.com

John Robert Powers Entertainment Company
27 E. Monroe #200
Chicago, IL 60603
312/726-1404 • 312/726-8019 - fax
www.johnrobertpowers.com
TV 1 • TV 2 • TV 3

Movement Theatre Laboratory
Dawn Arnold
2970 N. Sheridan #1021
Chicago, IL 60657
773/327-1572
The Movement Theatre Laboratory of The Moving Dock Theatre Company is an opportunity for actors to expand their study and application of various movement approaches to theatre. For information on how to become a part of the ensemble or about workshops offered by The Moving Dock, call 773/327-1572.

The Neo-Futurists
5153 N. Ashland
Chicago, IL 60640
773/275-5255
www.neofuturists.org
Neo-Futurist Performance Workshop
Advanced Neo-Futurist Performance Workshop
Both classes are studies in writing, directing and performing your own work.

New American Theatre
118 N. Main St.
Rockford, IL 61101-1102
815/963-9343

The North Shore Theatre of Wilmette
3000 Glenview Rd.
Wilmette, IL 60091
847/256-9694
Scene Study

Phoenix Rising Theatre
P.O. Box 4378
Wheaton, IL 60189-4378
312/409-2271 • 630/545-2087 - fax
www.enteract.com/~mmaning/Phoenix

Brenda Pickleman
535 N. Michigan #2914
Chicago, IL 60611
773/472-6550 • 630/887-0529
Using intensive on-camera scene study and a variety of teaching methods, this workshop is designed to train serious actors to successfully compete in the LA market for Film and Television. Workshops are held on Tuesday evenings in the heart of Chicago. Brenda Pickleman - 630/887-0529.

Piven Theatre Workshop
(See our ad on the following page)
927 Noyes
Evanston, IL 60201
847/866-6597 • 847/866-6614 - fax
Theatre Games • Story Theatre
Improv & Scene Study
Intermediate to Professional Scene Study

Plasticene
2122 N. Winchester #1F
Chicago, IL 60614
312/409-0400
www.plasticene.com
Summer Physical Theatre Intensive
Ongoing Workshops

Roadworks
1144 Fulton Market #105
Chicago, IL 60607
312/492-7150
312/492-7155 - fax
www.roadworks.org

Sarantos Studios
2857 N. Halsted
Chicago, IL 60657
773/528-7114 • 773/528-7153 - fax
Feature Film Acting
Scene Study
Monologue Preparation
On-Camera Auditioning
Acting for Beginners
We specialize in teaching proven techniques that allow you to be exciting and believable every time you perform or audition. For Theatre, TV, Commercials, Industrials, and Feature Film.
We invite you to observe a class free. Talk to our students about their rapid progress. See for yourself what we offer.

Scrap Mettle Soul
773/275-3999 • 773/561-3852 - fax
Story Gathering for Performance
Verbal and Physical Storytelling

Stage Actors Ensemble
656 W. Barry
Chicago, IL 60657
773/252-5433
members.aol.com/TSPChicago

Steppenwolf Theatre Company
758 W. North - 4th floor
Chicago, IL 60610
312/335-1888 x5603
312/335-0808 - fax
www.steppenwolf.org
The School at Steppenwolf (summer program)

Steven Ivcich Studio
The Professional Studio
5123 N. Clark
Chicago, IL 60640
773/343-5590
Professional Studio Program - 40 weeks of intensive training
Actors Workspace - 4-to-8 week classes

TinFish Productions
4247 N. Lincoln
Chicago, IL 60618
773/549-1888
www.Tinfish.org

Victory Gardens Theatre
2257 N. Lincoln
Chicago, IL 60614
773/549-5788 • 773/549-2779 - fax
www.victorygardens.org
Basic Acting
Introduction to Scenes & Monologues
Musical Theater • Speech & Movement
Dialects • Building a Character
Monologues • Scene Study
Improvisational Scene Study
Comedy Styles

Wisconsin Theatre Games Center
2397 Lime Kiln Rd.
Baileys Harbor, WI 54202
920/854-5072
Paul Sills One-Week Summer Improvisational Theatre Intensives

Kid's Classes

ALYO Children's Dance Theatre
P.O. Box 198672
Chicago, IL 60619
773/723-2596 • 773/723-7995 - fax

Beverly Art Center
2153 W. 111th
Chicago, IL 60643
773/445-3838 • 773/445-0386 - fax

BIZ-KIDZ
Young Actors Academy
708/243-4742
www.bizkidz.net
Professional, intensive audition and on-camera training and career guidance just for young performers ***and*** *their parents. Students' credits include: Film; television; Equity and community theater; live industrials and print. Reputable source of referral for casting. Visit www.bizkidz.net/page2castkidz.html to see talented young performers.*

Boitsov Classical Ballet
410 S. Michigan #300
Chicago, IL 60605
312/663-0844 • 312/939-2094 - fax

Borealis Theatre Company
P.O. Box 2443
Aurora, IL 60507
630/844-4928 • 630/844-5515 - fax

Chicago Academy for the Arts
1010 W. Chicago
Chicago, IL 60622
312/421-0202 • 312/421-3816 - fax
www.chicagoacademyforthearts.org

Chicago Moving Company
3035 N. Hoyne
Chicago , IL 60618
773/880-5402

Chicago Theatre Company
500 E. 67th
Chicago, IL 60637
773/493-0901 • 773/493-0360 - fax

CTM Productions
228 State St.
Madison, WI 53703
608/255-2080
www.theatreforall.com

Dancecenter North
540 N. Milwaukee
Libertyville, IL 60048
847/367-7970 • 847/367-7905 - fax
www.dancecenterNorth.com

DancInc
Nutrier West Center
7 Happ Rd.
Northfield, IL 60093
847/501-2024 • 847/501-3976

Eileen Boevers Performing Arts Workshop
595 Elm Pl. #210
Highland Park, IL 60035
847/432-8223 • 847/432-5214 - fax
www.appletreetheatre.com

Fieldcrest School of Performing Arts
11639 S. Ashland
Chicago, IL 60643
773/568-6706

Fleetwood-Jourdain Theatre
2010 Dewey Ave.
Evanston, IL 60201
847/328-5740 • 847/328-9093 - fax

Free Street Programs
1419 W. Blackhawk
Chicago, IL 60622
773/772-7248
www.freestreet.org

Golden's School of Dance
1548 Burgundy Pkwy.
Greenwood, IL 60103
630/540-0996 • 630/540-9650 - fax

Illinois Theatre Center
P.O. Box 397
Park Forest, IL 60466
708/481-3510 • 708/481-3693 - fax

It's Only A Stage
1847B W. Jefferson Ave.
Naperville, IL 60540
630/416-7974
www.onlyastage.com

Midwest Academy of Gymnastics
Body Xpressions Ltd.
30W315 Calumet Ave.
Warrenville, IL 60555
630/393-6225 • 630/393-6693 - fax
www.mwaogymnastics.org

The North Shore Theatre of Wilmette
3000 Glenview Rd.
Wilmette, IL 60910
847/256-9694

Northlight Theatre
9501 N. Skokie Blvd.
Skokie, IL 60076
847/679-9501
www.northlight.org

Oak Park Village Players
1006 Madison St.
Oak Park, IL 60302
708/524-1892

Phoenix Rising Theatre
P.O. Box 4378
Wheaton, IL 60189-4378
312/409-2271 • 630/545-2087 - fax
www.enteract.com/~mmaning/Phoenix

Piven Theatre Workshop
(See our ad on page 47)
927 Noyes
Evanston, IL 60201
847/866-6597 • 847/866-6614 - fax

Players Workshop of Second City
(see our ad on page 213)
2936 N. Southport
Chicago, IL 60657
773/929-6288 • 773/477-8022 - fax
www.intelli.com/pw

Shakespeare on the Green
Barat College - 700 E. Westleigh Rd.
Lake Forest, IL 60045
847/604-6344 • 847/604-6342 - fax
www.sotg.pac.barat.edu

Dance Classes

Academy of Movement and Music
605 Lake St.
Oak Park, IL 60302
708/848-2329 • 708/848-2391 - fax
Ballet, Jazz, Modern, Creative Movement, Spanish

American Dance Center Ballet Co.
10464 W. 163rd Pl.
Orland Park, IL 60462
708/747-4969 • 708/747-0424 - fax
Ballet, Jazz, Modern, Tap, Swing

Art Linkletter's Young World
1263 S. Main St.
Lombard, IL 60148
630/495-4940
Ballet, Jazz, Tap, Acrobat, Lyrical

Authentic Mid East Belly Dance
Jasmin Jahal
P.O. Box 56037
Chicago, IL 60656-0037
773/693-6300 • 773/693-6302 - fax
www.jasminjahal.com
Traditional Middle Eastern & Classical Egyptian Dance

Internationally famous performer/instructor Jasmin Jahal offers tasteful, authentic solo and group performances for private engagements, corporate events, theatre and film. Weekly dance classes and private lessons taught throughout Chicago and suburbs. Instructional and performance videos available. Recognized artist supported by Illinois Arts Council.

Ballet Chicago
185 N. Wabash #2305
Chicago, IL 60601
312/251-8833
312/251-8840 - fax
www.balletchicago.org
Ballet

Belle Plaine Studio
2014 W. Belle Plaine
Chicago, IL 60618
773/935-1890
773/935-1909 - fax
Ballet, Jazz, Modern, Tap, Belly Dance, Flamenco, NIA, Swing

Betsy Herskind School of Ballet
2740 W. Touhy
Chicago, IL 60645
773/973-6446
Ballet, Tap

Beverly Art Center
2153 W. 111th
Chicago, IL 60643
773/445-3838 • 773/445-0386 - fax
Ballet, Jazz, Modern, Tap

Boitsov Classical Ballet
410 S. Michigan #300
Chicago, IL 60605
312/663-0844 • 312/939-2094 - fax
Ballet - Vaganova Technique (Moscow Bolshoi Theatre system of training)

Boulevard Arts Center
6011 S. Justine
Chicago, IL 60636
773/476-4900 • 773/476-5951 - fax
Ballet, Modern, Tap, African

Celeste Dance Studio
9500 S. Avers
Evergreen Park, IL 60805
708/425-1122

Chicago Human Rhythm Project
2936 N. Southport #210
Chicago, IL 60657
773/296-0869 • 773/296-0968 - fax
www.humanrhythmproject.com
Adult tap instruction, all levels, specifically offered during their festival season in August.

Chicago Moving Company
3035 N. Hoyne
Chicago , IL 60618
773/880-5402
Modern, Aerobic Jazz, Creative Movement, Special Populations

Chicago Multicultural Dance Center
806 S. Plymouth
Chicago, IL 60605
312/461-0030
312/461-1184 - fax
Ballet, Jazz, Tap, Latin, West African

Chicago National Association of Dance Masters
5411 E. State St. #202
Rockford, IL 61108
815/397-6052
815/397-6799 - fax
www.cnadm.com
Workshops only; no ongoing classes.

Dance Arts, Ltd.
280 Palatine Rd.
Wheeling, IL 60090
847/459-9071
Ballet, Jazz, Modern, Tap, Hip-Hop

Dance Center Evanston
610 Davis St.
Evanston, IL 60201
847/328-6683
847/328-6656 - fax
Ballet, Jazz, Modern, Tap, Ballroom, Pilates

Dance Center of Columbia College
4730 N. Sheridan
Chicago, IL 60640
773/989-3310
773/271-7046 - fax
www.colum.edu
Ballet, Modern, Jazz, Tap, African

Dance Dimensions
595B N. Pinecrest Rd.
Bolingbrook, IL 60440
630/739-1195
Ballet, Jazz, Tap, Ballroom, Swing, Tumbling

Dance Therapy Center
Fine Arts Building
410 S. Michigan
Chicago, IL 60605
312/461-9826 • 312/461-9843 - fax
Ballet, Modern, Ballroom

Dancecenter North
540 N. Milwaukee
Libertyville, IL 60048
847/367-7970 • 847/367-7905 - fax
www.dancecenterNorth.com
Ballet, Jazz, Tap, Irish Step Dance, Social Dance, Urban Jazz

DancInc
Nutrier West Center
7 Happ Rd.
Northfield, IL 60093
847/501-2024 • 847/501-3976 - fax
Ballet, Jazz, Modern, Character, Flamenco, Hip-Hop, Pointe, Swing, Tap, Tumbling

Diana's Dance and Fitness Dynamics, Ltd.
Diana Duda
429 Park Dr.
Glenwood, IL 60425
708/755-8292 • 708/799-7613 - fax
Ballet, Jazz, Tap, Ballroom

Discovery Center
2940 N. Lincoln
Chicago, IL 60657
773/348-8120 • 773/880-6164 -fax
www.discoverycenter.cc
Ballet, Jazz, Modern, Tap, Bachta, Ballroom, Belly Dance, Contemporary Latin, Ethnic, Flamenco, Hip-Hop, Salsa, Social Dance, Swing, Tango

Dorothy's Stagecraft Academy
116 E. 115th
Chicago, IL 60628
773/821-6128
Ballet, Jazz, Tap, Acrobatic

Barbara Dubosq
1068 Hillcrest
Highland Park, IL 60035
847/831-3383
Ballet, Tap, Creative

Emergence Dance Theatre
804 1/2 Market
P.O. Box 186
DeKalb, IL 60115
815/758-6613
Ballet, Jazz, Modern, Tap

Evanston School of Ballet Foundation
1933 Central St. - 1st floor
Evanston, IL 60201
847/475-9225
Ballet

Fluid Measure Performance Company
6111 N. Paulina
Chicago, IL 60660
773/338-0519
Contact Improvisation Workshops, Summer Interdisciplinary Performance Workshops

Golden's School of Dance
1548 Burgundy Pkwy.
Greenwood, IL 60103
630/540-0996 • 630/540-9650 - fax
Ballet, Jazz, Tap, Ballroom, Clogging, Lyrical

Gus Giordano Dance Center
614 Davis
Evanston, IL 60201
847/866-9442 • 847/866-9228 - fax
Ballet, Jazz, Modern, Tap, Hip-Hop, Social Dance

Hedwig Dances
Administrative Offices
2936 N. Southport #210
Chicago, IL 60657
773/871-0872 • 773/296-0968 - fax
www.enteract.com\~hedwig
Modern, African, Butoh (Japanese Theatrical Dance form), Contemporary and World Dance, Latin, Physical Theatre Lab, Salsa, Spanish Flamenco, Swing, Visiting Artist Series

Jo's Footwork Studio
1500 Walker
Western Springs, IL 60558
708/246-6878
Ballet, Jazz, Modern, Tap, Hip-Hop, Musical Theatre

Joel Hall Dance Center
1511 W. Berwyn
Chicago, IL 60640
773/293-0900 • 773/293-1130 - fax
www.joelhall.com
Ballet, Jazz, Modern, Tap, Hip-Hop, African, Egyptian

Judith Svalander School of Ballet
83 E. Woodstock St.
Crystal Lake, IL 60014
815/455-2055
Ballet, Jazz, Modern, Tap, Character Dance, Drama, Musical Theatre, Pointe

Lou Conte Dance Studio
1147 W. Jackson
Chicago, IL 60607
312/850-9766 • 312/455-8240 - fax
Ballet, Jazz, Modern, Tap, Dance Fitness, Hip-Hop

Mayfair Academy of Fine Art
1025 E. 79th
Chicago, IL 60619
773/846-8180
Ballet, Jazz, Modern, Tap, Tumbling

Milwaukee Ballet
504 W. National Ave.
Milwaukee, WI 53204
414/643-7677 • 414/649-4066 - fax
www.milwaukeeballet.org
Ballet, Jazz, Modern, Spanish Character Dance

Muntu Dance Theatre of Chicago
6800 S. Wentworth #3E96
Chicago, IL 60621
773/602-1135 • 773/602-1134 - fax
African

Natyakalalayam Dance Company
2936 N. Southport #210
Chicago, IL 60657
773/296-1061 • 773/296-0968 - fax
www.hometown.aol.com/natyakala
Classical Indian Dance (Asian)

North Shore School of Dance
107 Highwood
Highwood, IL 60040
847/432-2060 • 847/432-4037 - fax
www.northshoredance.com
Ballet, Jazz, Modern, Tap, Hip-Hop

Old Town School of Folk Music
4544 N. Lincoln
Chicago, IL 60625
773/728-6000 • 773/728-6999 - fax
www.oldtownschool.org
Ballet, Jazz, Tap, African, Aztec, Belly, Breakdance, Flamenco, Flat-Foot, Hip-Hop, Hula, Indian, Irish, Latin, Mexican, Swing, Tango

Outabounds Performance Company
711 W. Main
Bensenville, IL 60106
630/860-0605

InterPlay Improvisation
Krystyna Parafinczuk
847/501-2024
Swing

Patterson School of Ballroom Dance
1240 Sunset Rd.
Winnetka, IL 60093
847/501-2523
Ballroom

Rockford Dance Company
711 N. Main
Rockford, IL 61103
815/963-3341 • 815/963-3541 - fax
www.rockforddancecompany.com
Ballet, Jazz, Modern, Tap, Ballroom, Tango Argentino

Royal Scottish Country Dance Society
Ree Grisham
3550 N. Lakeshore #227
Chicago, IL 60657
773/528-7824
Scottish Country

Ruth Page Foundation
School of Dance
1016 N. Dearborn
Chicago, IL 60610
312/337-6543 • 312/337-6542 - fax
www.ruthpage.com
Ballet, Jazz, Tap, Pilates

School of Performing Arts
200 E. 5th Ave. #132
Naperville, IL 60563
630/717-6622 • 630/717-5131 - fax
www.performing-arts.com
Ballet, Jazz, Modern, Tap, Hip-Hop

Shelley's School of Dance and Modeling, Ltd.
450 Peterson Rd.
Libertyville, IL 60048
847/816-1711
www.geocities.com/Broadway/Stage/2441
Ballet, Jazz, Modern, Tap, Hip-Hop, Lyrical, Musical Theatre, Pilates, Pointe

Barbara Silverman
773/267-3363
Ballet, Modern, Clogging, Square Dance

Emily Stein
773/868-9723
Ballet (pointe), Modern, History

Sara Stewart
6007 N. Menard
Chicago, IL 60646
773/763-6312

Teresa y los Preferidos
729 Lake Ave.
Wilmette, IL 60091
847/256-6614
Ballet, Flamenco

Tina Mangos Dance
773/282-5108
Ballroom, Movement for Performers, Latin, Swing

Von Heidecke School of Ballet
1239 S. Naper Blvd.
Naperville, IL 60540
630/527-1052 • 630/527-8427 - fax
Ballet, Pilates

Training

Stage Combat Classes

The Actors Gymnasium
Circus & Performing Arts School
Noyes Cultural Arts Center - 927 Noyes St.
Evanston, IL 60201
847/328-2795 • 847/328-3495 - fax
www.enteract.com/~actorgym

Your body is an instrument--we'll teach you to play it. A variety of physical performance skills, from trapeze to tap dance, juggling to mime. Professional-level classes, run jointly with the Lookingglass Theatre Company. Convenient Chicago and Evanston locations. SAFD stage combat certification workshops. Master classes with renowned performers.

Rachel Pergl
6658 N. Rockwell #1
Chicago, IL 60645
773/973-1073

R & D Choreography
7443 N. Hoyne #1N
Chicago, IL 60645
847/333-1494
www.theatrechicago.com/randd

R & D Choreography specializes in violence design, both onstage and on-camera. We offer fight choreography, special effects, and weapon rentals to help you achieve the zany slapstick, brutal combat, or acts of mayhem your production requires. We also conduct regular stage combat classes for the acting professional.

Modeling Classes

Model Image Center
1218 W. Belmont
Chicago, IL 60657
773/348-9349 • 773/348-9366 - fax
www.modelimagecenter.com

The Models Workshop
P.O. Box 3400
Chicago, IL 60654-0400
312/492-9991

Shelley's School of Dance and Modeling, Ltd.
450 Peterson Rd.
Libertyville, IL 60048
847/816-1711
www.geocities.com/Broadway/Stage/2441

Scriptwriting Classes

Center Theater's Training Program for Actors, Directors, Playwrights, and Singers
(See our ad on page 43)
1346 W. Devon
Chicago, IL 60660
773/508-0200 • 773/508-9584 - fax

Chicago Dramatists
1105 W. Chicago
Chicago, IL 60622
312/633-0630 • 312/633-0610 - fax

ETA Creative Arts
7558 S. South Chicago
Chicago, IL 60619
773/752-3955 • 773/752-8727 - fax

New Tuners Theatre
1225 W. Belmont
Chicago, IL 60657
773/929-7367

Victory Gardens Theatre
2257 N. Lincoln
Chicago, IL 60614
773/549-5788 • 773/549-2779 - fax
www.victorygardens.org

Coaches

Acting Coaches

Dawn Arnold
773/327-1572

BIZ-KIDZ
Young Actors Academy
708/243-4742
www.bizkidz.net
*Professional, intensive audition and on-camera training and career guidance just for young performers **and** their parents. Students' credits include: film; television; Equity and community theater; live industrials and print. Reputable source of referral for casting. Visit www.bizkidz.net/page2castkidz.html to see talented young performers.*

Belinda Bremner
773/871-3710
An audition is a job interview using someone else's words. The key to a successful audition is finding an author who tells your story in your words. Your choice of audition material speaks volumes. Decide what that message is and then craft your audition. Ideally suited for the well-trained actor looking for an edge.

Courtney Brown
3723 N. Southport
Chicago, IL 60613
773/878-3865
Brown is a fully certified teacher of the Alexander Technique who has practiced in Chicago for 8 years. He trained at the New Alexander School in London, where he worked with Margaret Goldie, Alexander's assistant for 20 years. Brown works with performing artists to achieve peak performance and self-coordination goals.

Dexter Bullard
2122 N. Winchester
Chicago, IL 60614
773/227-6487
Dexter Bullard is a Jefferson Cited director with ten years experience in casting and has taught acting and audition technique for over five years at University of Illinois, Columbia College, Actors' Center, and Audition Studio. Gain immediate results for auditions or breakthroughs in acting over a few sessions. Very affordable sliding scale.

Dale Calandra
773/508-0397
"Personal Training for the Total Actor"
Your Monologue is a SHOWCASE of your talent. ACT TO WIN! Contemporary to Classic, one-person shows, cold reading, on-camera, and callbacks. Over 500 actors privately coached since 1983. Creative Director, CTE's The Training Center; Artistic Director, Oak Park Festival Theatre.

Michael Colucci
Actor's Workshop
1350 N. Wells #F521
Chicago, IL 60610
312/337-6602 • 888/COLUCCI
312/337-6604 - fax
www.actorsworkshop.org
Michael specializes in the Ear-Prompter Intensive and A thru Z two-hour session, guaranteed to give the actor (not the beginner) competence and confidence in auditioning for industrial films. Likewise, a Monologue Intensive is available, where several selections are offered from which you choose and we develop one great piece. Since opening the Actors Workshop in 1991, Michael has worked with hundreds of actors in both these areas. (Commercial Technique also available.)

Ann Filmer
1539 N. Bell
Chicago, IL 60622
773/489-0843

Caitlin Hart
640 N. LaSalle
Chicago, IL 60610
773/381-9651
My coaching incorporates a Meisner approach to lay the groundwork for successful audition scenes and monologues. Structuring this background support allows you to behave with confidence and honesty at auditions. Monologues can be tailored to suit your needs. Presenting yourself professionally at auditions is also a focus. Credits include work in Chicago and NY. $50/hour.

Kevin Heckman
2600 W. Leland #3
Chicago, IL 60625
312/562-3748
Frightened of classical auditions? Nervous about working with Shakespeare? Learn to take control of your Shakespeare monologues by finding the clues he left for you. Kevin Heckman, veteran actor, director and teacher, offers private coaching on classical monologues. $25-35/hour.

Illinois Theatre Center
P.O. Box 397
Park Forest, IL 60466
708/481-3510 • 708/481-3693 - fax
Acting Workshop (by invitation only)
Advanced Acting Ensemble (permission of instructor only)
Beginning Acting for Adults

Lori Klinka
916 Rainbow Dr.
Glenwood, IL, 60425
708/709-0880 • 708/709-0881 - fax

Bob Kulhan
3638 N. Pine Grove #1
Chicago, IL 60613
773/296-4887
This is the first on-camera lab to incorporate the strengths of improvisation with the specifics of film and television auditions. Through genuine audition scripts and a realistic on-camera environment, you learn how to convey the meaning of the sides while bringing your personality to the audition. One-on-one or small groups only!

Ruth Landis, Inc.
773/463-3780 • 773/463-3683 - fax
A mind/body/spirit holistic approach to acting for theatre (monologues, scenes, cold reading), on-camera, and voice-over, striving to make auditioning and artistry a joyous experience, focusing on personal empowerment and relief of performance anxiety. Ruth has taught at Northwestern, Columbia, Roosevelt University, Victory Gardens and privately. $60.00 hourly.

Jaclyn Loewenstein
(formerly Greenberg)
2151 Ridge Ave. #2D
Evanston, IL 60201
847/866-8651

Michael Menendian
Raven Theatre
6931 N. Clark
Chicago, IL 60626
773/338-2177
STUDY PRIVATELY WITH RAVEN THEATRE ARTISTIC DIRECTOR MICHAEL MENENDIAN IN HOURLY SESSIONS ($30/session; 5 for $125). Whether fine-tuning existing monologues, developing new ones, and/or improving cold reading skills, Mr. Menendian works moment-to-moment with the actor to strengthen his/her grasp of craft and character development.

Janet B. Milstein
773/465-5804
Award-winning Acting Instructor at John Robert Powers, Janet has trained hundreds of actors, beginners to professionals. Her students continually get cast in Chicago theatre and have been signed by agents in Chicago, NY, and LA. Janet offers affordable private coaching in monologues and cold reading that will teach you the skills to audition powerfully and with confidence. Janet's book, ***111 One Minute Monologues****, will be released this spring by Smith and Kraus.*

Kurt Naebig
20 W. Hubbard
Chicago, IL 60610
630/495-7188 • 312/527-4566

Kathryn Nash
312/943-0167 • 312/943-0229 - fax
Acting - Voice - Speech Coach
Member - AEA, AFTRA, VASTA (Voice and Speech Trainers Association)
Private instruction specializing in:
Vocal techniques for stage and voice-overs.
Standard American diction.
Dialect acquisition and reduction.
Monologue coaching to integrate "kinesthetic, vocal, and emotional modes" within the acting process.

Cecilie O'Reilly
2023 N. Damen
Chicago, IL 60647
773/486-3649

Rick Plastina
1117 N. Taylor
Oak Park IL 60302
708/386-8270
Monologues and Dialogues: how to use an ear prompter.

Malcolm Rothman
3900 N. Lake Shore #12E
Chicago, IL 60613
773/281-4686
I provide intensive on-camera training and career guidance for experienced stage actors interested in getting into film, TV, and commercials. AEA-AFTRA-SAG actor with twenty years experience in Chicago and L.A. markets. Proven technique as taught by Amy Sunshine. No beginners. No contracts. No B.S.

Fredric Stone
5040 N. Marine #3A
Chicago, IL 60640
773/334-4196

A working professional actor/director with over 25 years experience (New York and Chicago) coaches actors in monologue and scene preparation for auditions - both contemporary and classical. He created and taught The Audition Workshop at Organic Theatre and currently teaches an 8-week Performing Shakespeare class at Victory Gardens Theatre.

Karen Vaccaro
1243 N. Damen
Chicago, IL 60622
773/201-0951

"The moment you lose yourself on stage marks the departure from truly living your part and the beginning of exaggerated false acting." Stanislavski

I can't say it any better than this. Together we create a space that is both disciplined yet nurturing. From the beginner to the working actor, you'll get the tools and the coaching needed to move your work and your career forward with grace and ease. Coaching for monologues - modern/classical/Shakespeare- career counseling and commercial copy. Credits include: Broadway, Off-Broadway, Steppenwolf, Goodman, Shakespeare Rep., Commercials, Television, Film.

Voice-Over Coaches

Helen Cutting
445 E. Ohio #1914
Chicago, IL 60611
312/527-1809

Helen Cutting is a 20-year veteran of the voice-over business. She has recorded thousands of television/radio commercials, promotions, animated videos, narrations, and has an English Theatre and training background.

Helen offers in-depth classes, private coaching in voice technique, demo tapes and consultations. All levels. Beginners welcome.

Charles Fuller
630/739-0044
630/739-3837 - fax

Sound Advice
(See our ad on page 59)
Kate McClanaghan
2028 W. Potomac #2 & 3
Chicago, IL 60622
773/772-9539 • 773/772-9006 - fax
www.voiceoverdemos.com

VoiceOver 101
Ray Van Steen
325 W. Huron #512
Chicago, IL 60610
312/587-1010 • 312/337-5125 - fax

Private, individual coaching sessions in voicing TV/radio commercials, narrations. Employs record/playback method in recording studio environment. Basics through production of voice-over demo. Van Steen is a published writer on the subject and has voiced thousands of commercials. Phone for free, no-obligation brochure. 312/587-1010.

Voice Over U
Sherri Berger
773/774-9559 • 773/774-9555 - fax
sherriberger.voicedemo.com

Sherri Berger has a sought-after ability to shape and/or renovate a performer's skill in the art of voice-overs. Using basic acting techniques, Sherri pinpoints a performer's strengths and weaknesses, keeps them in tune with trends, and helps them discover more interesting vocal nuances, styles and range capabilities.

Voices, Inc.
Charles Fuller
241 Douglas
Bolingbrook, IL 60440
630/739-0044
630/739-3837 - fax

Voices On
Thomas Test
1943 W. Belle Plaine
Chicago, IL 60613
773/528-7041

Your demo needs cutting-edge scripts and production values to stand out from the crowd. EVERY demo I've produced has resulted in agent representation for my students. Call Telly award-winning v/o talent Tom Test of "Voices On" at 773/528-7041 for private coaching, in-studio audition workshops, and demo production.

Dialect Coaches

Martin Aistrope
1243 N. Damen #2
Chicago, IL 60622
773/276-4665

Native Brit. Standard, Regional (Cockney, Scots, Irish, Yorks, Scouse, Geordie, etc.), Colonial (Aussie, NZ, SA, etc.). All technique and no music? Aaargh! Taped personal coaching, customized drill, facial exercises, tapes. You have a better ear than you think: Find out which one it is! Martin Aistrope, 773/276-4665.

Belinda Bremner
773/871-3710

An audition is a job interview using someone else's words. The key to a successful audition is finding an author who tells your story in your words. Your choice of audition material speaks volumes. Decide what that message is and then craft your audition. Ideally suited for the well-trained actor looking for an edge.

Kate DeVore
4451 N. Hamilton
Chicago, IL 60625
773/334-7203

Character-based dialect acquisition and coaching. The way we speak is an integral part of who we are; this principle informs technical coaching for sound changes, voice placement (resonance), and musicality of a dialect. Non role-specific dialect training also available, as is coaching in Standard American (accent reduction). Materials and personalized coaching tapes provided.

Cecilie O'Reilly
2023 N. Damen
Chicago, IL 60647
773/486-3649

Voice/Speech Coaches

Randy Buescher
Chicago/Naperville, IL
312/671-3181 • 708/352-0510

Randy Buescher Speech Level Voice Studio and Voice Therapy, Chicago/Naperville, 708-352-0510/312-671-3181. Can 98 Grammy Winners be wrong? Degreed in Music and Speech Pathology. All Styles.

Lia Corinth
847/328-4202

Kate DeVore
4451 N. Hamilton
Chicago, IL 60625
773/334-7203
Ten years experience as voice, speech and dialect coach; certified voice/speech pathologist specialized in performers' voice. Voice enhancement, exploration and development. Training in vocal projection, resonance, power, flexibility, ease and range. Vocal extremes (shouting and screaming) without injury. Vocal health and maintenance. Holistic approach to voice enhancement also available, incorporating energetic and complementary healing techniques to free and strengthen the voice.

Marina Gilman
5701 S. Dorchester
Chicago, IL 60637
773/955-0016
Marina Gilman is a certified Feldenkrais® Practitioner, licensed Speech and Language Pathologist, and holds an M.M. in Voice. She specializes in prevention and rehabilitation of voice professionals including singers, actors, and broadcast journalists. Her approach to teaching is a combination of somatic education and traditional voice training.

Richard Marriott
410 S. Michigan #920
Chicago, IL 60605
312/360-1728

Kathryn Nash
312/943-0167 • 312/943-0229 - fax
Acting - Voice - Speech Coach
Member- AEA, AFTRA, VASTA
(Voice and Speech Trainers Association)
Private instruction specializing in:
Vocal techniques for stage and voice-overs.
Standard American diction.
Dialect acquisition and reduction.
Monologue coaching to integrate "kinesthetic, vocal, and emotional modes" within the acting process.

Cecilie O'Reilly
2023 N. Damen
Chicago, IL 60647
773/486-3649

Professionally Speaking
(See our ad on page 61)
2033 W. Potomac - 2nd floor
Chicago, IL 60622
773/218-9183

Ann Wakefield
1500 N. LaSalle #3C
Chicago, IL 60610
312/751-9348

William Rush Voice Consultants
410 S. Michigan #528
Chicago, IL 60604
312/360-1039 • 630/620-1270
630/620-1271 - fax

Accompanists

Bobby Schiff Music Productions
363 Longcommon Rd.
Riverside IL 60546
708/442-3168
708/447-3719

Singing Coaches

Tamara Anderson
1023 Barberry Ln.
Round Lake Beach, IL 60073
847/546-5548 • 847/546-5717 - fax
Tamara has over 25 years of performance experience and has taught hundreds of beginner and professional students with her state-of-the-art vocal techniques. Get more out of your voice with personalized instruction. Realize your full potential by getting the tools, confidence and direction you need. Do you have a damaged voice, pitch problems, vocal fatigue, trouble getting the emotion across, stage fright, or just want to have a better, more versatile voice, while keeping it extremely healthy? E-mail: VOXDOC@aol.com

---

Bridget Becker
773/465-2086

Randy Buescher
Chicago/Naperville, IL
312/671-3181 • 708/352-0510
Randy Buescher Speech Level Voice Studio and Voice Therapy, Chicago/Naperville, 708-352-0510/312-671-3181. Can 98 Grammy Winners be wrong? Degreed in Music and Speech Pathology. All Styles.

Mark Burnell
2008C W. Potomac
Chicago, IL 60622
773/862-2665 • 773/862-2655 - fax
members.aol.com\burnell88\
Mark Burnell (773)862-COOL
Broadway, jazz, pop, rhythm & blues. Get your show together: repertoire, arrangements, demo recording. Prepare your audition: style, phrasing, transposition, rehearsal tapes. Work your chops: technique, flexibility, improvisation, ornamentation. MFA and 10 years with Carnegie Mellon Music Theatre Department. burnell88@aol.com

---

The Center For Voice
410 S. Michigan #635
Chicago, IL 60605
312/360-1111
A non-profit arts organization promoting singing through education and performance. Private lessons for all styles. Call for brochure.

Center Theater's Training Program for Actors, Directors, Playwrights, and Singers
(See our ad on page 43)
1346 W. Devon
Chicago, IL 60660
773/508-0200 • 773/508-9584 - fax

Dr. Ronald Combs
917 W. Castlewood
Chicago, IL 60640
773/271-8425

Lia Corinth
847/328-4202

Dancecenter North
540 N. Milwaukee
Libertyville, IL 60048
847/367-7970 • 847/367-7905 - fax
www.dancecenterNorth.com

DePaul University - Community Music Division
(See our ad below)
804 W. Belden
Chicago, IL 60614-3296
773/325-7262 • 773/325-7264 - fax
music.depaul.edu

Training

Kate DeVore
4451 N. Hamilton #3
Chicago, IL 60625
773/334-7203

David H. Edelfelt
1243 W. Foster
Chicago, IL 60640
773/878-SING
Through the use of solid vocal technique and unique coaching skills, I will guide you toward doing anything you wish with your voice, whether in Musical Theater, Classical or Cabaret, Jazz or Pop. I aim to enable you to allow every decision you make regarding your singing to be one of artistic choice, and not of technical or emotional limitation. 55 minute lessons for $55.

Marina Gilman
5701 S. Dorchester
Chicago, IL 60637
773/955-0016
Marina Gilman is a certified Feldenkrais® Practitioner, licensed Speech and Language Pathologist, and holds an M.M. in Voice. She specializes in prevention and rehabilitation of voice professionals including singers, actors, and broadcast journalists. Her approach to teaching is a combination of somatic education and traditional voice training.

Donald Knight
312/943-5339

Richard Marriott
410 S. Michigan #920
Chicago, IL 60605
312/360-1728

Music Workshop
Bob Kalal
4900 W. 28th Pl.
Cicero, IL 60804
708/652-4040
members.xoom.com\musicwkshop

Northwestern University School of Music
(ask for referrals)
711 Elgin Rd.
Evanston, IL 60208
847/491-7485
847/491-5260 - fax

Jilann Gabriel
410 S. Michigan #630
Chicago, IL 60605
800/831-3139 • 312/692-1703
773/237-0249

Old Town School of Folk Music
4544 N. Lincoln
Chicago, IL 60625
773/728-6000 • 773/728-6999 - fax
www.oldtownschool.org

Rebecca Patterson
3007 W. Eastwood
Chicago, IL 60625
773/588-0692
The focus of this studio is vocal technique. The approach is founded on principles of motion of tension-free singing, breath management, and expressive phrasing for all musical styles. Studio is conveniently located in Chicago's Ravenswood area, and students range from professional musicians to actors who are singing for the first time. Twenty years of teaching experience. Rebecca Patterson, 773/588-0692.

Rak Vocal & Healing Clinic
6056 W. Irving Park
Chicago, IL 60634
773/283-8349
Welcome to the RAK VOCAL & HEALING CLINIC where adult singers, actors and dancers become vocal athletes! Learn warm-ups/cool-down, preventive care, how to sing more healthfully when vocally-strained, and a basic technique to which you can apply any style of singing with strength, reliability, and charisma.

Patricia Rusk
1263 W. Foster
Chicago, IL 60640
773/784-7875

School of Performing Arts
200 E. 5th Ave. #132
Naperville, IL 60563
630/717-6622
630/717-5131 - fax
www.performing-arts.com

Sherwood Conservatory of Music
1312 S. Michigan
Chicago, IL 60605
312/427-6267
312/427-6677 - fax

Barbara Silverman
773/267-3363

Peggy Smith-Skarry
(See our ad on the following page)
1347 W. Winona
Chicago, IL 60640
773/728-5240

The Voice Works
Ruth Allyn
Near North, Chicago, IL 60610
312/944-3867

What a Voice Productions (The Vocal Studio)
(See our ad below)
Karyn Sarring
P.O. Box 577227
Chicago, IL 60657
773/769-6480
773/989-0033 - fax
www.whatavoice.com

William Rush Voice Consultants
410 S. Michigan #528
Chicago, IL 60604
312/360-1039
630/620-1270
630/620-1271 - fax

Wilmette Voice & Piano Studio
847/251-7449

Frank Winkler
1765 George Ct.
Glenview, IL 60025
847/729-1893

Instrument Coaches

Academy of Movement and Music
605 Lake St.
Oak Park, IL 60302
708/848-2329 • 708/848-2391 - fax

DePaul University - Community Music Division
(See our ad on page 63)
804 W. Belden
Chicago, IL 60614-3296
773/325-7262 • 773/325-7264 - fax
music.depaul.edu

Old Town School of Folk Music
4544 N. Lincoln
Chicago, IL 60625
773/728-6000
773/728-6999 - fax
www.oldtownschool.org

Northwestern University School of Music (Ask for referrals)
711 Elgin Rd.
Evanston, IL 60208
847/491-7485
847/491-5260 - fax

School of Performing Arts
200 E. 5th Ave. #132
Naperville, IL 60563
630/717-6622
630/717-5131 - fax
www.performing-arts.com

Sherwood Conservatory of Music
1312 S. Michigan
Chicago, IL 60605
312/427-6267 • 312/427-6677 – fax

Wilmette Voice & Piano Studio
847/251-7449

Movement Coaches

Courtney Brown
3723 N. Southport
Chicago, IL 60613
773/878-3865

Brown is a fully certified teacher of the Alexander Technique who has practiced in Chicago for 8 years. He trained at the New Alexander School in London, where he worked with Margaret Goldie, Alexander's assistant for 20 years. Brown works with performing artists to achieve peak performance and self-coordination goals.

Chicago Center for the Alexander Technique
Ed Bouchard
2216 W. Palmer #2R
Chicago, IL 60647
773/862-3320
773/235-9534 - fax

T. Daniel and Laurie Willets
c/o T. Daniel Productions
1047 Gage St.
Winnetka, IL 60093
847/446-0183
www.tdanielcreations.com

An ACTOR must gain the physical skills, imagination and confidence necessary to be as articulate with his Body as he is with Words. T. Daniel and Laurie Willets, internationally-acclaimed Mime and Theatre Movement performers, perform, consult, choreograph and teach for Stage, Film, Animation and Opera. Contact 847/446-0183.

Robin Lakes
1979 S. Campus Dr.
Evanston, IL 60208
847/491-7395 • 773/973-3929

Nana Shineflug
847/724-1931

Speech Therapy

Kate DeVore, M.A., CCC-SLP
4451 N. Hamilton
Chicago, IL 60625
773/334-7203

As a voice, speech and dialect trainer as well as a speech pathologist specialized in professional voice, Kate has created a unique combination of artistic and scientifically based techniques for vocal rehabilitation and speech training. She is also specialized in working with people who stutter, using similar principles to facilitate a feeling of ease and control in speech.

Center for Stuttering Therapy
9933 Lawler Ave.
Skokie, IL 60077
847/677-7473 • 847/677-7493 - fax
www.cfst.com

Krause Speech & Language Services
Sue Ellen Krause, Ph.D., CCC-SLP
233 E. Erie #815
Chicago, IL 60611
312/943-1927 • 312/943-2692 - fax

Professionally Speaking
(See our ad on page 61)
2033 W. Potomac - 2nd floor
Chicago, IL 60622
773/218-9183

Rak Vocal & Healing Clinic
6056 W. Irving Park
Chicago, IL 60634
773/283-8349
Welcome to the RAK VOCAL & HEALING CLINIC where adult singers, actors and dancers become vocal athletes! Learn warm-ups/cool-down, preventive care, how to sing more healthfully when vocally-strained, and a basic technique to which you can apply any style of singing with strength, reliability, and charisma.

Bonnie Smith, Ph.D., CCC-SLP
Division of Speech Pathology
University of Illinois
at Chicago Medical Center
1855 W. Taylor
Chicago, IL 60612
312/996-6520 • 312/996-1527 - fax
www.otol.uic.edu\divisions\speech.htm.

Universities *(with MFA's in Theatre)*

American Conservatory Theater
30 Grant Ave. - 6th floor
San Francisco, CA 94108
415/439-3250 • 415/834-3326 - fax
MFA's offered in Acting.

Arizona State University
Department of Theatre
P.O. Box 871003
Tempe, AZ 85287-1003
602/965-5359 • 602/965-5158 - fax
www.asu.edu/graduate
MFA's offered in Acting, Theatre for Youth and Scenography.

Boston University
School for the Arts
855 Commonwealth Ave. #470
Boston, MA 02215
617/353-3390 • 617/353-4490 - fax
http://web.bu.edu/SFA/
MFA's offered in Directing, Education, Theatre and Design.

Brandeis University
Department of Theatre Arts
Waltham, MA 02254-9110
617/746-3340 • 617/736-3408 - fax
www.brandeis.edu
MFA's offered Acting, Dramaturgy, Playwriting and Design.

California Institute of the Arts -- Theatre School
24700 McBean Parkway
Valencia, CA 91355
805/253-7853 • 805/255-0690 - fax
MFA's offered in Acting, Directing, Directing for Theatre, Video & Cinema, Design, Management and Technical Direction.

Columbia University
Hammerstein Center/Theatre
School of the Arts, Columbia University
New York, NY 10027
212/854-3408 • 212/854-3344 - fax
www.columbia.edu/cu/arts
MFA's in Acting, Directing, Dramaturgy, Playwriting and Management.

DePaul University
The Theatre School at DePaul University
2135 N. Kenmore
Chicago, IL 60614
773/325-7999 • 800/4DEPAUL
ttsweb.tht.depaul.edu
MFA's offered in Acting, Directing, Costume Design, Lighting Design and Set Design.

Eastern Michigan State University
Department of Comm. & Theatre Arts
124 Quirk
Ypsilanti, MI 48197
313/487-1153 • 313/487-1484 - fax
www.emich.edupublic/cta/theatre_Home_page.html
MFA's offered in Theatre for the Young.

Florida State University
School of Theatre 239 FAB
Florida State University
Tallahassee, FL 32306-2008
904/644-6795 • 904/644-7408 - fax
www.fsu.edu\~Theatre\
MFA's offered in Acting, Directing, Music Theatre, Costume Design, Design/Technical Theatre, Lighting Design and Scene Design.

Illinois State University
Department of Theatre
Campus Box 5700
Normal, IL 61761
309/438-8783 • 309/438-7214 - fax
www.orat.ilstu.edu/theatre
MFA's offered in Acting, Directing and Design.

Indiana University
Dept. of Theatre & Drama
Theatre 200
Bloomington, IN 47405
812/855-4503 • 812/855-4704 - fax
www.fa.indiana.edu/~thtr
MFA's offered in Acting, Directing, Playwriting, Costume Design, Lighting Design, Set Design and Theatre Tech.

Louisiana State University
Department of Theatre
217 Music and Dramatic Arts Bldg.
Baton Rouge, LA 70803-2525
504/388-3531 • 504/388-4135 - fax
MFA's offered in Acting and Directing.

Mankato State University
Dept. of Theatre Arts, Box 5
Mankato, MN 56002-4800
507/389-2118 • 507/389-2922 - fax
www.mankato.msus.edu
MFA's offered in Acting, Directing and Design/Tech.

Michigan State University
Department of Theatre
149 Auditorium Building
East Lansing, MI 48824
517/355-6690 • 517/355-1698 - fax
http://pilot.msu/theatre/unit
MFA's offered in Acting and Production Design.

National Theatre Conservatory
1050 13th St.
Denver, CO 80204
303/893-4000
www.denvercenter.org/edu
MFA's offered in Acting.

Northern Illinois University
School of Theatre Arts
DeKalb, IL 60115
815/753-1335 • 815/753-8415 - fax
MFA's offered in Acting, Directing and Design/Tech.

Northwestern University
Theatre Department
1979 S. Campus Dr.
Evanston, IL 60208
847/491-3170 • 847/467-2019 - fax
www.nuinfo.nwu.edu/speech/departments/theatre.html
MFA's offered in Directing and Stage Design.

Ohio State University
Department of Theatre
1849 Cannon Dr.
Columbus, OH 43210
614/292-5821 • 614/292-4818 - fax
MFA's offered in Acting, Directing and Design/Tech.

Ohio University
School of Theatre
307 Kantner Hall
Athens, OH 45701
614/593-4818 • 614/593-4817 - fax
MFA's offered in Acting, Directing, Playwriting, Design, General, Production and Tech.

Pennsylvania State University
School of Theatre Arts
103 Arts Building
University Park, PA 16802-2900
814/865-7586
MFA's offered in Acting, Directing, Design and Tech.

State University of New York/Purchase
Conservatory of Theatre Arts & Film
735 Anderson Hill Rd.
Purchase, NY 10577
914/251-6830 • 914/251-6300 - fax
MFA's offered in Directing/Stage Management and Stage Design/Theatre Tech.

Purdue University
Department of Visual and Performing Arts
1376 Stewart Center
West Lafayette, IN 47907
765/494-3074 • 765/496-1766 - fax
www.sla.purdue.edu/theatre/acting.html
MFA's offered in Acting, Directing, Scenography and Technology.
Just 2 hours south of Chicago. Graduate MFA programs in Acting, Production Design & Technology (Costume, Scenery, Lights, Sound, Theatre Engineering, Technical Theatre); MA Program in Stage Management. Assistantships with tuition waiver plus salary up to $10,000/year. Member: U/RTA, NAST, ACTF. More info: www.sla.purdue.edu/theatre/ or e-mail theatre@purdue.edu. EA/EOU.

Roosevelt University
Theatre Program
430 S. Michigan
Chicago, IL 60605-1394
312/341-3719 • 312/341-3814 - fax
www.roosevelt.edu
MFA's in Directing/Dramaturgy, Musical Theatre and Performance.

Southern Illinois University
Department of Theatre
Carbondale, IL 62901-6608
618/453-5741 • 618/453-7582 - fax
www.siu.edu/~mccleod/
MFA's offered in Directing and Playwriting.

Southern Methodist University
Theatre Division
1164 Owens Art Center
Dallas, TX 75275
214/768-2558
www.smu.edu/~meadows/
MFA's offered in Acting, Directing and Design.

University of Alabama
Dept. of Theatre & Dance
Box 870239
Tuscaloosa, AL 35487-0239
205/348-5283
www.asf.net
MFA's offered in Acting, Directing, Playwriting/Dramaturgy, Costume Design, Costume Design/Production, Set Design/Technical Production and Management/Arts Administration.

University of Arizona
Theatre Arts Department
University of Arizona
Tucson, AZ 85721
520/621-7007
520/621-2412
www.arizona.edu
MFA's offered in Acting, Directing and Design/Tech.

University of California - Los Angeles
Department of Theatre UCLA
Los Angeles, CA 90024-1622
310/825-7008 • 310/825-3383 - fax
www.tft.ucla.edu
MFA's offered in Acting, Directing, Playwriting and Design & Production.

University of California, San Diego
Department of Theatre and Dance
La Jolla, CA 92093-0344
619/534-1046
MFA's offered in Acting, Directing, Dramaturgy, Playwriting, Design and Stage Management.

University of Cincinnati
College-Conservatory of Music
P.O. Box 210096
Cincinnati, OH 45221-0096
513/556-5803 • 513/556-3399 - fax
www.UC.edu/www/ccm
MFA's offered in Acting, Directing, Musical Theatre, Costume Design, Lighting Design, Make-up & Wig Design, Scenic Design, Sound Design and Stage Management.

University of Delaware
Professional Theatre Training Program
Mitchell Hall, RM 109
Newark, DE 19716
302/831-2201
www.udel.edu/theatre
MFA's offered in Acting, Stage Management and Technical Production.

Linenwood College
Department of Performing Arts
209 S. Kingshighway
St. Charles, MO 63301
314/949-4949 • 314/949-4910 - fax
MFA's offered in Acting, Directing and Design/Technical Theatre.

University of Florida
Department of Theatre
Hume Library
Gainesville, FL 32611
904/392-2038
MFA's offered in Performance and Design/Technology.

University of Houston
School of Theatre
Houston, TX 77204-5071
713/743-3003 • 713/749-1420 - fax
MFA's offered in Acting, Directing, Costume Design and Scenic Design.

University of Illinois, Urbana-Champaign
Dept. of Theatre
4-122 Krannert Center
500 S. Goodwin Ave.
Urbana, IL 61801
217/333-2371 • 217/244-1861 - fax
www.uiuc.edu/providers/kcpathaater/theat.html
MFA's offered in Acting and Design/Management/Tech.

University of Iowa
Dept. of Theatre Arts 107 TB
Iowa City, IA 52242-1705
319/335-2700
www.uiowa.edu
MFA's offered in Acting, Directing, Playwriting, Design and Stage Management.

University of Massachusetts
Department of Theater
Room 112 - Fine Arts Center
Amherst, MA 01003
413/545-3490 • 413/545-4312 - fax
MFA's offered in Directing, Dramaturgy, Costume Design, Lighting Design and Scenic Design.

University of Michigan
Dept. of Theatre & Drama
2550 Frieze Build.
Ann Arbor, MI 48109-1285
734/764-5350 • 313/763-5097 - fax
www.theatre.music.umich.edu
MFA's offered in Directing, Playwriting and Design.

University of Missouri-Kansas City
5100 Rockhill Rd.
Kansas City, MO 64110
816/235-2784 • 816/235-5367 - fax
MFA's offered in Acting and Design/Technology.

University of Nebraska-Lincoln
Dept. of Theatre Arts & Dance
215 Temple Building, 12th & R Sts.
Box 880201
Lincoln, NE 68588-0201
402/472-2072
MFA's offered in Acting and Design/Tech.

University of North Carolina
Department of Dramatic Art
CB#3230, Graham Mem. 052A
Chapel Hill, NC 27599-3230
919/962-1132 • 919/966-2611 - fax
MFA's offered in Professional Actor Training Program, Costume Technology and Technical Production.

University of Oregon
Dept. of Speech & Theatre Arts
216 Villard Hall
Eugene, OR 97403-1231
503/346-4171 • 541/346-1978 - fax
http://darkwing.oregon.edu/~theatre
MFA's offered in Costume Design, Lighting Design and Scenery Design.

University of Southern California
School of Theatre
Los Angeles, CA 90089-0791
213/740-1289 • 213/740-8888 - fax
www.usc.edu/dept.theatre/DramaNet
MFA's offered in Acting, Directing, Playwriting and Design.

University of Texas at Austin
Department of Theatre & Dance
College of Fine Arts
Austin, TX 78712
512/471-5793
MFA's offered in Acting, Creative Drama/ Theatre for Children & Youth, Directing, Playwriting, Design and Theatre Tech.

University of Washington
School of Drama
Box 353950
Seattle, WA 98195-3950
206/543-5140 • 206/543-8512 - fax
http://artsci.washington.edu/drama/schdram1.html
MFA's offered in Acting, Directing and Design/Tech.

University of Wisconsin-Madison
Theatre and Drama Department
6173 Vilas Hall
821 University Ave.
Madison, WI 53706-1497
608/263-2329 • 608/263-2463 - fax
http://polyglot.lss.wisc.edu/tnd/theatre.html
MFA's offered in Acting, Costuming, Design and Technology.

University of Wisconsin-Milwaukee
Professional Theatre Training Prog.
P.O. Box 413
Milwaukee, WI 53201
414/229-4947 • 414/229-2728 - fax
www.uwm.edu
MFA's offered in Acting, Costume Production, Stage Management and Technical Production.

University/Resident Theatre Association (U/RTA)
1560 Broadway #414
New York, NY 10036
212/221-1130 • 212/869-2752 - fax
www.urta.com
Graduate School Auditions • Contract Management Program • Post-Graduate Audtions

A national organization providing useful and friendly services to candidates seeking professional MFA training in all theatre disciplines, and to graduate schools and theatre companies. Assisting students interested in U/RTA member programs; management help for groups employing professional artists; career services for recent MFA graduates and more. Membership not required for most services.

Wayne State University
Theatre Department
3225 Old Main
Detroit, MI 48202
313/577-3508
www.comm.wayne.edu/theatre
MFA's offered in Acting, Costuming, Lighting Design, Scenic Design, Stage Management and Theatre Management.

Western Illinois University
Browne Hall
900 W Adams St.
Macomb, IL 61455
309/298-1543
www.wiu.edu
MFA's offered in Acting, Directing and Design.

Yale University
P.O. Box 208325
New Haven, CT 06520
203/432-1507 • 203/432-9668 - fax
www.yale.edu./drama
MFA's offered in Acting, Directing, Playwriting/Dramaturgy/Dramatic Criticism, Design, Technical Design/Production and Theatre Management.

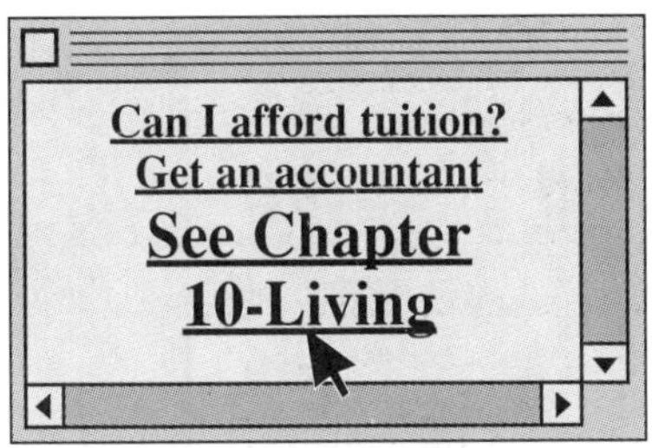
Can I afford tuition?
Get an accountant
See Chapter
10-Living

The Actor's Tools

The things you never knew you'd need.

Shakespeare's Motley Crew's "The Roaring Girl" – pictured (left to right): Don Bender, Jonathan Watkins, William Sidney Parker, Duane Sharp

Photographer Checklist

A good headshot is one of the most important investments an actor can make. It's your calling card, introduction and logo all rolled into one. As a result, it's important to be careful when choosing a photographer to ensure that the money you spend gets you the best shots possible.

1. Research

This is a big investment, so you want to do your research carefully. Though it may be tempting, DON'T SKIMP!! Your headshot is your introduction to many casting people. You want it to look professional. A great deal is one that gets you great shots. Look for photographers whose style you like or who sound appealing to you. Some places to check:

PerformInk
This Book
Act One Studios–Act One has a portfolio of many photographers' work.

References

If a friend has had a good experience with a photographer, or if an agent recommends someone, check him or her out. Don't take this reference as gospel, though. What works for your friend may not work for you.

2. Consultation

Any legitimate photographer should offer a free consultation. Look for the following things:

Space

Are you comfortable with the space the photographer shoots in?

Personality

Do you get along with the photographer? Do they listen to you and what you want to do? Are you able to be yourself?

Portfolio

Look at the photographer more closely. Have they shot anyone who's similar to you in appearance? How are those shots? Do all the shots look the same, or does the photographer seem to change his/her style with each subject?

3. Makeup Artist

You may want to hire a makeup artist as well. The photographer may have someone available that they like to work with. Do research. Any makeup you use should enhance your look without changing it. In the end you want to look like you.

4. The Shoot

The day finally arrives. What can I do to be sure of having the best session possible?

Sleep

It's important to be well rested. Schedule your shoot at the time of day when you are at your best.

Clothes

Bring a lot of choices. In particular, bring clothes that show your shape without being too tight or revealing. One photographer recommends bringing clothing that is darker than your skin tone. Above all, bring clothes that you're comfortable in.

Music

Bring music that you love. It'll help you maintain positive energy and a positive mood.

5. Choosing Your Shot

I've got my proof sheets back, but how do I choose between all these tiny shots?

Get a Loupe

Though it may sound like a wolf of some sort, a loupe is actually a small eye piece that will help you get a better idea of what a shot will look like blown up.

Get Advice

See what shots your agent likes. If you have an experienced actor friend, see what they like.

Get a Concept

Know what sort of image you're looking to project and choose shots that reflect that. What are you trying to sell, and how are you going to project that?

Get Some Shots

If necessary, spend the extra money to get extra shots blown up. You'll never know exactly how a shot will look until it's 8" by 10".

Over

6. Retouching

If your shot's almost perfect—if one hair's out of place or if a wrinkle in your sweater is marring an otherwise perfect shot—get it retouched. This is a process, done either by hand or computer, that will remove those imperfections. Retouching should leave you looking like you, however. In the end, the shot has to represent how you look.

7. Reproduction

Now that you've chosen your shots, you have to get them reproduced.

Style

Matte finishes with a border are currently in style in Chicago. Ask your photographer and/or agent for their recommendations.

Font

Even the font your name is in can help express yourself. Print your name out in a bunch of different ones to find one that you like.

Lithographs

Lithographs are made by breaking a picture into dots, like printing a photograph in a newspaper. On the positive side, it's cheaper. On the negative, the quality is not as high. Lithographs might be useful for certain types of mass mailings, but most agents prefer the traditional photographic process.

8. Postcard

Finally, in addition to standard headshots, you may want to make a postcard. Postcards are used for invitations to agents and directors, thank you notes and other "Remember me?" sort of purposes. Postcard photos can be much more wacky than traditional headshots and can even use more than one photograph. Anything that will help them remember you is suitable.

Photographers

Linda Balhorn
400 E. Randolph #1008
Chicago, IL 60601
312/263-3513

Basil Fairbanks Studio
Noel Grigalunus
4908 N. Glenwood
Chicago, IL 60640
773/907-9567 • 773/907-0050 - fax

Brad Baskin
850 N. Milwaukee
Chicago, IL 60622
312/733-2192
www.bradbaskin.com

Sherry Bell
847/918-0263
305/604-9907 • 847/913-0070 - fax

Bianco Scotti Productions
2458 W. 38th
Chicago, IL 60632
312/301-9373

Peter Bosy
6435 Indian Head Trail
Indian Head Park, IL 60525
708/246-3778 • 708/246-1080 - fax
www.peterbosy.com
Working with me builds character! I collaborate, coordinate and create the very best images for you to look the part. The promotional ads I work on for Chicago Shakespeare Theater prove my point. If you need more proof, visit my website at www.peterbosy.com or call 708/246-3778.

Camera I
Joe Weinshenker
3946 N. Monticello
Chicago, IL 60618
773/539-1119

Guy J. Cardarelli
119 W. Hubbard - 3rd floor
Chicago, IL 60610
312/321-0694
708/452-8844

Scott Chambers
2107 W. Grand
Chicago, IL 60612
312/850-0262 • 312/850-0285 - fax

Christopher Jacobs Studio
1443 W. Grand
Chicago, IL 60622
312/563-0987 • 312/563-0588 - fax
www.jacobs-photography.com

Mary Clare
1201 Laura Ln.
Lake Bluff, IL 60044
847/680-3686

Classic Photography, Inc.
John Karl Breun
38 South Main St. #2A
Mount Prospect, IL 60056
847/259-8373 • 847-259-8474 - fax
www.classicphoto.com

Keith Claunch
415 W. Huron - 2nd floor
Chicago, IL 60610
773/612-3983

Andrew Collings
(See our ad on page 80)
1840 W. Hubbard #3B
Chicago, IL 60622
312/455-1791
www.andrewcollings.com

Costume Images
3634 W. Fullerton
Chicago, IL 60647
773/276-8971 • 773/276-0717 - fax
www.costume-images.com

Daniel Byrnes Photography
113 W. North
Chicago, IL 60610
312/337-1174
Actors, Models, Dancers, Musicians: Whether your needs are for headshots, portfolios, or promotional photos, we have the experience to give you individualized images to be remembered. 20 years experience in Chicago and Los Angeles. Ask about our Scene Stealers Portfolios. VISA and Mastercard accepted.

David Renar Studio
320 N. Damen
Chicago, IL 60612
312/226-0001
www.renar.com

Dan DuVerney
1937 W. Division - 1st floor
Chicago, IL 60622
773/252-6639

Edda Taylor Photographie
Courthouse Square #304
Crown Point , IN 46307
219/662-9500

Linn Ehrlich
312/209-2107

Elan Photography
5120 Belmont #H
Downers Grove, IL 60515
630/960-1400 • 630/969-1972 - fax
www.elanphotography.com

Dale Fahey
773/973-5757

Furla Photography & Video
1440 Waukegan Rd.
Glenview, IL 60025
847/724-1200 • 847/729-3888 - fax

Gerald Peskin Photography
681 Academy Dr.
Northbrook, IL 60062
847/498-0291

Jai Girard
3428 N. Janssen
Chicago, IL 60657
773/929-2625

Jennifer Girard
1455 W. Roscoe
Chicago, IL 60657
773/929-3730
773/871-7762
773/871-2308 - fax

Steve Greiner
1437 W. Thomas
Chicago, IL 60622
773/227-4375 • 773/227-4379 - fax

Daniel Guidara
773/745-6442

Images by Onate
Dan Onate
3500 Midwest Rd.
Oak Brook, IL 60522
708/496-0961
630/655-2212

Deon Jahnke
228 S. 1st St.
Milwaukee, WI 53204
414/224-8360 • 414/224-8356 - fax
www.execpc.com\~deon

JLB Photography
18031 Dixie Hwy.
Homewood, IL 60430
312/339-3909
708/799-0719

Gary Jochim
1470 W. Huron #2F
Chicago, IL 60622
312/738-3204

Paladino Photography
105 E. Burlington
Riverside, IL 60546
708/447-2822

Joel DeGrand Photography
2715 S. Archer #2
Chicago, IL 60608
312/674-0900 • 312/674-0901 - fax
www.degrand.com

John Cascarano Photography
319 N. Western
Chicago, IL 60612
312/733-1212 • 312/733-2715 - fax

Joseph Amenta Photography
555 W. Madison #3802
Chicago, IL 60661
773/248-2488

The Actor's Tools

Joshua Owens Photography
(See our ad on page 85)
8240 N. Harding
Skokie, IL 60076
847/673-9446 • 312/851-3118
www.joshuaowensphotography.com
Variety and spontaneity, not to mention a bit of fun; these are the keys to getting a great photograph. One that actually works for you. Whether you're brand new or just feel it's time to express your development, if you're looking for a unique photo experience, call.

Laurie Locke
4018 S. Oak Park Ave.
Stickney, IL 60402
708/749-2444

Mike McCafrey
Photography
Fashion & Acting Head Shots/Portfolios
312.222.9776

Max Photography
P.O. Box 14620
Chicago, IL 60614
773/477-6548

Brian McConkey
(See our ad on page 81)
312 N. May #6J
Chicago, IL 60607
312/563-1357 • 312/563-1615 - fax

Michael Brosilow Photography
(See our ad on page 83)
1370 N. Milwaukee
Chicago, IL 60622
773/235-4696 • 773/235-4698 - fax

Michael McCafrey Photography
(See our ad on this page)
109 W. Hubbard
Chicago, IL 60610
312/222-9776

Mike Canale Photography
614 Davis St.
Evanston, IL 60201
847/864-0146
$169.00 Headshots. Satisfaction guaranteed. Located in the Giordano Dance Center, one block from CTA & Metra stops. Established 1980.

Rick Mitchell, Inc.
(see our ad on page 86)
652 W. Grand
Chicago, IL 60610
312/829-1700

Papadakis Photography
17 Lexington Rd.
South Barrington, IL 60010
847/428-4400 • 847/428-4403 - fax
www.papadakisphotography.com
Specializing in people photography, especially children. We shoot ads, hire talent, and help connect talent with agents. We work with all 40 agents and casting directors. We have helped talent go on to shoot print ads, commercials, pilots, TV and feature films. Call for a free marketability evaluation!

Patrick Harold Productions
1757 W. Augusta
Chicago, IL 60622
312/226-3831 • 312/226-3832 - fax

Paul Sherman Photography
213 N. Morgan
Chicago, IL 60607
312/633-0848 • 312/666-1498 - fax
www.paulshermanphotos.com

Payton Studios
Reginald Payton
117 S. Morgan #204
Chicago, IL 60607
312/432-1001 • 312/432-0225 - fax
www.paytonstudios.com

Pete Stenberg Photography
(See our ad on page 74)
225 W. Hubbard - 6th floor
Chicago, IL 60610
312/644-6137
312/644-9728 - fax
www.petestenberg.qpg.com

Photographic Creations
Robert D. Wright
15 Stratford Ct.
Indian Head Park, IL 60525
708/246-8043

Suzanne Plunkett
3047 N. Lincoln #300
Chicago, IL 60657
773/477-3775 • 773/477-4640 - fax

Robert Erving Potter III
(See our ad on page 82)
Chicago Photographer
2056 W. Superior
Chicago, IL 60612-1314
312/226-2060
www.chicago-photographer.net

Pret a Poser Photography
231 George St.
Barrington, IL 60010
847/382-2211 • 847/842-0494 - fax

Proctor & Proctor Photography
409 N. Racine
Chicago, IL 60622
312/829-5511 • 312/829-5514 - fax
www.tspphoto.com

Isabel Raci
773/486-1980 • **773/862-4608**

Rubinic Photography
319 N. Western
Chicago, IL 60612
312/733-8901 • 312/733-8902 - fax
www.rubinic.com

Gerber/Scarpelli Photography
1144 W. Fulton Market
Chicago, IL 60607
312/455-1144 • 312/455-1544 - fax

Shag Studios
1545 N. Larrabee #2N
Chicago, IL 60610
312/943-1718

Sima Imaging
Sid Afzali
1821 W. Hubbard #301
Chicago, IL 60622
312/733-1788 • 312/733-6890 - fax

Kenneth Simmons
3026 E. 80th St.
Chicago, IL 60617
773/684-7232

Triangle Studio
3445 N. Broadway
Chicago, IL 60657
773/472-1015 • 773/472-2201 - fax

Tyrone Taylor Photography
1143 E. 81st
Chicago, IL 60619
773/978-1505

Vic Bider Photography
1142 W. Taylor
Chicago, IL 60607
312/829-5540

G. Thomas Ward
1949 W. Leland
Chicago, IL 60640
773/271-6813
www.nationaltalent.com

Wayne Cable Photography
312 N. Carpenter
Chicago, IL 60607
312/226-0303 • 312/226-6995 - fax

David A. Weinstein & Associates
773/486-8850 • 773/486-7678 - fax

Jean Whiteside
6410 N. Glenwood #1S
Chicago, IL 60626
773/274-5545

Winkelman Photography
P.O. Box 531
Oak Park, IL 60303-0531
312/953-2141

Steven Wright
1545 N. Larrabee
Chicago, IL 60610
312/943-1718

Yamashiro Studio
2643 N. Clybourn
Chicago, IL 60614
312/280-4970 • 773/883-0453 - fax
www.yamashirostudio.com

Photo Reproductions

A&B Photography
650 W. Lake - 2nd floor
Chicago, IL 60661
312/454-4554
312/454-1630 - fax

ABC Pictures
(See our ad below)
1867 E. Florida
Springfield, MO 65803
417/869-3456
417/869-9185 - fax
www.abcpictures.com

Artisan Printing & Lithography
445 W. Erie
Chicago, IL 60610
312/337-8400
312/337-5631 - fax

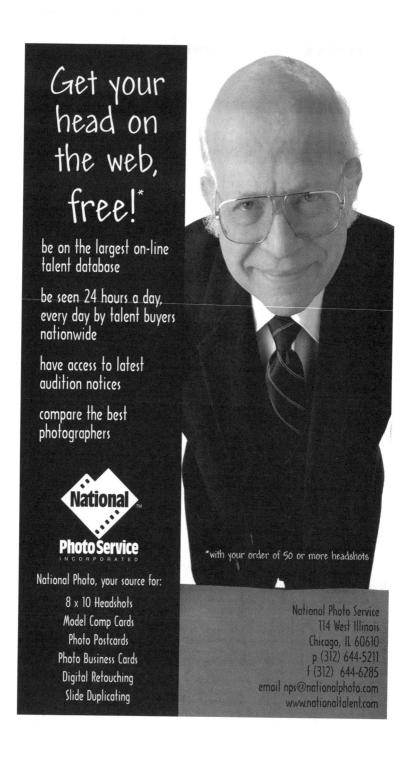

Bodhis Photo Service
112 W. Grand
Chicago, IL 60610
312/321-1141 • 312/321-3610 - fax

Composites International
12335 S. Keeler Ave.
Alsip, IL 60803
708/597-3449 • 708/597-3421 - fax

Ideal Photos of NYC
155 W. 46th St. - 2nd floor
New York, NY 10036
800/929-5688 • 212/386-2106 - fax
www.idealphotosofnyc.com
Why pay more?
Due to our HIGH volume we can offer you more for less! Call for free samples and an order form. Ask about our $44 for 100 8 x 10 Reproduction Special. We specialize in mail orders. POSTCARDS-8X10's-COLOR-B/W-RETOUCHING-RESUMES ON BACK OF PHOTOS-BUSINESS CARDS-MAILERS-ONE STOP FOR ALL YOUR PROMOTING NEEDS!

National Photo Service
(See our ad on page 88)
114 W. Illinois
Chicago, IL 60610
312/644-5211 • 312/644-6285 - fax
www.nationalphoto.com

Photoscan
646 Bryn Mawr St.
Orlando, FL 32804
800/352-6367
407/839-5029
www.ggphotoscan.com

Quantity Photo
Rich Pace
119 W. Hubbard - 2nd floor
Chicago, IL 60610
312/644-8290 • 312/644-8299 - fax
www.quantityphoto.com

Photo Retouching

John Bresnahan
3320 N. Clifton
Chicago, IL 60657
773/248-7211

Bob Faetz Retouching
203 N. Wabash #1320
Chicago, IL 60601
312/759-0933 • 312/759-0944 - fax

G. Mycio Digital Imaging
333 N. Michigan #715
Chicago, IL 60601
312/782-1472 • 312/782-9874 - fax

Irene Levy Retouching Studios
300 N. State #3431
Marina Towers
Chicago, IL 60610
312/464-0504 • 312/464-1665 - fax

Retouching Company
573 W. Polk
Chicago, IL 60607
312/263-7445 • 312/922-2086 - fax
www.enteron.net

Makeup Artists

Sharleen Acciari
1007 W. Webster
Chicago, IL 60614
773/248-1273

Bianco Scotti Productions
2458 W. 38th
Chicago, IL 60632
312/301-9373

Cat'Ania's Hollywood Make-Up & Hair
170th Torrence Ave.
2 River Place #L
Lansing, IL 60438
708/889-9800 • 708/889-9802 - fax
Makeup, Hair, Cases, Set Bags & Chairs. 24 hour delivery service to your set location & more...

Cheryl Channings
54 E. Oak - 2nd floor
Chicago, IL 60611
312/280-1994 • 312/280-1929 - fax
www.channings.com

Che Sguardo Makeup Studio
500 N. Wells
Chicago, IL 60610
312/527-0821
888/858-9012

Cathy Durkin
1749 N. Wells #1106
Chicago, IL 60614
312/787-0848

Femline Hair Designs, Inc.
3500 Midwest Rd.
Oak Brook, IL 60522
630/655-2212

Duncan Forbes
317 S. Oak Park Ave. #104
Oak Park, IL 60302
708/848-2996

Marcus Geeter
655 W. Irving Park #207
Chicago, IL 60613
773/975-8242 • 773/296-2905 - fax

Robyn Goldman
312/751-8994

Anna Intravatolo
11350 Behrns
Melrose Park, IL 60164
847/455-2596 • 847/455-5772 - fax

Blair Laden
1864 Sherman Ave.
Evanston, IL 60201
847/328-1177

Jerry Malik
312/760-2515 - pgr.

Marianne Strokirk Salon
361 W. Chestnut
Chicago, IL 60610
312/944-4428 • 312/944-4429 - fax
www.mariannestrokirk.com

Marilyn Miglin Institute
112 E. Oak
Chicago, IL 60611
800/662-1120 • 312/943-1184 - fax
www.marilyn-miglin.com

Tammy McEwen
630/226-9092

Darcy McGrath
312/337-1353

Media Hair & Makeup Group
Maureen Kalagian
708/848-8400

Model Image Center
1218 W. Belmont
Chicago, IL 60657
773/348-9349 • 773/348-9366 - fax
www.modelimagecenter.com

Sandy Morris
773/549-4951

Nouvelle Femme
1157 Wilmette Ave.
Wilmette, IL 60091
847/251-6698

Shelly Rolf
630/262-1142 • 630/262-0461 - fax

Nancy P. Stanley
773/871-1396

Syd Simons Cosmetics, Inc.
6601 W. North Ave.
Oak Park, IL 60302
877/943-2333
708/660-0266
www.sydsimons.com

Transformations by Rori
146 N. Oak Park Ave.
Oak Park, IL 60301
708/383-8338 • 708/383-6796 - fax

Transformations by Rori
110 S. Arlington Heights Rd.
Arlington Heights, IL 60005
847/454-0600

Jamie S. Weiss
1800 W. Roscoe #404
Chicago, IL 60657
773/472-9665

A Look at the bad side of Resumés

Look with a spot
I damn him.

By Kevin Heckman

The resumé that is glued, stapled or otherwise affixed (hopefully) to the back of your headshot is a key piece of your presentation. No one gets hired in this business based on their resumé, but a good one garners more respect and a bad one can lose you a job.

For information on what should go into a resumé, check out (appropriately) our checklist. If you'd like to know some of the things that shouldn't, read on.

Actually, these particular points I mention aren't all big no-no's, though some are. I also include things I or other directors have simply found strange. Each of these oddities has appeared in some form on actual resumés.

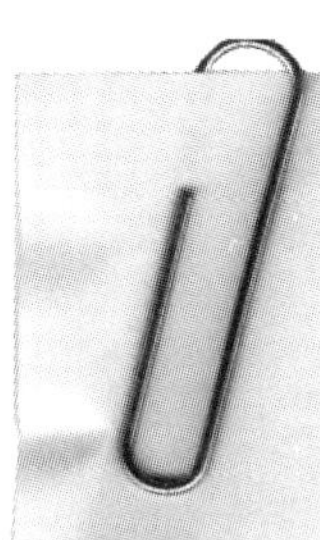

Nadia E. Phektev

EMC

Height: 5'7"
Hair: Ochre
Eyes: Hazel
Voice: High Tenor

The EMC thang

I've never understood why actors list their EMC (Equity Membership Candidate) status under their name. I assume it's a spin-off of listing your union memberships there, but union membership affects casting and EMC doesn't. EMC's gather weeks by working as a non-Equity actor in certain Equity houses. Once they accumulate 50 weeks, they have to join the union with their next Equity job or drop their EMC status. The only situation in which EMC could influence casting is if Nadia has close to 50 weeks. Otherwise, she's just emphasizing something that doesn't matter.

Call that actor...

Wow, Nadia gave a great audition. I should definitely give her a call. Many directors separate your headshot and resumé from the cover letter that accompanied it. If your resumé doesn't have contact info, no one will contact you. Of course, many actors don't list an address or their home phone numbers as a security precaution, but you've got to give casting people some way to reach you.

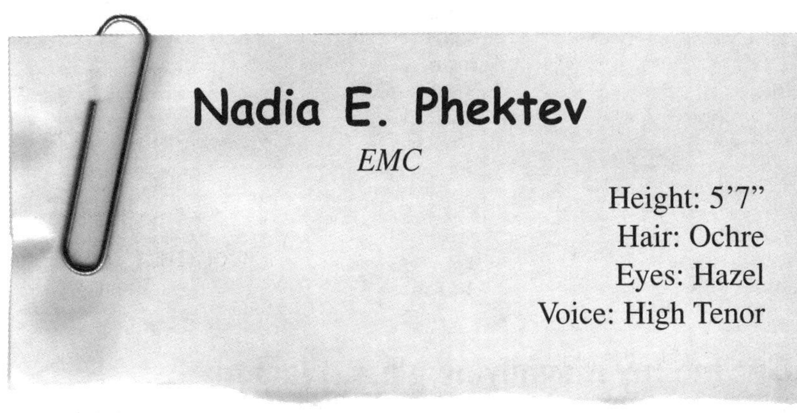

What does she look like?

If a casting director gets 200 headshots and resumés over a three-day span, and if two percent of the headshots are attached to their accompanying resumés with only a paper clip, what are the odds that that paper clip will successfully keep those resumés with their headshots? If you chose E. Not Good, you're correct!! Those resumés will probably get tossed. Staple, glue, whatever. Just make sure your resumé stays attached to your picture.

Production	Role	Theatre
Ten Little Indians	Tonto	Misaligned Theatre
You're a Good Man Charlie Brown	Calvin	Griffin Ascending
I'm 25 and Who the Fuck Cares	Bette	Stage Left
Dark at the Top of the Stairs	The Electrician	Goomdan Theater
Red Noses	The Pediatrician	Off-Stage Right

Who produced this show?

What's wrong with this picture? Only that Stage Left didn't produce *I'm 25 and Who the Fuck Cares.* It went up at Stage Left, but was produced by Irrelevant Players. Needless to say, if this resumé shows up at Stage Left, this actor's probably not going to get called in. Furthermore, any director who's familiar with Stage Left is probably going to think that this actor's lying about their work. Not the image she wanted to project.

Production	Role	Theatre
Ten Little Indians	Tonto	Misaligned Theatre
You're a Good Man Charlie Brown	Calvin	Griffin Ascending
I'm 25 and Who the Fuck Cares	Bette	Stage Left
Dark at the Top of the Stairs	The Electrician	Goomdan Theater
Red Noses	The Pediatrician	Audience Right Theatre
Tight-Ass Androgynous	The Queen	Theatre Pyu
Glass Meringue	Chef Tom	The Hyperactives
Six Degrees of Being Apart	Sydney Poitier	Eating Crow Theater
Billy Joe and the Remarkably Hued Overcoat	Billy Joe	Downtown Hilton Theater
Goddamn Car	Driver	Well-Known Window Productions
Always Cross-Hatched	Binky	Regal Porgie Playhouse
A Collection of Blue Hominids	The Blue One	Nettles Road Theatre

Get me my magnifying glass, Watson

The fact is, many directors look more closely at your training and skills than they do your credits. There's no reason to cram every show you've ever done on your resumé. Choose those credits that put you in the best light. Include name theatres, well known shows or anything that got good press. You may even want to have different resumés for different genres: classical work, musicals, children's theatre, etc. Then you can emphasize work that particularly suits you for that genre.

Education & Training
B.A.-Theatre/Astrology–Mulligan University
Physical Theatre–Plastic Bean Performance Group
Vocal Performance–Camilla Rosen

Special Skills
Driver–Moped, Stage Combat, Basic Tumbling, Dialects (New York, Texas, Deep South, Western Pennsylvania), Puppetry, Winking at Boys

Well isn't that special

Actors go to all sorts of lengths to be sure their resumé will be noticed. In this case, the actor has printed her resumé on cloud paper. Unfortunately, clouds or flowers or pink neon paper are more likely to upstage your resumé than call attention to it. They'll remember the paper but not the person. Present yourself as a professional. If your resumé feels sparse, do student film, take class, or work for one of Chicago's dozens of small theatres who might see your potential build your resumé. A cheap attention grabber can annoy casting people and that will hurt instead of help.

Additionally, beware of the cute special skill. First of all, be sure it's a skill. "Winking at boys" isn't really that difficult, and listing it won't necessarily impress anyone. Also, be sure you can do whatever it is the moment they ask. If you list "Belch the Pledge of Allegiance" as a skill, you'd better be able to do it right there. Special Skills can help you get the job, but it's also part of your presentation. If you get too cutesy, casting people are less likely to treat you as a professional.

Chances are, most of these errors or oddities aren't going to make or break your chances at getting the part, but your resumé introduces you and it should introduce you as a professional actor. If you've done that, you're one step closer to convincing a director you should be seriously considered for the part.

Resumé Checklist

Your resumé is often the most important piece of material a casting director or agent will receive from you. Present yourself in the best light possible. Highlight your strengths. Be sure that it's easy to read. And don't forget to include:

1. **Your name**
   This should be at the top and in the largest font.

2. **Your stats**
   Height, weight, hair and eye color are all standard. Don't include your age or age range. They'll figure that out themselves.

3. **Your beeper or contact number**
   Obviously you want to be reachable. Don't include your address unless they specifically ask for it. You never know who'll get their hands on your resumé. Some agencies won't want your number on the resumé. They want all bookings to go through them. If you do have your number on a resumé and you get a call that should go through your agent, refer it to your agent. Work leads to work.

4. **Room for an agency stamp or sticker**
   Once you get representation, you don't want to have to completely redesign your resumé!

5. **For theatre, film, etc.**
   List production name to the left

6. **Your role in the middle**
   Theatre, studio or production company to the right

7. **For film, also indicate type of work (i.e. "Day Player" or "Principal")**
   You may have been brilliant in that independent film, but the agent/director may never have seen it. Listing "Queen Anne" on your resumé doesn't tell them anything, but indicating it was a principal does.

8. Training

Either list

Areas of training
Corresponding teachers

Or

Schools or studios
Classes taken

Use whichever method shows you off best. If you've had impressive teachers, be sure to mention their names. If you've trained at schools that are recognizable, mention them.

9. University degrees

10. Special skills

11. Dialects

12. Sports (Indicate level of skill)

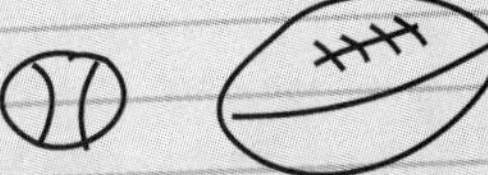

13. Languages spoken (Indicate fluency)

14. Odd skills or talents (Be sure you can do it!!)

Anything that doesn't fit into the above categories can go here. A lot of actors get cute in this section. That's fine, but if you list "Choking dog impressions" you'd better be able to impersonate a choking dog on a moment's notice.

15. Commercials

Write "Commercial list available upon request"

This keeps you from getting into the sensitive and confusing issue of product conflict until you have to.

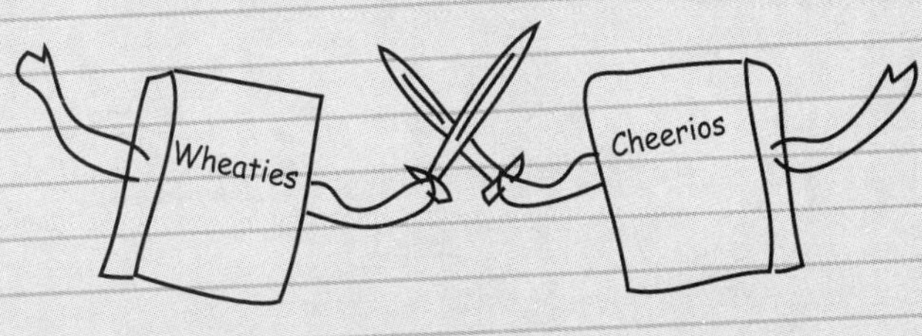

Cover Letter Checklist

This is often your first introduction to an agent or director. Remember your audience; they see dozens of these letters each day, so you want to be sure that yours is to the point and presents you in a good light. There are a few things you can do to ensure this.

1. **Confirm the Names**

   How would you feel getting a letter that's intended for you, but misspells your name?

2. **Keep it Short**

   Remember, they see dozens of these letters and aren't interested in reading your life story.

3. **Contents**

   Name, Number and Address

   You must include your basic stats: name, address and contact numbers on your cover letter. Don't assume that they'll refer to the information on your headshot; make it as easy for them as possible.

   It's OK to Name-Drop

   If you know someone who's represented by the agent, mention that (s)he speaks well of that agent. Keep it appropriate. Mentioning that you met John Lennon's cousin once is probably not going to help you.

   Give Referrals

   If there's a director or teacher that will speak well of you, mention them. Be sure to OK this with the individual in question first.

   Talk About Your Present Work

   Are you doing a good show? Taking an exciting class? Auditioning for anything interesting? Mention it. Anything that indicates that you're pursuing your craft will make you look better.

   What Are Your Goals?

   How can this particular agency help you get where you want to go? Keep this brief and fairly specific.

Resumé Services

Act I Bookstore
2540 N. Lincoln
Chicago, IL 60614
773/348-6757 • 773/348-5561 - fax
800/55PLAYS
www.act1books.com

Act I Bookstore serves everyone from Chicago to Sao Paolo to Istanbul for its theatre and film book needs. You can find thousands of plays, acting books, screenplays, agent listings, monologues, musicals, audition notices, reading copies of shows currently auditioning, a professional resumé service, theatre games, and many other books for actors, directors, writers, producers, designers, teachers and filmmakers. Open Mon-Wed 10-8 and Thur-Sun 10-6. The best online bookstore for theatre and film is www.act1books.com.

Bob Behr
Resumés by Mac
4738 N. LaPorte
Chicago, IL 60630
773/685-7721 • 773/283-9839 - fax

CastNet
5757 Wilshire Blvd #124
Los Angeles, CA 90036
888/873-7373 • 323/964-1050 - fax
www.castnet.com

Ink Well
112 W. Illinois
Chicago, IL 60610
312/644-4700 • 312/644-4703 - fax

Trade Papers

Act One Reports
640 N. LaSalle #535
Chicago, IL 60610
312/787-9384 • 312/787-3234 - fax
www.actone.com

Updated listings of agencies, casting directors, photographers, and industry related information.

American Theatre
355 Lexington Ave.
New York, NY 10017
212/697-5230 • 212/557-5817 - fax
www.tcg.org

National theatre periodical containing news, features, and articles.

Audition News
P.O. Box 250
Bloomingdale, IL 60108
630/894-2278 • 630/894-8364 - fax

Audition notices for the greater Midwest.

Backstage
1515 Broadway - 14th floor
New York, NY 10036-8986
212/536-5368
800/437-3183 - subscriptions
www.backstage.com

The theatrical trade paper for the east coast.

Backstage West
5055 Wilshire Blvd. - 5th floor
Los Angeles, CA 90036
323/525-2356 • 323/525-2354 - fax
www.backstagewest.com

The theatrical trade paper for the west coast.

Breakdown Services, Ltd.
1120 S. Robertson Blvd. - 3rd floor
Los Angeles, CA 90035
310/276-9166 • 310/276-8829 - fax
www.breakdownservices.com

Creates cast breakdowns for film, TV, theatre and commercials.

Callboard
870 Market St. #375
San Francisco, CA 94102
415/430-1140 • 415/430-1145 - fax
www.theatrebayarea.org
The theatrical trade paper for the San Francisco area.

Casting News
P.O. Box 201
Boston, MA 02134
617/787-2991
The theatre and film trade paper for Boston and Eastern Massachusettes.

CastNet
5757 Wilshire Blvd #124
Los Angeles, CA 90036
888/873-7373 • 323/964-1050 - fax
www.castnet.com

Equity News
Actors Equity Association
165 W. 46th
New York, NY 10036
212/719-9570 • 212/921-8454 - fax
Union news and updates for members.

Hollywood Reporter
5055 Wilshire Blvd.
Los Angeles, CA 90036
323/525-2150 • 323/525-1583 - fax
www.hollywoodreporter.com

The National Casting Guide
888/332-6700
www.pgdirect.com
Resource directory for the acting industry on a national basis.

Ross Reports Television and Film
1515 Broadway - 14th floor
New York, NY 10036
800/817-3273
212/536-5178 • 212/536-5294 - fax
www.backstage.com/rossreports
Updates on production and casting in feature film and television.

Screen Magazine
16 W. Erie - 2nd floor
Chicago, IL 60610
312/664-5236 • 312/664-8425 - fax
www.screenmag.com
Chicago's film trade paper.

Show Music Magazine
Goodspeed Opera House
Box 466 - Goodspeed Landing
East Haddam, CT 06423-0466
860/873-8664 • 860/873-2329 - fax
www.goodspeed.org

Side Splitters
P.O. Box 5353
Wheaton, IL 60189
630/942-9710
SIDE SPLITTERS, Chicago's only comedy entertainment magazine, is dedicated to promoting comedy community members who are working here or elsewhere in the areas of standup, improv, film, t.v, radio or theatre. Side Splitters also offers performer-friendly ad rates and is a valuable networking tool. Available in clubs, theatres. Phone 630-942-9710.

Theatre Directories
P.O. Box 510
Dorset , VT 05251
802/867-2223 • 802/867-0144 - fax
800/390-2223
www.theatredirectories.com
Publishes SUMMER THEATRE DIRECTORY, REGIONAL THEATRE DIRECTORY and more.

TheatreChicago.com
P.O. Box 25179
Chicago, IL 60625
312/203-6385
www.TheatreChicago.com
TheatreChicago.com is Chicago's definitive online theatre resource. With a searchable production schedule, advertising, job postings, interviews, reviews, and directories for theatre companies, performers, technicians and many other related professionals and services, TheatreChicago.com is one-stop shopping for theatre professionals and patrons alike. And most of it's absolutely free-of-charge!

Variety
P.O. Box 16507
North Hollywood, CA 91615-6507
800/323-4345 - (weekly)
800/552-3632 - (daily)
www.variety.com

Answering Services

Burke Communications
P.O. Box 4152
Oak Park, IL 60303-4152
708/383-8580
708/386-1336 - fax
www.magicallone.com

Beepers

Ameritech
800/MOBILE-1

Comm One Wireless
1437 W. Taylor
Chicago, IL 60607
312/850-9400 • 312/850-9442 - fax

Electronic Beepers Inc.
61 E. Washington
Chicago, IL 60602
312/332-6024

MCI Worldcom
800/571-6682
312/781-6030

Metrotone Paging
3321 N. Milwaukee
Chicago , IL 60641
773/777-4555 • 773/777-2810 - fax

PageMart
800/864-4357 • 888/304-9899 - fax
www.pagemart.com

PortaCom
531 S. Dearborn
Chicago, IL 60605
312/939-PAGE • 312/939-7759 - fax

Skynet
800/577-4SKY

Skytel
800/456-3333

SmartBeep
800/BEEP-199

The Sound Advantage
2911 N. Clark
Chicago, IL 60657
773/404-1288 • 773/404-1291 - fax

Cell Phones

Ameritech
800/MOBILE-1

AT&T
888/344-3332

Cellular One
800/CELLONE

Comm One Wireless
1437 W. Taylor
Chicago, IL 60607
312/850-9400
312/850-9442 - fax

Metrotone Paging
3321 N. Milwaukee
Chicago , IL 60641
773/777-4555
773/777-2810 - fax

Nextel
800/NEXTEL9

MCI Worldcom
800/571-6682
312/781-6030

PrimeCo
800/774-6326

Skynet
800/577-4SKY

The Sound Advantage
2911 N. Clark
Chicago, IL 60657
773/404-1288
773/404-1291 - fax

Makeup Supplies

All Dressed Up Costumes
150 S. Water
Batavia, IL 60510
630/879-5130 • 630/879-3374 - fax
www.alldressedupcostumes.com

Broadway Costumes, Inc.
1100 W. Cermak
Chicago, IL 60608
312/829-6400 • 312/829-8621 - fax
www.broadwaycostumes.com

Cat'Ania's Hollywood Make-Up & Hair
170th Torrence Ave.
2 River Place #L
Lansing, IL 60438
708/889-9800 • 708/889-9802 - fax
Chicagoland's Newest & Finest Industry Cosmetic Center & Beauty Salon, Cat'Ania's Hollywood Make-Up & Hair offers a Complete Line of Professional Cosmetics, Beauty Products & Accessories for the Television, Theatre & Motion Picture Industry. We are dedicated to servicing the Midwest. ***Come Celebrate Our Grand Opening!*** *During the New Year 2000. Where You'll Find IMAN, RCMA, Patti LeBelle, Taut, Tom & Tina Aromatherapy, Kryolan, Ben Nye, La Femme, other fine cosmetic lines, and fragrances. Also available Purellair, Paul Mitchell, Modern Elixirs, American Crew, d:fi, Jungle Care, Wigs, Hair Pieces, Tools of the Trade, Make-Up & Hair Cases, Skin & Hair Care Products, BeautySalon, Delivery and 24 Hour Service & More...*

Center Stage
497 Rt. 59
Aurora, IL 60504
630/851-9191

Che Sguardo Makeup Studio
500 N. Wells
Chicago, IL 60610
312/527-0821 • 888/858-9012

Chicago Hair Group
734 N. LaSalle
Chicago, IL 60610
312/337-4247
Focusing primarily on wigs.

Fantasy Costumes Headquarters
(see our ad on page 106)
4065 N. Milwaukee
Chicago, IL 60641
773/777-0222
800/USA-WIGS
773/777-4228 - fax
www.fantasycostumes.com

Grand Stage Lighting Company
630 W. Lake
Chicago, IL 60661
312/332-5611 • 312/258-0056 - fax

Josie O'Kain Costume & Theatre Shop
2419B W. Jefferson St.
Joliet, IL 60435
815/741-9303 • 815/741-9316 - fax
www.josieokain.com

Razzle Dazzle Costumes
1038 Lake St.
Oak Park, IL 60301
708/383-5962 • 708/383-0069 - fax

Riley's Trick & Novelty Shop
6442 W. 111th
Worth, IL 60482
708/448-0075 • 708/448-0999 - fax
www.rileystrickshop.com

Syd Simons Cosmetics, Inc.
6601 W. North Ave.
Oak Park, IL 60302
877/943-2333 • 708/660-0266
www.sydsimons.com

Stage Weapons

Arms and Armor
1101 Stinson Blvd. NE
Minneapolis, MN 55413
612/331-6473
www.armor.com

Center Firearms Co.
10 W. 37th St.
New York, NY 10018
212/244-4040
212/947-1233 - fax

Sheet Music

Act I Bookstore
2540 N. Lincoln
Chicago, IL 60614
773/348-6757 • 773/348-5561 - fax
800/55PLAYS
www.act1books.com
Act I Bookstore serves everyone from Chicago to Sao Paolo to Istanbul for its theatre and film book needs. You can find thousands of plays, acting books, screenplays, agent listings, monologues, musicals, audition notices, reading copies of shows currently auditioning, a professional resumé service, theatre games, and many other books for actors, directors, writers, producers, designers, teachers and filmmakers. Open Mon-Wed 10-8 and Thur-Sun 10-6. The best online bookstore for theatre and film is www.act1books.com.

Carl Fisher Music
333 S. State
Chicago, IL 60604
312/427-6652 • 312/427-6653 - fax

Lighting Rental

Chicago Spotlight, Inc.
1658 W. Carroll
Chicago, IL 60612
312/455-1171 • 312/455-1744 - fax
www.chicagospotlight.com

Designlab
806 N. Peoria - 2nd floor
Chicago, IL 60622
312/738-3305 • 312/738-2402 - fax
www.designlab-chicago.com

Grand Stage Lighting Company
630 W. Lake
Chicago, IL 60661
312/332-5611 • 312/258-0056 - fax

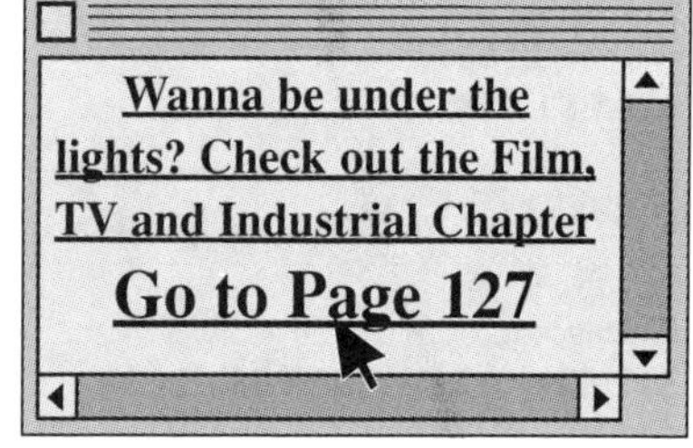

Wanna be under the lights? Check out the Film, TV and Industrial Chapter
Go to Page 127

Dance Supplies

American Dance Center Ballet Co.
10464 W. 163rd Pl.
Orland Park, IL 60462
708/747-4969 • 708/747-0424 - fax

Big N Little Shoes
3142 W. 111th
Chicago, IL 60655
773/239-6066

Dance & Mime Shop
643 W. Grand
Chicago, IL 60610
312/666-4406

Dance Arts, Ltd.
280 Palatine Rd.
Wheeling, IL 60090
847/459-9071

Illinois Theatrical
P.O. Box 34284
Chicago, IL 60634
773/745-7777 • **800/745-3777**
800/877-6027 - fax

Kling's Theatrical Shoe Company
218 S. Wabash - 8th floor
Chicago, IL 60604
312/427-2028 • 312/427-3929 - fax

Leo's Dancewear
1900 N. Narragansett
Chicago, IL 60639
773/745-5600 • 773/889-7593 - fax

Motion Unlimited
218 S. Wabash - 8th floor
Chicago, IL 60604
312/922-3330 • 312/922-7770 – fax

Costume Shops

All Dressed Up Costumes
150 S. Water
Batavia, IL 60510
630/879-5130 • 630/879-3374 - fax
www.alldressedupcostumes.com

Bead Different
214 E. Chicago Ave.
Westmont, IL 60559
630/323-1962

Beatnix
3400 N. Halsted
Chicago, IL 60657
773/281-6933

Beverly Costume Shop
11628 S. Western
Chicago, IL 60643
773/779-0068 • 773/779-2434 - fax

Broadway Costumes, Inc.
1100 W. Cermak
Chicago, IL 60608
312/829-6400 • 312/829-8621 - fax
www.broadwaycostumes.com

Cat'Ania's Hollywood Make-Up & Hair
170th Torrence Ave.
2 River Place #L
Lansing, IL 60438
708/889-9800 • 708/889-9802 - fax
Prosthetics, SPFX Supplies & Halloween Masks & Makeup, Stage and Film Make-Up Workshops.

The Actor's Tools

Center Stage
497 Rt. 59
Aurora, IL 60504
630/851-9191

Chicago Costume Company
1120 W. Fullerton
Chicago, IL 60614
773/528-1264 • 773/935-4197 - fax
www.chicagocostume.com

Cindy Makes Things
2000 W. Carroll
Chicago, IL 60612
312/829-0099 • 312/829-0998 - fax
www.cindymakesthings.com

Dance & Mime Shop
643 W. Grand
Chicago, IL 60610
312/666-4406

Facemakers, Inc.
140 Fifth St.
Savannah, IL 61074
815/273-3944 • 815/273-3966 - fax

Fantasy Costumes Headquarters
(see our ad below)
4065 N. Milwaukee
Chicago, IL 60641
773/777-0222
800/USA-WIGS
773/777-4228 - fax
www.fantasycostumes.com
e-mail: info@fantasycostumes.com

Flashy Trash
3524 N. Halsted
Chicago, IL 60657
773/327-6900 • 773/327-9736 - fax

Hubba Hubba
3309 N. Clark
Chicago, IL 60657
773/477-1414

Josie O'Kain Costume & Theatre Shop
2419B W. Jefferson St.
Joliet, IL 60435
815/741-9303 • 815/741-9316 - fax
www.josieokain.com

Leo's Dancewear
1900 N. Narragansett
Chicago, IL 60639
773/745-5600 • 773/889-7593 - fax

A Lost Eras Costumes & Props
Charlotte Walters
1511 W. Howard
Chicago, IL 60626
773/764-7400 • 773/764-7433 - fax

Razzle Dazzle Costumes
1038 Lake St.
Oak Park, IL 60301
708/383-5962 • 708/383-0069 - fax

Show Off
1472 Elmhurst Rd.
Elk Grove Village, IL 60007
847/439-0206 • 847/439-0219 - fax

Task Force Military
2341 W. Belmont
Chicago, IL 60618
773/477-7096

Victorian Emphasis
918 Green Bay Rd.
Winnetka, IL 60093
847/441-6675

Thrift Stores

Ark Thrift Shop
3345 N. Lincoln
Chicago, IL 60657
773/248-1117

Ark Thrift Shop
1302 N. Milwaukee
Chicago, IL 60622
773/862-5011

Brown Elephant Resale
3651 N. Halsted
Chicago, IL 60657
773/549-5943

Brown Elephant Resale
3939 N. Ashland
Chicago, IL 60657
773/244-2930

Chicago's Recycle Shop
5308 N. Clark
Chicago, IL 60640
773/878-8525

Disgraceland
3338 N. Clark
Chicago, IL 60657
773/281-5875

Kismet Vintage Clothing and Furniture
2923 N. Southport
Chicago, IL 60657
773/528-4497

Little City Resale Shop
1720 W. Algonquin
Palatine, IL 60067
847/221-7130 • 847/358-3291 - fax

Ragstock
812 W. Belmont - 2nd floor
Chicago, IL 60657
773/868-9263 • 773/868-6819 - fax
www.ragstock.com

Right Place
5219 N. Clark
Chicago, IL 60640
773/561-7757

Sale Barn Square
971 N. Milwaukee
Wheeling, IL 60090
847/537-9886
www.salebarnsquare.com

Salvation Army Thrift Store
General Number
773/477-1771
www.salvationarmy.org

Time Well
Consignment Furniture
2780 N. Lincoln
Chicago, IL 60614
773/549-2113
www.chicago-antiques.com/time_well.htm

Unique Thrift Store
3224 S. Halsted
Chicago, IL 60608
312/842-8123

Libraries

Harold Washington Public Library
Chicago Public Libraries
400 S. State
Chicago, IL 60610
312/747-4300
www.chipublib.org

Newberry Library
60 W. Walton
Chicago, IL 60610
312/943-9090

North Suburban Library System
847/459-1300
www.nslsilus.org

Stock Montage
104 N. Halsted #200
Chicago, IL 60661
312/733-3239 • 312/733-2844 - fax
Library of stock stills

Bookstores

Act I Bookstore
2540 N. Lincoln
Chicago, IL 60614
773/348-6757 • 800/55PLAYS
773/348-5561 - fax
www.act1books.com
Act I Bookstore serves everyone from Chicago to Sao Paolo to Istanbul for its theatre and film book needs. You can find thousands of plays, acting books, screenplays, agent listings, monologues, musicals, audition notices, reading copies of shows currently auditioning, a professional resumé service, theatre games, and many other books for actors, directors, writers, producers, designers, teachers and filmmakers. Open Mon-Wed 10-8 and Thur-Sun 10-6. The best online bookstore for theatre and film is www.act1books.com.

Afterwords Bookstore
23 E. Illinois
Chicago, IL 60611
312/464-1110
www.abebooks.com/home/afterwords

Barbara's Bookstore
1350 N. Wells
Chicago, IL 60610
312/642-5044 • 312/642-0522 - fax

Barbara's Bookstore
700 E. Grand
Chicago, IL 60611
312/222-0890

Barnes and Noble Bookstore
659 W. Diversey
Chicago, IL 60614
773/871-9004 • 773/871-5893 - fax
www.bn.com

Borders Books, Music & Cafe
830 N. Michigan
Chicago, IL 60610
312/573-0564
www.borders.com

Borders Books & Music
2817 N. Clark
Chicago, IL 60657
773/935-3909
www.borders.com

Feedback Theatrebooks
P.O. Box 220
Brooklin, ME 04616
207/359-2781 • 207/359-5532 - fax
Publishes books dealing with theatre.

Showfax
800/886-8716
www.showfax.com

Unabridged Books
3251 N. Broadway
Chicago, IL 60657
773/883-9119 • 773/883-9559 - fax

Casting Hotlines

The latest auditions are put on these hotlines first. The Audition Hotline and Casting Call Hotline are updated twice weekly.

Casting Call Hotline
2944 N. Broadway
Chicago, IL 60657
976-CAST • 773/529-9040
773/935-3951 - fax
www.redhenproductions.com/castcall

Illinois Filmboard Hotline
312/427-FILM

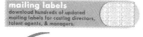

Talent and Casting Agencies

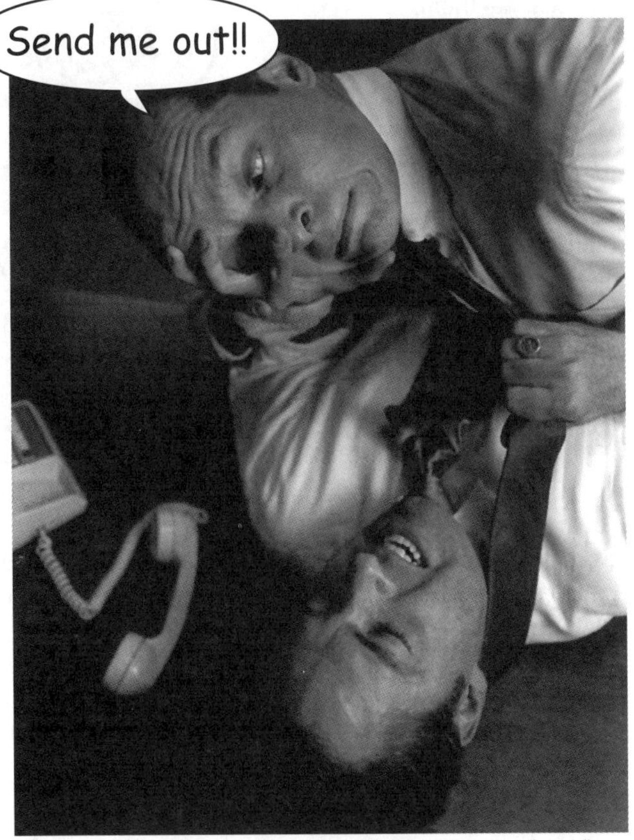

The Aardvark's "Descent: A Darwinian Comedy" – pictured (top to bottom): Mark Ulrich, Robert Bailey.

Developing a Healthy Relationship with Your Agent

if you know That I do fawn
on men and hug them hard,

And after scandal them;
hold me dangerous.

By Tab Baker

A good talent-agent relationship is like flagging a taxi to get around in an unknown city.

Realize that the driver has made a substantial investment to get a taxi and is driving to make money. You, likewise, have made a substantial investment and need to get to your destination to make money. They make money when you arrive. During the ride, you don't have to have a great chat with the driver, but common courtesies are simple; but if you're both in a chatty mood, chat away. If either of you is all about business or not having the greatest day, respect that. The primary thrust of this analogy is: **You need to get somewhere, so you hire someone to drive you.** Yes, you could drive yourself, but the expense of owning or renting a car in this foreign city is too rich for your budget (as would be the expense of maintaining contact with all of the casting people your agent submits to via phone, fax, FedEx, messenger and mail—every day).

The question is: which taxi to flag down?

Choose Your Agent Intelligently

You rightfully expect a well-maintained taxi and a knowledgeable driver. You agree to pay the driver to **get you there safely, by the most efficient route and for a fair price.** You wouldn't take a taxi that had smoke coming from the engine or a bad smell in the interior. And you would question the driver if he seemed to be taking a circuitous route or was exceptionally rude to you. This same sensibility applies with agents—whether you are multi-listed and flagging down the first taxi to pull up or exclusive and at a point where you hire a service to drive you.

Know Where You Want To Go

I can't emphasize enough the importance of **knowing where you want to go.** The taxi driver can't get you there by circling the block until you decide whether you want to go to the airport or the train station—neither can your agent. And truth be told, there are lots of other fares waiting for a ride who have already decided where they want to go.

Here are some other tips for having a good relationship with your agent:

1. Every Agency is a business, just as you are.

Your objective is not to become friends with your agent or "schmooze" your way into stardom. Admittedly, both of these can be great perks, but your primary objective is to develop a healthy business relationship that is **mutually beneficial**.

2. Every person within the Agency is human, just as you are.

You have bad days and good ones—as do they. Pay attention to the vibe. It's not "butt-kissing" to send a thank-you note after a booking or to **sincerely ask** your agent how they are feeling if they seem to be having a bad day. But if it's not sincere, save the energy, take care of business and graciously leave.

And in the name of multi-universal deities, treat the receptionist with respect! Piss them off and your calls could always go to voice-mail or your resumé might never make it to an agent's desk. The receptionist truly has the power to put things in the "maybe" pile.

3. Learn their skills, as you expect them to know yours.

You may be tremendously talented in one area and not so hot in another—as are they. **Learn the responsibilities of people in the agency.** The agent who handles stage probably won't be able to answer your on-camera question accurately, and asking the wrong person clearly shows that you haven't taken much time to do your homework.

4. You carry the weight as the business who hires and pays.

You contract the agency to submit you for auditions, arrange times, negotiate contracts and intercede if there are problems on the job. In exchange for this service, **you pay them**—10 percent of your income from the job (up to 20 percent if it is print work).

You, as a business, execute all of the contracts. Pay attention and ask questions about the responsibilities your business is committing to—**before you sign!** It is your responsibility to speak up when you feel the services you contracted for were not delivered. And you and the agent mutually share the power to terminate the agreement if the terms agreed to are not being met.

5. If you don't know, ask.

If you are executing a contract directly with a client, check with your agent first. Every agent in the city can tell horror stories of a "Must-Join" who never asked the meaning of Taft-Hartley, signed a contract and then didn't have money to join the union on the day of a shoot. Even though the agent may intercede, the final weight is on you. **It makes you both look bad**, loses money for your business and, consequently, theirs.

6. Keep people informed.

Good execution of business usually leads to continued improvement in your product. However, it doesn't do much good if no one knows that your product is **"New and Improved."**

Before you get a drastic hair change, factor the cost of new headshots into the expense of the style.

Mail postcards to keep people apprised of jobs you have done or are doing. Don't be disappointed if they don't come to see your show; the point is to keep them informed and keep your growing product in the top of their minds.

Call in before you go out of town. Creating a situation where your agent makes a commitment based on misinformation from you is one of the surest ways to destroy a potentially healthy relationship.

Not every agency is a perfect match for everyone. Even though your best college friend recommended this agency because she has a great relationship and gets bookings all of the time, it may not be the same for you at this agency. If you get a strange "vibe" from the initial meeting with the agency (or even after you've been there for a while) ask the "human beings" (who are the agents) if there is a way to make the business relationship work better. If you've been clear and realistic in your statement of where you want to go, and they have been forthright in the people whom they desire to represent, the conversation should be fairly straightforward.

Be thorough…Be sincere…Good luck.

Getting an Agent Checklist

Dealing with your agent(s) is a full-time job, but if you do it well, it can be lucrative. Keep these steps in mind when seeking an agent:

1. Mailing

Materials

Your mailing should include a headshot and resumé, a cover letter and a self-addressed, stamped envelope. Refer to the checklists for headshots and resumés for more info.

Research

Different agencies do different things. Some focus on minority talent. Some are union, some aren't. Some handle theatrical bookings. Some have offices both here and in L.A. Check them out through this book and Act I Reports before you start submitting.

2. Audition

I Should Bring...

Have at least 25 headshots and resumés with you and ready to go. If they want to represent you, you should be ready.

My Pieces

Have two or three pieces ready, even if they only want one. They'll probably put you on tape, so choose pieces that are suited to film. All these pieces should be contemporary; few agents care whether or not you can handle Shakespeare.

3. Relationship

Multi-Listing vs. Exclusivity

Most agents will not want to sign you exclusively at first. They'll wait until they've worked with you and decided that you're worth the commitment. One exception to this is C.E.D., which only signs talent exclusively. In the meantime, you can sign with as many agents as you want. This is very different from L.A. or New York, where all talent is signed exclusively.

Blah Blah

Checking In

Every agency has different policies for checking in. Follow them. You want to remind your agents that you exist without irritating them. To this end, call with specific questions, not general chit-chat (e.g., "I was just calling to make sure you had enough pictures and resumés" is much more palatable than "Hey! How ya' doin'?"). Don't drop by, unless that's the specific preference of the agent. Remember, they're busy trying to get you work. There's fine line to follow here between keeping your face in their head and making them want to issue a restraining order. Use common sense.

Communicate

Let them know how an audition went. Keep them posted on the shows you do, the classes you take and the projects you're working on. Most importantly, let them know when you're going out of town (otherwise known as "booking out"). Nothing irritates an agent more than calling an actor and finding out they're on tour for the next month.

Union Status

It's up to you to keep track of your union status. If your next union job means you have to join, let your agent know.

Commission

An agent can only take 10 percent on a union job. They can take 20 percent for print work. If the gig is non-union, the agency can take more than 10 percent, and many do. Pay attention to the percentage your agent takes, particularly if you notice it changing. Incidentally, if an agent takes over 10 percent on a union job, they're breaking the law.

Ring, Damnit!

4. Booking

Be Available

Keep your pager with you. If your agent wants to send you out, they may want to send you out right now.

Get the Info

Be sure you know where the audition is, when they're expecting you, whether there's copy, what you should wear, when it shoots, etc. Your agent may be in a hurry to get off the phone, but if you don't know these things you're going to look bad at the audition.

5. Exclusivity

Benefits

Being exclusive is more prestigious, and you usually get more attention. The agency has invested in you, so they're more likely to try to get you work.

Problems

Be sure you like your agency and the people you're dealing with before you go exclusive. You're stuck with them. Also, inform other agencies that represent you of your decision promptly.

6. Collecting

It's your responsibility to collect from your agent. Keep track of what they owe you. This can be a difficult game to play, as many actors don't want to anger their agent by bugging them for money. However, they do have a responsibility to pay you. If you need to know what your legal rights are, you can start by calling Joyce Markmann at the Illinois Department of Labor. Also check out "Actors Don't Have to Be Victims" in the UNIONS chapter.

7. Scams

No agent should ever insist that you get headshots with a particular photographer or that you take classes from a particular studio. They can recommend, but they can't insist. Similarly, they shouldn't charge you a fee to sign with their agency. These are all scams designed to take advantage of inexperienced actors. If this happens, or if you're placed in any other situation that makes you uncomfortable, find another agent.

Talent Agencies

Ambassador Talent
333 N. Michigan #910
Chicago, IL 60601
312/641-3491
SAG/AFTRA/AFM franchised
Registration Policy: Send headshot and resumé. Agency will call if interested. All ages.

Aria Model and Talent Management
1017 W. Washington #2C
Chicago, IL 60607
312/243-9400 • 312/243-9020 - fax
SAG/AFTRA/Equity franchised
Co-Owners - Mary Boncher, Marie Anderson Boyd
On-Camera, TV, Film - Tracy Stewart-Kaplan
Registration Policy: Actors/models must submit resumé photo/composite by mail. Agency will contact you if interested. No voice-over or screenwriters. Open call Fri 4-4:30 p.m.

Arlene Wilson Models
430 W. Erie #210
Chicago, IL 60610
312/573-0200
www.arlenewilson.com
AFTRA/SAG/Equity franchised
On-Camera - Peter Forster, Anna Jordan
Voice-Over - Anna Jordan
Registration Policy: Submit headshot and resumé by mail first. The agency will contact you if interested.

Baker & Rowley
17 N. Loomis #2J
Chicago, IL 60607
773/252-7900 • 312/243-4953 - fax
AFTRA/SAG franchised
On-Camera, Film, Print, Voice-Over, Tradeshow, Promotions - Diane Rowley, Richard Baker, Roberta Kablach
Commercial and Film - A. Ashley Hoff
Theatre, Musical Theatre - Emily Golan
Registration Policy: Send one headshot and resumé and voice demo with a S.A.S.E. Agent will contact you if interested. Multi-cultural representation. Open registration Tuesdays 12-2pm. No other drop-ins.

Big Mouth Talent
935 W. Chestnut #415
Chicago, IL 60622
312/421-4400 • 312/421-4403 - fax
Brooke Tonneman
Registration Policy: Send headshot and resumé with a S.A.S.E. Agency will call if interested. All ages.

CastNet
5757 Wilshire Blvd #124
Los Angeles, CA 90036
888/873-7373 • 323/964-1050 - fax
www.castnet.com

CED (Cunningham, Escott, DiPene)
1 E. Superior #505
Chicago, IL 60611
312/944-5600 • 312/944-5694 - fax
SAG/AFTRA/Equity franchised
On-Camera, Stage - Diane Herro Sanford
Industrial and Commercial - Nate Tico
Voice-Over - Gina Mazza
Registration Policy: Send photo/resumé, demo. Agent will call if interested. Representing only exclusive clients.

ChicagoActors.com
4933 W. Louise St. #1
Skokie, IL 60077
847/674-2277
www.chicagoactors.com
Chicago's Source for Talent - our state-of-the-art internet database provides actors with a resource to place their headshot and resumé on-line for industry professionals to look at worldwide. Additionally, resources, links, audition notices and local theatrical reviews are available for actors. Actors can now register their contact information and a thumbnail headshot on-line for FREE.

Elite Model Management
58 W. Huron
Chicago, IL 60610
312/943-3131 • 312/943-2590 - fax
AFTRA/SAG/Equity franchised.
TV, Stage, Film - Maureen Brookman, Maryann Drake, Todd Turina
Industrial Film - Nancy Kidder
Voice-Over - Joan Sparks
Registration Policy for Actors: Mail or drop off two pictures and resumés. The appropriate agent will contact you within six to eight weeks if interested. No walk-ins.

Emilia Lorence Ltd.
325 W. Huron #404
Chicago, IL 60610
312/787-2033 • 312/787-5239 - fax
AFTRA/SAG/Equity franchised
President - Judy Kasner
On-Camera - Nick DeBok, Jackie Grimes, Judy Kasner
Industrial, Film - Nick DeBok, Jackie Grimes, Judy Kasner
Voice-Over - Jackie Grimes
TV - Judy Kasner
Open registration on Mon., Wed., Fri., 2:30pm- 4pm. Closed daily between 12:00 & 2:00. Actors should bring 3 headshots and resumés. Voice-over talent should submit a tape. Agency will call for reading at a later date if interested.

ETA, Inc.
7558 S. South Chicago Ave.
Chicago, IL 60619
773/752-3955 • 773/752-8727 - fax
SAG/AFTRA franchised
Registration policy: Mail composites and resumés to Joan P. Brown, who will contact you if interested.

Geddes Agency
1633 N. Halsted #400
Chicago, IL 60614
312/787-8333 • 312/787-6677 - fax
AFTRA/SAG/Equity franchised
Film, TV, Theatre - Elizabeth Geddes, Paula Muzik, Erica Daniels
Commercial, Industrial - Polly Rich,
Voice-Over - Beth-Ann Zeitler
Registration Policy: Actors must submit headshot and resumé by mail only. Agency will call if interested.

Harrise Davidson & Associates
65 E. Wacker #2401
Chicago, IL 60601
312/782-4480 • 312/782-3363 - fax
AFTRA/SAG/Equity franchised
President - Harrise Davidson
Commercial and Film - Gina Wake
Industrial Film - Jeanie Moeslein
Registration Policy: No drop-ins. Registration for actors and actresses on Wednesdays from 3pm to 4pm. Children and models please send photos; agency will contact you if interested. When registering, bring two headshots with resumés attached.

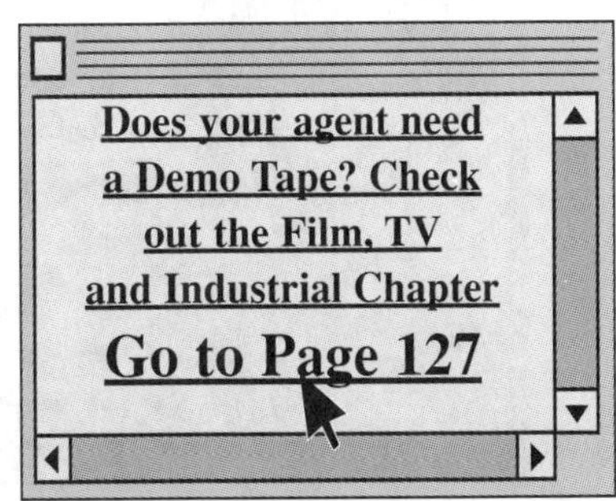

Does your agent need
a Demo Tape? Check
out the Film, TV
and Industrial Chapter
Go to Page 127

Latin Choice Entertainment
Choice Modeling - Modeling Division
1120 N. LaSalle #10J
Chicago, IL 60610
312/787-4790 • 312/787-7432 - fax
www.latinchoice.com
President - Karyn Suarez
Registration Policy - Ethnic Types preferred, but all types considered and represented. Send headshots/composites and/or snapshots by mail first with S.A.S.E. The agency will contact you if interested. Ages 16 and up. All models must send photos to Choice Modeling division. No drop-ins.

Lily's Talent Agency, Inc.
5962 N. Elston
Chicago, IL 60646
773/792-1160 • 773/792-0939 - fax
AFTRA/SAG/Equity franchised
President - Lily Ho
On-Camera - Sara Strezepek
Registration Policy: Actors must submit two headshots and resumés and S.A.S.E. by mail. Include phone number and statistics. Agency will respond if interested.

Linda Jack Talent
230 E. Ohio #200
Chicago, IL 60611
312/587-1155 • 312/587-2122 - fax
AFTRA/ SAG franchised
Voice-Over - Linda Jack, Jamie Marchi
On-Camera - Mickey Grossman, Linda Bernasconi, Stacy Schafer
New Talent Submissions - Stacy Schafer
Registration policy: Submit by mail.

McBlaine & Associates, Inc.
805 Touhy Ave.
Park Ridge, IL 60068
847/823-3877
President - Mary Poplawski
Voice-Over, Industrial, Commercial, Film, Children, New Faces - Kristin Runfeldt, Paige Ehlman, Brett Ehlman
Registration Policy: No drop-ins. Send a headshot and resumé with a S.A.S.E.

McCall Model & Talent
6930 South Shore #1
Chicago, IL 60649
773/256-1264 • 773/256-1279 - fax
AFTRA/SAG franchised
Voice-Over, Commercial Print,
Industrials - Rochelle McCall
Registration Policy: Appt. only. Send headshot or color snapshot (preferred).

Nicosia Entertainment Enterprises
(See our ad on page 120)
305 W. Hackberry Dr.
Arlington Heights, IL 60004
847/392-9259
708/348-2306-pgr.
Registration Policy: H/R, demo tapes, video. Send S.A.S.E. No phone calls. Audition Policy: Will call if interested.

Norman Schucart Enterprises
1417 Green Bay Rd.
Highland Park, IL 60035
847/433-1113
AFTRA/SAG franchised
TV, Industrial Film, Print, Live Shows -
Norman Schucart, Nancy Elliott
Registration Policy: New talent should first submit headshot/composite and resumé with phone number by mail (include S.A.S.E. postcard). If interested, the agency will arrange to interview you in Chicago.

North Shore Talent, Inc.
454 Peterson Rd.
Libertyville, IL 60048
847/816-1811
847/816-1819
847/816-1717 - fax
On-Camera, Voice-Over, Print,
Promotion, Convention, Runway -
Sherrill Tripp
Registration Policy: Talent check-in line 847/816-1819. Submit headshot, resumé and any marketing materials (non-returnable). Agency will call if interested. Registration by appointment only. No drop-ins.

Nouvelle Talent
P.O. Box 578100
Chicago, IL 60657
312/944-1133
AFTRA/SAG/Equity franchised
TV, Film, Trade Show - Ann Toni Sipka
Trade Show - Carlotta Young
Registration Policy: Send picture and resumé. Agency will contact you if interested.

Premiere Model & Talent Management
27 E. Monroe #200
Chicago, IL 60603
312/726-8089 • 312/726-8019 - fax
www.premiereagency.com
Shay Mathew - Agency Director
Registration Policy: Open call Thursday from 1- 2 pm.

Sa-Rah Talent
222 S. Morgan #2C
Chicago, IL 60607
312/733-2822
AFTRA/SAG franchised
Voice-Over, Print, Commercial, Film,
Industrial - Jacquelyn Conard
Registration Policy: Mail photo and resumé with S.A.S.E. Agency will contact you. No drop-ins.

Salazar & Navas, Inc.
760 N. Ogden #2200
Chicago, IL 60622
312/666-1677
AFTRA/SAG franchised
On-Camera, Voice-Over, Film,
Commercial Print - Myrna Salazar, Trina Navas
Registration Policy: Hispanic/Latin types preferred, but all types considered and represented. New talent seen on Tuesday, 12-4pm.

Shirley Hamilton, Inc.
333 E. Ontario #302B
Chicago, IL 60611
312/787-4700 • 312/787-8456 - fax
AFTRA/SAG/Equity franchised
President - Shirley Hamilton
Vice President - Lynn Hamilton
TV, Film, Voice-Over - Hillary Weigel, Laurie Hamilton
Registration Policy: Registration by mail only with S.A.S.E. Actors must submit headshot and resumé. Agency will contact by mail if interested.

Stewart Talent
58 W. Huron
Chicago, IL 60610
312/943-3131
AFTRA/SAG/Equity franchised
TV, Stage, Film - Maureen Brookman, Maryann Drake, Todd Turina
Industrial Film - Nancy Kidder
Voice-Over - Joan Sparks
Print - Kathy Gardner
Children - Kathy Gardner, Sheila Dougherty
Commercials - Sheila Dougherty
Registration for Actors: mail or drop-off two pictures and resumés. The appropriate agent will contact you within six to eight weeks if interested. No walk-ins.

Suzanne's A-Plus
108 W. Oak
Chicago, IL 60610
312/642-8151
312/803-1368 - Talent Information
AFTRA/SAG/WGA franchised
On-Camera - Robert Schroeder, Nancy Tennicott, Aime Richardson
Children - Aime Richardson
New Faces - Julie Becker
Registration Policy: Actors must submit photo and resumé Attn: "on-camera" and agency will contact you in six to eight weeks if interested. Models call Monday to come in on Tuesday. Open call for models Tuesday 11-12pm sharp.

TRC Productions
4433 W. Touhy Ave. #301
Lincolnwood, IL 60712
847/763-1256 • 847/982-6868 - fax
Registration Policy: Phone or submit headshot and resumé by mail.

Voices Unlimited
541 N. Fairbanks #2850
Chicago, IL 60611
312/832-1113
AFTRA/SAG franchised
Voice-Over - Linda Bracilano, Susan Davies
Registration Policy: Voice-over talent should submit commercial and/or narrative tape, two minutes or less, with resumé. An agent will contact you if interested.

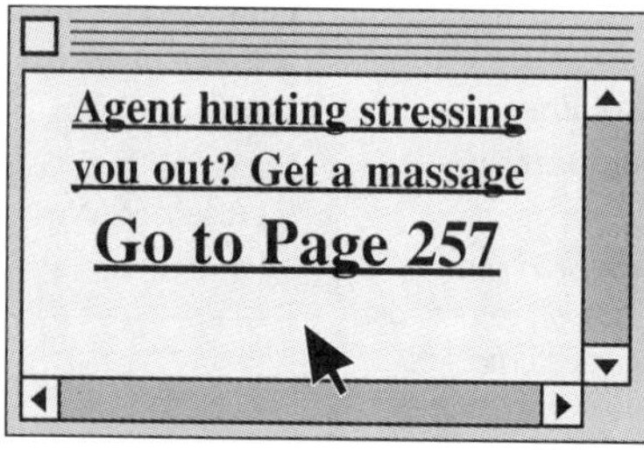

Agent hunting stressing you out? Get a massage
Go to Page 257

Talent Agencies – Milwaukee

Arlene Wilson Talent, Inc.
807 N. Jefferson #200
Milwaukee, WI 53202
414/283-5600 • 414/283-5610 - fax
www.mindspring.com/~arlene
AFTRA franchised
President - Michael Stothard
Voice-Over, On-Camera, Broadcast
Director - Carol Rathe
Registration Policy: Open call for actors Wed. 1:30-3pm. Must have current headshots and resumés or voice demo. May also send materials.

Jennifer's Talent Unlimited, Inc.
740 N. Plankinton #300
Milwaukee, WI 53203
414/277-9440
AFTRA franchised
President - Jennifer L. Berg
Registration Policy: Actors must submit a headshot and resumé. Agency will contact you if interested.

Lori Lins, Ltd.
7611 W. Holmes
Green Field, WI 53220
414/282-3500
AFTRA/SAG franchised
Booker - Lori Lins, Jenny Siedenberg, Betty Anthoine
Registration Policy: Actors must submit headshot and resumé. Agency will respond if interested.

Tradeshow Agencies

Best Faces
1152 N. LaSalle #F
Chicago, IL 60610
312/944-3009 • 312/944-7006 - fax
Registration Policy: Send materials Attn: Judy Mudd. Agency will contact you if interested.

Claire Model & Talent Management, Inc.
P.O. Box 1028
Wheeling, IL 60090
847/459-4242 • 847/459-0001 - fax
Registration: Send headshot and resumé to Clarisse Rosenstock.

Concept Model Management, Inc.
219 Eisenhower Lane
Lombard, IL 60148
630/686-6410
www.conceptmodels.com
Exclusive talent only. 17-24 years in age. No walk-ins. Send photo and resumé/ composite card. Agency will call if interested.

Corporate Presenters
(A division of Karen Stavins Enterprises)
attn: New Talent
Three Illinois Center
303 E. Wacker - Concourse
Chicago, IL 60601
312/938-1140 • 312/938-1142 - fax
Registration Policy: Submit composite or headshot. Agency will contact if interested. Narrators, hosts/hostesses and models booked for trade shows, conventions, special promotions and variety acts. 17 years and older.

Group, Ltd.
2375 E. Tropicana, Suite E
Las Vegas, NV 89119
702/895-8926
Registration: Submit headshot and resumé to Vegas office. Will contact if interested.
You can register via email at groupvegas@aol.com

Nouvelle Talent
P.O. Box 578100
Chicago, IL 60657
312/944-1133
Registration Policy: Send picture and resumé. Agency will contact you if interested.

Temporary Professionals
625 N. Michigan #600
Chicago, IL 60611
773/622-1202 • 773/622-1303 - fax
Registration policy: Submit headshot and resumé. Will contact if interested.

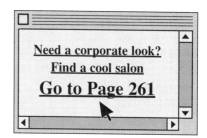

Need a corporate look?
Find a cool salon
Go to Page 261

Casting Directors

Actors are generally welcome to submit one headshot and resumé and keep in touch with post cards. Never call a casting director; it will only hurt your chances of ever getting work through that individual.

All City Casting
P.O. Box 577640
Chicago, IL 60657-7640
773/588-6062
Registration Policy: Send headshot/ resumé Attn: June Pyskacek.

Beth Rabedeau Casting
920 N. Franklin, #205
Chicago, IL 60610
312/664-0601 • 312/207-6917 - fax
Registration Policy: Send headshot and resumé Attn: Beth Rabedeau.

Brody, Tenner, Paskal
20 W. Hubbard #2E
Chicago, IL 60610
312/527-0665 • 312/527-9085 - fax
Registration Policy: Send materials Attn: Rachel Tenner, Casting Director, Mickie Paskal, Casting Director.

Simon Casting
1512 N. Fremont #202
Chicago, IL 60622
312/202-0124 • 312/202-0128 - fax
Registration Policy: Send headshot and resumé Attn: Claire Simon.

Communications Corporation of America
(See our ad above right)
Fred Strauss - Executive Producer
P.O. Box 14262
Chicago, IL 60614-0262
773/348-0001 • 773/472-6557 - fax
Casts entire productions. Specialized projects Illinois Film Board member
Submission Policy: Will take submissions through mail. No walk-ins, no calls. Send to Fred Strauss Communciations.

David O'Connor Casting
1017 W. Washington #2A
Chicago, IL 60607
312/226-9112
Registration Policy: Send headshot and resumé Attn: David O'Connor, Carrie Buhl, Sarah Reule.

HollyRik Heitz Casting
920 N. Franklin #205
Chicago, IL 60610
312/664-0601 • 312/664-3297 - fax
www.HollyRik.com
Registration Policy: Send materials Attn: Rik Kristinat.

Holzer & Ridge Casting
773/549-3169
Registration Policy: For registration information, call 773/549-3169.

Jane Alderman Casting
833 W. Chicago #103
Chicago, IL 60622
312/563-1566 • 312/563-1567 - fax
Registration Policy: Send headshot/ resumé Attn: Jane Alderman.

JAZ Casting
3617 N. Kedvale
Chicago, IL 60641
312/343-8111
Registration Policy: Send materials Attn: Jennifer Rudnicke.

Kordos & Charbonneau
P.O. Box 420
Wilmette, IL 60091
847/674-4775
Registration Policy: Send headshot and resumé Attn: Richard Kordos or Nan Charbonneau.

Segal Studio
1040 W. Huron
Chicago, IL 60622
312/563-9368
Registration Policy: Send headshot and resumé Attn: Jeffrey Lyle Segal.

Extras Casting

Holzer & Ridge Casting
773/549-3169
Registration Policy: For registration information, call 773/549-3169.

K.T.'s
P.O. Box 577039
Chicago, IL 60657-7039
Registration Policy: Send 6 pictures or composites. Include on resumé phone number, address, social security number, height, weight, hair and eye color, age (or age range), car color and make.

Karen Peake Casting
1212 S. Michigan #1002
Chicago, IL 60605
312/360-9266
Registration Policy: Send S.A.S.E to get registration information.

McCall Model & Talent
6930 South Shore Dr. #1
Chicago, IL 60649
773/256-1264 • 773/256-1279 - fax
AFTRA/SAG franchised
Registration Policy: Appt. only. Send headshot or color snapshot (preferred).

ReginaCast
P.O. Box 585
Willow Springs, IL 60480
312/409-5521
Registration Policy: Send a current photo with your age and height and a 9X12 S.A.S.E.

Literary Agents

Stewart Talent
58 W. Huron
Chicago, IL 60610
312/943-3131
Literary Submissions: Send 2 page synopsis/summary and letter of inquiry with S.A.S.E. to Stewart Talent, Attn: Literary Division. Agency will contact you if interested.

Film, TV and Industrials

Barabbas' "The Whiteheaded Boy" produced by Performing Arts Chicago

Cutting a Demo Tape

For I have neither wit,
nor words, nor worth,

Action nor utterance,
nor the power of speech

To stir men's blood.

By Katie Ayoub

Demo tapes are essential for voice-over work. The tape represents your talent. The professionals listening to your tape are busy and spare just about two minutes for you to impress them. Your demo has to pop, it has to be tight and it has to sound professional.

Most importantly, your demo tape should represent you. Know your demographic and know your skill set, then layer it into your product. Most of the coaches agree that a demo tape should run a maximum of two minutes. (Coach Sherri Berger notes that the current trend in LA is an even zippier one to one and a half minute tape.) The demo should consist of actual or virtual national or regional radio ads, not your cousin Eddie's made up copy of a car dealer's sizzling sale; professional product is the key here.

Catching an Agent

You've rolled up your sleeves and produced a dynamo demo tape. Now you want an agent to hear it, pick up the phone and beg you to let them represent you. Better yet, you want to be on their CD. The agent's CD is ground zero. It is a compilation of their best talent. The precious CD gets sent to the ad agencies who then say, "We'll take track number three. Here's a bazillion dollars."

Before your eyes glaze with images of paying off your student loans, let's backtrack to getting an agent.

"We do, eventually, listen to all of the tapes that we get," says Debby Kotzen, a voice-over agent with CED. "It should be professionally produced. If we like them we call them in, talk to them, find out where they are. We audition them. Cold reads are crucial," continues Kotzen.

That last sentence echoes in every discussion we have about voice-overs. CED likes the demo to be no more than one and a half minutes, which is the trend in LA. And regarding the controversy over head shots: "No headshots unless you're submitting on-camera as well."

Talent agent Linda Jack advises, "Actors need to remember that, for voice-over work, they need to concentrate on communication coming through the voice, not the body." Length of tape? "A minute to a minute and a half." Headshots? "Headshots are worthless to me."

Linda Bracilano, talent agent with Voices Unlimited, stresses the importance of the cold read. "We are looking for incredible cold readers. If you can't produce in the studio...well, that's not good," she says. The agency listens to all of the demo tapes. "No priority, we just go through the pile." Length of tape? "Less is more. Voice-over demo tapes are only used to get an agent. You really have to be on the agent's CD now."

Bracilano cautions actors to really think before making the tape. "Demo tapes are so expensive, you have to know that you're good. It has to be something that you have to do, not just something to make extra money or you won't make it," she stresses. Headshots? "No." Also, do not drop into her office.

"Have some training first," advises Jackie Grimes of Emilia Lorence. "The market is inundated with unmarketable voices." Length of demo? "As long as it's not more than two minutes, I'll listen to it. We want variety on the tape, if they can do it," she stresses.

Demo Tapes

Audio One, Inc.
(See our ad below)
Ray Van Steen
325 W. Huron #512
Chicago, IL 60610
312/337-5111 • 312/337-5125 - fax

Bobby Schiff Music Productions
363 Longcommon Rd.
Riverside, IL 60546
708/442-3168 • 708/447-3719 - fax

Bosco Productions
(See our ad on page 132)
160 E. Grand - 6th floor
Chicago, IL 60611
312/644-8300

Dress Rehearsals Studios, Ltd.
312/829-2213 • 312/829-4085 - fax
www.chicagostudios.com

Music Workshop
Bob Kalal
4900 W. 28th Pl.
Cicero, IL 60804
708/652-4040
members.xoom.com\musicwkshop

Renaissance Video
130 S. Jefferson
Chicago, IL 60661
312/930-5000 • 312/930-9030 - fax
www.whateverwerks.com

Sound Advice
(See our ad on page 59)
Kate McClanaghan
2028 W. Potomac #2 & 3
Chicago, IL 60622
773/772-9539 • 773/772-9006 - fax
www.voiceoverdemos.com

Sound/Video Impressions
110 S. River Rd.
Des Plaines, IL 60016
847/297-4360 • 847/297-6870 – fax

VoiceOver 101
Ray Van Steen
325 W. Huron #512
Chicago, IL 60610
312/587-1010 • 312/337-5125 - fax
Private, individual coaching sessions in voicing TV/radio commercials, narrations. Employs record/playback method in recording studio environment. Basics through production of voice-over demo. Van Steen is a published writer on the subject and has voiced thousands of commercials. Phone for free, no-obligation brochure. 312/587-1010.

Voice Over U
Sherri Berger
773/774-9559
773/774-9555 - fax
sherriberger.voicedemo.com
Sherri Berger has a sought-after ability to shape and/or renovate a performer's skill in the art of voice-overs. Using basic acting techniques, Sherri pinpoints a performer's strengths and weaknesses, keeps them in tune with trends, and helps them discover more interesting vocal nuances, styles and range capabilities.

Voices On
Thomas Test
1943 W. Belle Plaine
Chicago, IL 60613
773/528-7041
Your demo needs cutting-edge scripts and production values to stand out from the crowd. EVERY demo I've produced has resulted in agent representation for my students. Call Telly award-winning v/o talent Tom Test of "Voices On" at 773/528-7041 for private coaching, in-studio audition workshops and demo production.

Voices, Inc.
Charles Fuller
241 Douglas
Bolingbrook, IL 60440
630/739-0044 • 630/739-3837 - fax

Reels

Absolute Video Services, Inc.
715 S. Euclid
Oak Park, IL 60302
708/386-7550 • 708/386-2322 - fax
www.absolutevideoservices.com

Allied Digital Technologies
1200 Thorndale Ave.
Elk Grove Village, IL 60007
847/595-2900 • 847/595-8677 - fax

Argonne Electronics
7432 N. Milwaukee
Niles, IL 60714
847/647-8877

Cinema Video Center
211 E. Grand
Chicago, IL 60611
312/644-0861 • 312/644-2096 - fax
www.networkcentury.com

ELB's Entertainment, Inc.
Eugene Barksdale
2501 N. Lincoln Ave. #198
Chicago, IL 60614-2313
800/656-1585 • 312/401-7178 - fax
www.elbsentertainment.com

Film to Video Labs
5100 N. Ravenswood #200
Chicago, IL 60640
773/275-9500 • 773/275-0300 - fax
www.ftvlabs.com

Intervideo Duplication Services
3533 S. Archer
Chicago, IL 60609
773/927-9091 • 773/927-9211 - fax
www.historicvideo.com

VOICE OVER DEMO TAPES
*Private Coaching & Directing
*Full service professional recording studios
*Scripts Cassette and CD Duplication J-cards
BOSCO PRODUCTIONS
(312) 644-8300
160 E Grand Chicago IL 60611
Fax (312) 644-1893 E-mail radioact1@aol.com
www.BoscoProductions.com

Master Images Video Duplication
112 Carpenter Ave.
Wheeling, IL 60090
847/541-4440

Northwest Teleproductions
142 E. Ontario
Chicago, IL 60611
312/337-6000 • 312/337-0500 - fax
www.nwtele.com

Renaissance Video
130 S. Jefferson
Chicago, IL 60661
312/930-5000 • 312/930-9030 - fax
www.whateverwerks.com

Sound/Video Impressions
110 S. River Rd.
Des Plaines, IL 60016
847/297-4360 • 847/297-6870 - fax

Video Replay, Inc.
118 W. Grand
Chicago, IL 60610
312/467-0425 • 312/467-1045 - fax
www.videoreplaychicago.com

Using an Ear Prompter

Come on my right hand,
for this ear is deaf,

And tell me truly what
thou think'st of him.

By Katie Ayoub

Ear prompters help actors with their lines. They also help them with their bank accounts. Pros in ear prompter technique land lots of on-camera industrial work, which some refer to as the bread and butter of the Chicago actor.

An ear prompter plays back a recorded script in the talent's ear. The equipment can be wireless or wired. Both can be customized to the ear, which is important in trapping sound meant only for the benefit of the actor.

"It's kind of like patting your head and rubbing your stomach at the same time," says Steve Merle of Act One Studios. "You have to get so comfortable with the technical part that you can forget about it and get back to acting."

Ear prompters give on-camera talent cadence and help with enunciation. For the client, they're more cost-effective than teleprompters; actors supply their own ear prompters.

"The thing to avoid is what we call the 'ear prompter stare' where the actor is concentrating on hearing the voice in his head," says Merle.

Act One offers two ear prompter courses—a basic nine-week course and an advanced five-week course. Other ear prompter classes are offered by Rick Plastina and Michael Colucci.

Rick Plastina
708/386-8270
1117 N. Taylor
Oak Park IL 60302
Two hour session $150 monologues and dialogues, how to use ear prompter

---

"I teach everything about using the ear prompter for monologues and dialogues," says Rick Plastina. "The hardest thing for actors to overcome is not making it sound like a script." According to Rick, a piece should look like memorized material rather than repeated words. Brando uses one on all of his films. Nicholson used one on Hoffa. "If you use it well, no one should ever know that you're using the ear prompter."

Film, TV & Industrials

Ear Prompters

Credible Communication, Inc.
(See our ad below)

Instant Memory™ Ear Prompting Systems
155 Little John Trail NE
Atlanta, GA 30309
404/892-0660
www.ear-prompter.com

Sargon Yonan
67 E. Madison #1415
Chicago, IL 60603
312/782-7007 • 312/782-7529 - fax

Acting on Film

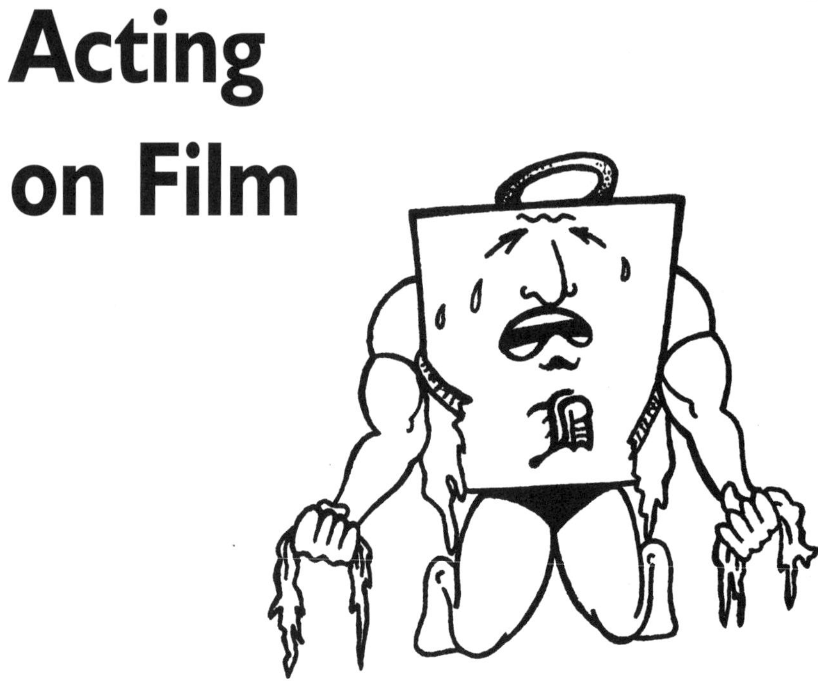

If you have tears, prepare to shed them now.

You all do know this mantle. I remember

The first time ever Caesar put it on.

By Adrianne Duncan

So…you wanna be in the movies? So do I, and I hope to give you some tips on how to do a good job once you are cast. I'd like to share what I learned while working on *The Chameleon,* the independent SAG feature shot this October in Michigan.

Even though I had been on sets many times, I knew I would need to learn about preparing for a lead role, and so I read. A lot. Three of the books I highly recommend, and from which much of this article is drawn, are **Acting in Film** by Michael Caine, **The Camera Smart Actor** by Richard Brestoff and **Secrets of Screen Acting** by Patrick Tucker.

"Acting in Film" is a series of observations and advice by Caine, the actor who starred in such films as *Alfie, Sleuth* and *Educating Rita*—to name three out of over 100. **The Camera Smart Actor** takes the reader through a typical first day on a set and explains the various functions of the crew, which is immensely helpful. **Secrets of Screen Acting** is one of the best books on film acting technique I've ever read. Tucker is a British director and tends to work more technically. Some of his advice sounds as though it would produce artificial results, but it is invaluable and works in practice.

Acting in film is about preparation. Too many actors expect that they will get on a set and be told what to do and how everything works. Most likely, you won't. You are a freelance professional who has been hired to do a specific job, and you should know what that job entails and how it fits into everyone else's job.

Don't expect that the director will give you some magical insight about how to play the character. That's not really their job. Most of what they will tell you is technical— and remember, the director is thinking in terms of the story and how you fit into it, not just about you. Any acting direction you get on a set is GRAVY.

Part of your job as an actor is to make everyone else's life easier: the director, by knowing your lines and having explored your role and made strong choices before getting on the set; the editor, by making sure your continuity is as perfect as it can be; the first AD (assistant director), by making sure they know where you are at all times.

There are two types of continuity—technical and emotional—and both are important. Technical continuity involves doing the same thing in the same way on every take. In *The Chameleon*, there is one scene in which I had to eat a bagel and drink orange juice. I choreographed for myself on which syllables I would take a bite of bagel, pick up the glass, take a sip of juice, put the glass down and so on. This helps the editors, who like to cut on a movement so that the audience will be distracted by the motion and not notice the abruptness of the cut. If you're constantly doing different actions or are moving differently, it limits the editor's options. Again, you are trying to make their lives easier. A fringe benefit is that better continuity means more chances of you being the one they cut to and stay on.

Emotional continuity involves matching your emotions and mood from scene to scene. This is important, as scenes are shot out of sequence. You should get something on the set called a "day out of days," which is a schedule of which scenes are being shot on which days (which is always subject to change). Make a time frame for yourself, both as an actor to stay organized and as a character to stay chronologically in the story. As a lead character, this is even more important since you will be carrying a large portion of the story and you need to make sense. You as the actor need to be flexible and ready for any change—that's why the timeline and any notes you can make to help yourself are such great tools.

A common misconception is that film acting is always smaller and more subtle than stage acting, when in fact the opposite is often true. Sure, in a close-up you can do a lot of acting with your eyes alone, but in a wide or a master shot you need to use your entire body to act—any less and your performance will be missed. In those types of shots you need to physicalize, not internalize. Adjusting to size of shot is an area that Patrick Tucker elaborates upon in **Secrets of Screen Acting.** Always ask the DP (director of photography) or director what the size of the shot is. You can also tell the size of the shot by how far away the boom operator is holding the mike. The boom operator wants to keep the mike right over the edge of the frame—as close as possible to pick up the sound but not to enter into the picture. You should always be aware of the size of the shot so that you can adjust your acting accordingly.

You need to adjust vocally according to size of shot as well. Remember the principle of the boom moving farther away as the shot gets wider? Your voice should follow this principle as well. In film, you do not want to over-project. Nothing sounds more artificial than a loud, over-articulated performance. Think of sucking the mike into you, rather than pushing your voice out toward the mike. Yes, in post-production they can take your voice down if you're too loud, but you will lose the intense emotional qualities you can gain by pulling in vocally.

Another area to be aware of that also goes against the "less is more" principle is reaction shots. The footage that most likely will wind up as a reaction shot is of you listening while the other character in the scene is talking. However, you have to give some kind of reaction to cut to. Even though you may feel like you are listening and reacting, it may not necessarily look like it. You have to do more with your face, not less. Listen with all of your senses and your whole body. Physicalize your reactions, but don't let your acting show.

Another great trick that Tucker gives in **Secrets of Screen Acting** is bringing your hands up into the shot. Again, this sounds artificial, but be aware of the communicative powers of your hands. If you can motivate your hands up into the frame (at key points - not all the time), the shot (and you) will be far more compelling.

Every film set is different. Depending upon the people involved, you will probably be treated according to the atmosphere on the set and the size of your role. My advice is to be nice to everyone all of the time, no matter how you are treated. Be professional and prepared. Bring wardrobe that could be used for your character— you never know how good or bad the wardrobe person can be, or how big the wardrobe budget is. Be proficient at doing your own makeup—again, you may be better than the makeup artist. This goes for men too—bring powder for shine and foundation or concealer for skin tone. Bring a portable alarm clock—you never know when the power could go out. Bring a book. Work out if you can. Calls tend to be early in the morning—try to get up half an hour early and warm up physically and vocally. Get sleep and eat right.

While you are shooting, you may be asked if you want to watch dailies. Dailies, or rushes, are rough cuts of the scenes that have already been shot and which many directors watch every day. As far as watching dailies goes, this is an issue on which actors feel differently. I didn't watch my dailies, and I'm not sure if I ever would. It is hard to be objective about your work and, when you are in the middle of the process, self-criticism could hamper your performance.

Finally, once you have done your preparation, familiarized yourself with technical terms, done your reading and research, gotten healthy and physically fit—relax! Be in the moment and concentrate on the other actors in the scene with you. Listen. React. Work moment-to-moment. The camera can read anything false. Concentrate on the relationship you have with the other character in the scene—that's what will be interesting. Know how to work with the camera, but ultimately forget about it. And try not to put too much pressure on yourself.

I read a great quote from Al Pacino in which he talks about "the courage, not just to fail, but to be utterly boring, like Brando did. They're not called 'keeps,' they're called 'takes.' Actors think you have to keep everything!" Acting in film is a blast. Take pride in your ability and your craft; treat yourself as a professional and others will return the favor.

Heading West

Far from this country
Pindarus shall run,

Where never Roman
shall take note of him.

By Tab Baker

Los Angeles—home of swimming pools and movie stars. And home to many aspiring actors. Before heading west and competing in such a saturated market, you should ask yourself the following questions:

Is Los Angeles the place for your product?

The clear objective in choosing a city is placing your product in the best market to sell your wares. Los Angeles is not the place to go if you seek a career in theatre; it's an on-camera town. Live theatre in L.A. seems to exist as a forum for finding on-camera talent. Also, Los Angeles is a union town: If you are looking to be paid for your services, a union card is a must.

The current market is tremendously fixated on attempting to capture the 18-34 year old segment of our population. As a result, 20-somethings are highly visible in the medium. This is a tremendous plus if you are: under 30, over 5'9", white and male. However, the downside is that at every audition there is a glut of people who look like you. If you are over 40, under 5'5", black and female, the roles are not nearly as plentiful. However, the upside is that fewer people are called to audition for a given role.

The under-30 male may have a greater quantity of auditions, but he must work fervently to separate himself from the pack. The over-40 female must work incessantly to increase the number of opportunities. Los Angeles has a place for both products—but **focused marketing** is demanded in each case to increase the odds.

When are you, as an actor, ready to go?

This business is a game of odds. You increase your odds by improving your product. You increase your odds by intelligently studying the market and knowing where your product fits. You increase your odds by joining organizations and hiring people who help strategically administer and position your product (e.g,. agent, accountant, manager, lawyer).

Most significantly (and optimistically), each time you receive a "no" for a job, the odds increase for the next reply to be a "yes." Be prepared to be turned down a lot. Accept the fact that extended, high-stakes risks and large investments of your own capital are part and parcel of this industry. (Making a cross-continental move definitely qualifies as a high-stakes risk of your investment!)

Some strong “musts” to **hedge your bets** for a committed and extended stay:

- Have a regular source of income.
- Have a car or be prepared to buy one.
- Know how to read a map.
- Have a SAG card or stay home until you get one.
- Know the meaning of the term “franchised agent.”
- Have a pager or cell phone with voice mail.
- Be prepared for the expense of shooting new headshots.
- Purge the industrials off your resumé.
- Have an active credit card (with a low balance) and an ATM card.
- Maintain a strong friendship/family base.

Prepare for a lifestyle change

Call it what you will: "ground wire," "wake-up call" or "point of reference," there is a strong need to know that there are people whom you trust who will be honest with you. When it seems you can do no wrong and everyone you do business with uses a sing-songy ‘fab-u-lous" to describe you—the friend/family base can help you keep a grasp on reality. Or conversely, if it seems you can’t buy your way into an audition, your karma is down and your mantra won’t work—there is someone who knows that a good "little Johnny" joke or a cup of Earl Grey will warm your spirits.

Earthquakes, riots, smog and non-stop commuting aside, “native” Californians joke that Midwesterners always complain about the lack of good pizza, seasonal changes or encountering Santa on the boulevard or garland on palm trees. These subtle changes in lifestyle that seem so simple can cause depression if there is no strong friend/family base.

Remember this:

- A move to Los Angeles as an actor is not just a change in location, it is a complete lifestyle change.
- Friendship withdrawal can be immobilizing.
- If you don't have a strong idea of who you are, then the city and industry will spin you like a top until you fall over.

Is your business strong enough to make the move?

Treat yourself as a business. Heading west as an actor is a corporate relocation without corporate perks.

If you're planning to relocate your business as an actor (or operate a Midwest and West Coast division) you would be well advised to do exploratory trips. Be clear in your mind when you are going on an "exploratory mission" and when you are making "the move." That way you will be clear with family, employers, agents and casting directors here.

If your trip is an exploratory one, make it that. You should be exploring and networking, not auditioning. Even if you manage to get a meeting with an agent on your first trip, the agent won't be very interested in representing someone who lives in Chicago. And you aren't prepared to move. It's a frustrating waste of time for both businesses.

The function of the exploratory trip is to learn the lay of the land. Find your way around. Learn the freeway systems. Fill in the blanks that articles like this can leave you with. Check out potential neighborhoods where you would like to rent. See how far it is from the Valley to West Hollywood. Look at the availability of "money jobs." Find out where the union offices are…etc, etc.

Make a budget and stick to it! And remember that it is a tax-deductible business trip. When budgeting, don't forget to include the cost of renting a car—don't put the extra weight of transportation-sharing on the friend who has let you bunk in his or her place. Include the cost of a gift for your friend. Consider timing your trip with a friend who wants to explore as well and check out a share deal on a hotel. Include the cost of three meals a day—eating out is more expensive in LA.

For your first exploratory trip—fly. There is no benefit to saving the airfare in exchange for arriving exhausted from a non-stop three day drive The advantage to booking a cheap airfare with serious restrictions is that you must commit in advance to the trip and the length of stay, or pay serious penalties. The drawback is that you might miss a Chicago booking because of the inflexibility of your airline ticket.

The exploratory trips will help to increase your odds. When you feel the odds are in your favor—make the leap.

Take a deep breath and stay true to self.

Unions and Organizations

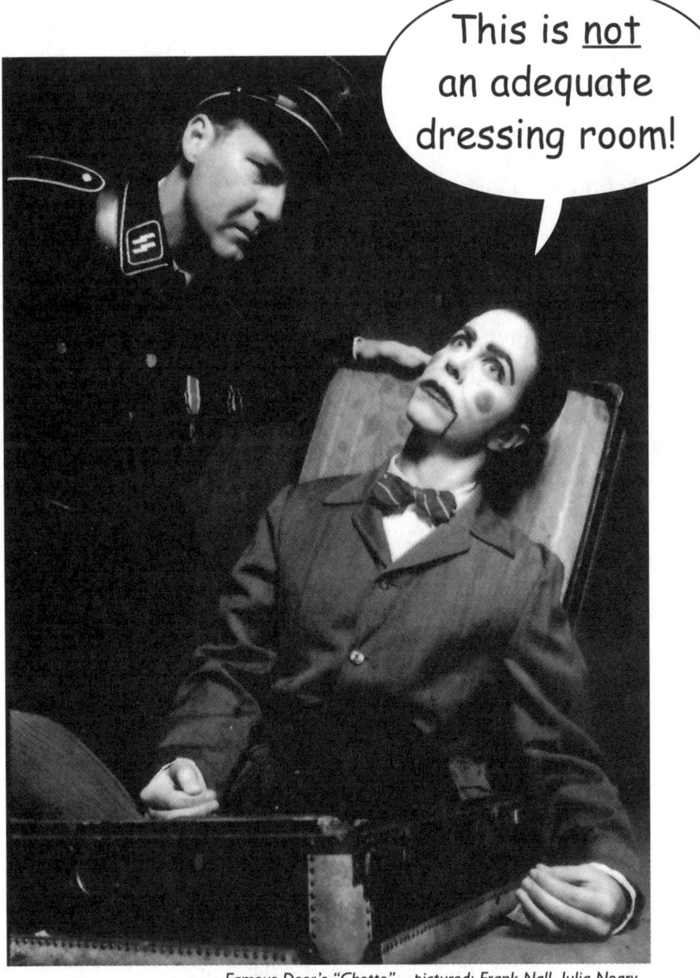

Famous Door's "Ghetto" – pictured: Frank Nall, Julia Neary – photo: Brad Miller

Actors Equity Association

But those that understood him smil'd at one another and shook their heads; but for mine own part, it was Greek to me.

By Carrie L. Kaufman

If you're at all familiar with theatre in New York or Los Angeles, you know that getting your Equity card is the first and foremost priority on young actors' minds. People do summer theatre as much for the Equity points as for the experience. They will find anything to get that Equity card.

Not in Chicago.

Non-Equity theatre rules in Chicago. There are, at any given time, over 200 theatres in this city and only 40 or so are Equity. Of those, over 40 percent are Tier N, which is, for all intents and purposes, the stage between Equity and non-Equity.

This is not to say that actors can't, or shouldn't, join **Actors Equity Association.** But you must be wise about where your career is going and if you are ready to make the commitment. Once you join, you cannot do non-Equity theatre again unless you drop out of the union, forfeiting your dues and entrance fee and any benefits you may have accrued.

Actors need to consider the types of roles they can realistically be cast in. If you're a quirky, specialty character type, would it be wise to take that Goodman Equity contract and shut off the few future roles available by closing the non-Equity door? On the other hand, are there millions of people just like you who could be offered a non-Equity contract for less money in an Equity show and still be available to do non-Equity theatre?

While you're talking to yourself, consider this: In the last decade Actors Equity in Chicago has bent over backwards to embrace small theatre companies, giving their members many more opportunities to work. The Chicago Area Theatre (CAT) contract has seven tiers with, among other things, different salary structures and casting requirements. Most exciting is the Tier N contract, which has made it possible for small, low-budget theatres to hire Equity actors on a show by show basis. (See below for a complete rundown of Equity contracts frequently used in the Chicago area.)

If you are faced with the decision whether or not to join Equity, remember, if a company thinks you're good enough to turn Equity, they'll probably think you're good enough to cast in the future.

Membership

There are three ways to join Actors Equity Association:

1) Get cast in an Equity show and sign an Equity contract.

2) Be a member in good standing of one of the eight unions that make up the 4-A's (Associated Actors and Artists of America). The sister unions are: **AFTRA** (the American Federation of Television and Radio Artists), **SAG** (the Screen Actors Guild), **AGMA** (the American Guild of Musical Artists), **AGVA** (the American Guild of Variety Artists), **SEG** (Screen Extras Guild), **HAU** (the Hebrew Actors Union), **APATE** (Association of Puerto Rican Artists and Theatrical Employees) and **IAG** (the International Artists Guild).

3) Join the Equity Membership Candidate Program.

The first avenue is possible, but rare.

The second is up to the other unions.

The **Equity Membership Candidate Program** (EMC) gives non-Equity actors the chance to work in Equity theatres and earn points toward Equity membership. The first step is getting cast for a non-Equity role by an Equity theatre who participates in the program. That's where summer theatre comes in.

Once you enroll and pay your $100 fee (which will go toward your initiation fee once you join the union), you earn points for each week you work in an Equity show until you reach 50 weeks, when you can join the union. At that point, you cannot be hired by an Equity theatre unless they sign you to an Equity contract. It is not unusual for a non-Equity actor to reach 50 weeks and then drop out of the EMC program so they don't have to join Equity. At that point you can re-join EMC, but you have to pay another $100 and start again from scratch.

The **initiation fee** for joining Actors Equity Association is $800. Members also must pay **semi-annual dues** totaling $78 and pay 2 percent of their gross salary for each Equity contract they sign.

Benefits

Equity members have access to a **health plan**, a **vision care plan** and **dental plan.** Equity actors can be eligible for one year of health benefits if they complete 10 Equity work weeks in a 12 month period. They have to keep working 10 weeks or more each following year to maintain health benefits.

Other benefits are a bit less tangible, but make up the backbone of Equity's existence. All producers must post a **bond**, for instance, for each show so Equity members can get paid if the show closes early. The union also administers a **pension plan** and provides **workers' comp.** Actors under Equity contracts must be given certain breaks at certain periods of time, and the work space must be of a certain standard. Actors also can't work more than so many hours in a day or week. If you supply a costume piece, you must, under Equity rules, be paid rental for that costume by the theatre.

I could go on. It's a union.

Contracts

Equity theatres in the Chicago area work under four basic types of contracts: **CAT** (Chicago Area Theatre), **LORT** (League of Resident Theatres), **Dinner Theatre** and **Children's Theatre.**

CAT

The Chicago Area Theatre contract came to being in the mid-1980's as a more flexible alternative to other Equity contracts. It is divided into seven tiers which specify, among other things, different salary arrangements and shows per week. Each tier has a standard minimum salary and benefits, but often theatres negotiate their own. Every tier but Tier N requires at least one Equity actor, plus an Equity stage manager. Tier

N requires the stage manager be an Equity Membership Candidate. Tiers 2 - 6 require understudies, though the understudies do not have to be Equity members. An Equity understudy who is required to be there all the time would be paid the same as an Equity actor. An understudy who is hired on a "stand-by" basis would be paid a salary equivalent to three tiers down from the tier the show is working under. For instance, a stand-by understudy for a Tier VI theatre would be paid a Tier III salary, which would go up when the understudy went on. CAT theatres can be for-profit or non-profit.

Here is a brief rundown of the CAT tiers and their weekly salaries:

Tier 6: up to eight performances a week with a minimum salary of $591.75 for actors and $707.50 for stage managers.

Tier 5: up to eight performances a week with a minimum salary of $493 for actors and $577 for stage managers.

Tier 4: up to seven performances a week with a minimum salary of $417.25 for actors and $478.75 for stage managers.

Tier 3: up to six performances a week with a minimum salary of $289.50 for actors and $336.75 for stage managers.

Tier 2: up to five performances a week with a minimum salary of $211.25 for actors and $243.50 for stage managers.

Tier 1: up to four performances a week with a minimum salary of $137.50 for actors and $168.50 for stage managers.

Tier N: up to four performances a week with a minimum salary of $136.50 for actors, with no requirement to hire an Equity stage manager or understudies or contribute to the health insurance fund. In addition, Tier N theatres must do 50 percent of their season as Equity shows. Tier N work weeks do not count towards an actor's eligibility for health care benefits.

In addition, CAT contracts offer a **"More Remunerative Employment"** MRE clause. Essentially, if an actor gets a higher paying job — say a national commercial — then the theatre is required to let the actor do the commercial and put on an understudy in his stead until the job ends. This was a recognition that actors in Chicago earn their bread and butter from on-camera work and that if theatres wanted to attract actors who might earn more, they needed to promise them time off when the opportunities came up. The MRE is applicable to all CAT contracts, including CAT N. It is not applicable to many other Equity contracts. LORT and Dinner Theatre contracts, for instance, don't have MREs.

LORT

The **League of Resident Theatres** is a membership organization of non-profit regional theatres around the U.S. Guthrie is LORT. Arena Stage is LORT. Basically, the anchor regional theatre in any city is probably a member of LORT and therefore under a LORT Equity contract. LORT contracts with Equity permit touring and cover musical and non-musical theatre. Salary and contract requirements are based on the theatre's budget and box office grosses. There are five levels: A, B+, B, C & D. Theatres may employ a resident company but are not required to do so. Chicago has three LORT contract theatres: **Goodman, Northlight** and **Court.**

Dinner Theatre

Chicago is the birthplace of dinner theatre. Over 35 years ago, William Pullinsi took some inheritance money and started Candlelight Dinner Playhouse, inventing the concept of dinner theatre. Candlelight, sadly, closed its doors in 1997, but the concept lives on all over the country. Most of the dinner theatres in the Chicago area are in the suburbs and most focus their attention on musical theatre. Happy is easier to digest. There are six tier structures under the Dinner Theatre contract. Salary is based on seating capacity. Actors Equity must approve any dinner theatre in Chicago (and New York City, Los Angeles County or San Francisco). Dinner does not have to be served in the same room as the show. This puts theatres such as **Marriott Theatre at Lincolnshire** — which often sells restaurant/theatre packages — under this contract.

Theatre for Young Audiences

TYA is the contract for children's theatre in Chicago. Actors can be hired on a weekly contract or a per-performance contract. Performances generally don't begin after 7 p.m. and may not exceed 90 minutes in length. The contract allows for "associated artist activity," such as classes and workshops with students. Both local and overnight touring are permitted. This contract is used both for resident companies who have an outreach program and for companies that make their livings touring to schools. Actors can make decent supplementary income doing children's theatre in Chicago.

AFTRA & SAG

By Carrie L. Kaufman

Actors can get pretty steady work in commercials, industrials, voice-over and film in Chicago. Most of it's paid. Some of it's paid well. Almost all of it is union.

The **American Federation of Television and Radio Artists** (AFTRA) and the **Screen Actors Guild** (SAG) are the other two performer unions. They are closely related. In fact, in Chicago, AFTRA and SAG are run out of the same office under one executive director. They are, like all unions, run by an elected board of members.

Whether or not a production is covered by AFTRA or SAG is quite complicated and is one of the reasons union members have been clamoring for a merger for decades.

SAG covers all movies and all animation, regardless of the medium. If a movie is shot on film, it's SAG. If it's shot on digital video, it's still SAG. It's SAG even if it is only released on TV.

AFTRA covers radio and vocal recording, as well as broadcast news people. It also covers awards shows and soap operas.

Union jurisdiction gets murky when it comes to commercials, industrials (workplace videos), basic cable and non-prime-time programming or syndicated programming. Officially, it's up to the producer to decide which contract to use. In cities where AFTRA and SAG are administered out of the same office, jurisdiction over television commercials and industrials is determined by the medium used. Commercials and industrials in Chicago, for instance, are SAG if they are shot on film and AFTRA if they are shot on video.

Membership

Joining AFTRA and SAG is fairly easy, though not cheap. You can join AFTRA at any time by simply paying the initiation fee and half a year's dues. For SAG, you first have to get cast under a SAG contract. That means you land your first big commercial (for convenience sake, let's say it's shot on film and is SAG), or even local SAG commercial, or you get the role of the young doctor who comes into the hospital room and says, "It's late. Everybody out," in the latest Bruce Willis flick. Once you get that contract, you are eligible to join SAG. But you don't have to join right away.

As you're signing that contract, you will likely hear — from your agent or the casting director, or even the production coordinator — two words: **Taft-Hartley.** "You're Taft-Hartley now, so you'd better call the union," the production coordinator will say as she bumps you up from an extra to a speaking role.

The Taft-Hartley Act is one of the laws that covers unions and is also known as the National Labor Relations Act. Essentially, it says that a union can't require somebody to join until 30 days after their first day of employment. For a steel worker, that's a month after they're hired. For an actor, that could be years after they get their first job.

Once you get that first SAG job, you have 30 days to take as much union work as you can land without joining the union. If you land a union job 31 days after your first, though, you immediately have to join the union.

This is when actors get in trouble. **The initiation fee for SAG is currently $1,192.** That number is the equivalent of two day rates in a theatrical film or television show. Minimum yearly dues are $100, to be paid in twice yearly installments — the first in addition to the initiation fee when you join. **The initiation fee for AFTRA is currently $1,000.** Minimum yearly dues are $116, to be paid in twice yearly installments. Dues for both unions are based on an actor's earnings.

So, you've spent all the money you made two years ago doing SAG jobs under the Taft-Hartley 30-day protection. Now you have to fork over $1,237 to the union *before you even step on the set.* Don't have it? Too bad. You should have put it away two years ago in anticipation of having to join.

Contracts

There are multiple SAG and AFTRA contracts for various aspects of the business. I am not going to list them here. Under some contracts, you might just get paid a session fee. Under others, you might get paid a session fee plus residuals, with more to be negotiated after the sale of the production. SAG and AFTRA have books on this.

Product Conflict

If the ad agency stops running a commercial, they still might have to pay you. Under rules governing **product conflict,** an actor under contract to do a commercial for one type of product — such as a Nissan — cannot turn around and do a commercial for a competitive product — such as the Ford F150. Remember, image is everything, and neither ad agencies nor their clients want that cuddly, yet enigmatic man the public is so identifying with to show up selling a competitive product.

In that case, the advertiser must pay the actor a **holding fee** to keep the actor from being in a competitive commercial. The holding fee, paid every 13 weeks, is equivalent to the session fee. For nice national campaigns, the agency and client might pay the fee for a few years.

Now, suppose you did a non-union commercial for the MaidRite Hamburger Shack back in your hometown of Waterloo, Iowa in the summer of 1990. Then you get cast in a national Burger King commercial. Great, right? Sorry. You're out of luck. That MaidRite commercial was non-union. Unless your contract specified otherwise, they may still be running the commercial. Even if they aren't, they don't have to pay you anything to hold the commercial, and they could run it any time. In fact, if the owner of the store sees your face coming across his TV screen every hour or so, he might decide to take your old commercial out of the can and exploit your newfound familiarity.

Chances are, if you make a non-union commercial, you can never do a union commercial for the same type of product. Period. You may, if you want to pay the legal bills, go back and draw up a contract with the non-union client to not use the commercial again. You may have to pay the non-union client a hefty sum in order to do so.

If you ignore that MaidRite commercial and take the Burger King job, then someone from Burger King notices your younger face on a local TV station in Iowa, the trouble you can get into is enormous. The production company may simply be able to cut you out of the Burger King commercial and you'll have to forfeit any fees you may have earned. If they can't do that, and the Burger King bigwigs and the ad agency decide to pull the commercial, *you could be liable for all of the expenses incurred to put that commercial together.* Everything. The entire production — hundreds of thousands of dollars — could be charged to you.

Similar consequences can ensue if you did a union commercial for McDonald's in 1990 and have simply "forgotten" about those checks McDonald's is still paying you in holding fees.

That said, if you do a union commercial for McDonald's and they stop paying you holding fees, they cannot run that commercial again without hiring you again. Then you are free to do the Burger King commercial. This is one obvious advantage of working under a union.

Benefits

AFTRA and SAG are unions and give their members the same benefits as any union, including pension, retirement and health plans.

Actors must earn $7,500 in a 12-month period to get one year of health insurance. To keep it, they have to make at least $7,500 a year thereafter.

On a set, AFTRA and SAG negotiate everything from meals and bathroom breaks to overtime. There are myriad rules, and it would behoove any actor to call the AFTRA/SAG office to find out what they are.

If an actor is on a shoot and something comes up that is questionable — say the production manager says everybody is working overtime and not getting paid overtime rates — it's not a union actor's responsibility to argue. Tell the production manager that it's all right with you if it's all right with your union and your agent, then get on the horn and call either one. Let them do the arguing for you.

Joining a union is never an easy process. There are rules and regulations galore. Sometimes it might seem as if they get in the way. But all the rules are there to protect the members, and actors need all the protection they can get.

Unions

Actors Equity Association
203 N. Wabash #1700
Chicago, IL 60601
312/641-0393 • 312/641-6365 - fax
www.actorsequity.org

American Federation of Television & Radio Artists (AFTRA)
1 E. Erie #650
Chicago, IL 60611
312/573-8081 • 312/573-0318 - fax
www.aftra.com

Directors Guild of America
400 N. Michigan #307
Chicago, IL 60611
312/644-5050 • 312/644-5776 - fax
www.dga.org

Screen Actors Guild (SAG)
1 E. Erie St., #650
Chicago, IL 60611
312/573-8081 • 312/573-0318 - fax
www.sag.org

Actors Don't Have to be Victims

By all the gods that
Romans bow before,
I here discard my sickness.

By Carrie L. Kaufman

Acting is a brutal business. Teachers and casting directors will tell you that actors have to control of what they can control and let go of the rest. This is good advice, because there's little actors can control.

Still, actors don't have to be victims. You should be treated with the respect with which any professional treats a fellow professional. You should also, of course, give that respect and act professionally. But when the line is crossed, actors don't have to sit there and take it.

Where that line is drawn is up to you. You must decide what you're willing to take and when you're willing to fight back.

Unions

Unions are there to protect members from all sorts of indignities, from pay disputes to harassment. If you are a member of AFTRA, SAG or Actors Equity Association, call them. Even if you're not a member, call them. Your complaint might fall under their jurisdiction. If not, they can help you get to the proper agency.

If you walk into a casting director's office and he or she makes a lewd remark about you or asks you to take off your shirt for the audition, call your union and your agent. Don't assume that you're being too sensitive. Sometimes there are legitimate reasons for this (such as soap or bra commercials), but those instances are rare. In any case, if auditioning nude is legitimate, your agent will be notified and you will have that information before you even accept the audition. There will also be all sorts of precautions, such as only necessary personnel in the room, including at least one other woman (if you're a woman). There should be no surprises.

SAG also can help if your agent hasn't paid you in a timely fashion, or if she takes out more than 10 percent from your pay (or 20 percent for print). Usually, this happens with non-union franchised agents, but SAG can point you in the right direction to file a complaint.

Employment Issues

Illinois Department of Labor
160 N. LaSalle - 13th floor
Chicago, IL 60601
Joyce Markmann (agent questions)
312/793-1817
Wage Claim Division (for employment compensation)
312/793-2808

The Department of Labor is the agency that handles disputes between employers and employees—or their agents. There are two basic divisions in the Department of Labor that actors need to know about. The first is Joyce Markmann's division.

Remember that name. If you've been wronged and you need an ally, call Joyce Markmann. She is a no-nonsense woman who has a passion for getting people who take advantage of others. She is the best friend an actor has in state government.

Markmann deals with problems with agencies—even bogus ones. If your agent starts taking 25 percent out of your check, call Joyce. She'll look up their file and tell you what they've told the state they charge in commission. If it's only 10 percent, she'll get in touch with the agent and get them to pay you the other 15 percent. She also might start disciplinary action if she gets too many complaints.

The same is true for agents who pay slowly or not at all. Say you did a commercial months ago and still haven't gotten paid. You call your agent and they tell you the client hasn't paid them. Then you run into someone who was on that same commercial—booked through another agency—and they tell you they got paid over a month before. Call Joyce Markmann.

Especially call Joyce if you run into an agent who doesn't seem to be licensed. Markmann is full of stories about people who have been taken advantage of. Stories about so-called "agents" calling young mothers in by telling them their kid is just perfect for modeling or commercials, then charging them $800 to take the kid's picture or video tape—and telling them they have to come back in six months to do the same thing because the kid has grown. Nothing ever happens to the headshot or video tape. The kid is never sent out on any jobs. And even if he was sent out, the mother still needn't have paid. Agents get paid by the client after they get you the job. Actors should never pay to get a job.

If your dispute is directly with an employer and it deals with your pay, call the Wage Claim Division of the Department of Labor. They step in when an actor is paid less than they were hired for or when an actor is not paid at all (if, in fact, the theatre or production company has agreed to pay in the first place).

If you feel you've been wronged in your pay, file a complaint with the Wage Claim Division. They will send a letter to the employer. When they get the employer's response, they will compare your claim to their response and either dismiss it or send it to the next level—a hearing. If the employer is found liable in the hearing, he or she has a certain amount of time to pay. If the employer still doesn't pay, Wage Claim then sends it to the Attorney General's office, where legal proceedings are begun. For this last phase to take place, actors need to stay in touch with the Department of Labor after an employer is found liable. The department has no way of knowing if the employer has fulfilled his or her obligations unless you tell them.

The Equal Employment Opportunity Commission
National Office
1801 L Street, N.W.
Washington, D.C. 20507
202/663-4900
TDD: 202/663-4494
www.eeoc.gov

Chicago District Office
500 West Madison #2800
Chicago, IL 60661
312/353-2713
TDD: 312/353-2421

The EEOC protects against discrimination in the workplace. If you feel you've been sexually harassed, call the EEOC and make a complaint. If you feel you've been dismissed because of your race, call the EEOC. There are laws that protect you, and the commission will check out your story. Chances are, you aren't the only one who has complained.

In cases of sexual discrimination—including harassment and pregnancy—you can also call the Women's Bureau, which has regional offices all over the country. The Chicago office of the Women's Bureau is at 312/353-6985. They cover the Illinois, Indiana, Michigan, Minnesota, Ohio and Wisconsin areas.

The Women's Bureau is not an enforcing agency. They are a resource for information and statistics on women in the workplace. But they can give you advice or point you in the right direction if you feel you've been wronged.

Department of Human Rights
100 W. Randolph #10-100
Chicago, IL 60601
312/814-6200
www.state.il.us.dhr

The Illinois Department of Human Rights deals with any sort of discrimination in the work force. They are essentially the state alternative to the EEOC. If you've been fired because you're pregnant, call them. If you've been fired because you're over 40, they can help. If you've been fired or not hired because you're African-American or Hispanic or have an unfavorable military discharge or an arrest record, call them.

They are also the place to call if you've been the victim of sexual harassment.

You will need to go to the department's offices to file a complaint, which consists of filling out a four-page form and going through an interview. Plan to spend half a day there.

After your complaint is filed, the employer will be notified and given time to respond. In the meantime, Human Rights, with your help, will try to find other people who may have gone through the same things you have, in order to build a stronger case.

After the employer responds, you and the employer are brought into the same room for a fact-finding conference. Then everything is turned over to the Department of Human Rights' legal department. If they find "substantial evidence" that discrimination has occurred, they will send it over to the Human Rights Commission, which takes legal action.

Consumer Issues

Illinois Attorney General
100 W. Randolph
Chicago, IL 60601
312/814-3000
(Check the white pages for specific departments.)

The Office of the Attorney General deals with consumer issues. If you pay to get your headshots reproduced and the company goes bankrupt after it has cashed your check, call the Attorney General's office.

The Attorney General also will go after an employer who has not paid an employee and has been found liable by the Illinois Department of Labor (see above).

Better Business Bureau
Chicago Office
330 N. Wabash
Chicago, IL 60611
312/832-0500

The Better Business Bureau deals with contracts and obligations. If you paid a photographer to take your headshot but the film came out totally black, and he won't give you your money back, call the Better Business Bureau (as well as the Attorney General's office).

If, however, that same photographer asks you to pose nude or if an agent starts yelling and screaming obscenities at you, the Better Business Bureau will be of no help. They may be sympathetic, but they do not deal with matters of behavior.

Turn the page for a list of other helpful Organizations.

Similar Organizations

Chicago Access Corporation
322 S. Green #100
Chicago, IL 60607
312/738-1400 • 312/738-2519 - fax
www.cantv.org

Chicago Dance Coalition
410 S. Michigan #819
Chicago, IL 60605
312/419-8384

Chicago Federation of Musicians
Local 10 208 AFM
175 W. Washington
Chicago, IL 60602
312/782-0063 • 312/782-7880 - fax
www.livemusichicago.com

Chicago Film Office
1 N. LaSalle #2165
Chicago, IL 60602
312/744-6415 • 312/744-1378 - fax
www.ci.chi.il.us/wm/specialevents/filmoffice/

Chicago National Association of Dance Masters
5411 E. State St. #202
Rockford, IL 61108
815/397-6052 • 815/397-6799 - fax
www.cnadm.com
Workshops only; no ongoing classes.

Illinois Film Office
100 W. Randolph - 3rd Floor
Chicago, IL 60601
312/814-3600 • 312/814-8874 - fax
www.commerce.state.il.us

National Dinner Theatre Association
P.O. Box 726
Marshall, MI 49068
616/781-7859 • 616/781-4880 - fax
www.ndta.com

University/Resident Theatre Association (U/RTA)
1560 Broadway #414
New York, NY 10036
212/221-1130 • 212/869-2752 - fax
www.urta.com
Graduate School Auditions
Contract Management Program
Post-Graduate Audtions
A national organization providing useful and friendly services to candidates seeking professional MFA training in all theatre disciplines, as well as to graduate schools and theatre companies. Assisting students interested in U/RTA member programs, management help for groups employing professional artists, career services for recent MFA graduates, and more. Membership not required for most services.

Women in the Director's Chair
941 W. Lawrence #500
Chicago, IL 60640
773/907-0610 • 773/907-0381 - fax
www.widc.org

Women's Theatre Alliance
P.O. Box 64446
Chicago, IL 60664-0446
312/408-9910
www.wtac.org

Theatres

Lid Productions " Kapoot" – pictured: Dan Griffiths, Stephen Eric Chipps – photo: Jason Tugman

Equity Theatres

Obviously, there are a ton (figuratively) of theatres in Chicago, both Equity and non. Keep the following in mind when using these listings. (1) Check the contact person for a headshot and resumé – it's not always the artistic or managing director. The contact name is right under Equity or non-Equity in the body of the listing. (2) If you're calling a theatre's administrative line, be sure it's for a good reason. Larger companies, particularly, will not be very tolerant of unnecessary questions. (3) Pay attention to the mission of the company and their union status when sending out headshots. If a company doesn't use non-Equity actors and you're not in the union, don't send a headshot. If you aren't interested in doing the sort of shows that a company produces, don't submit to them. Use this information to find the theatres with which you want to work.

The Aardvark
Ann Filmer - Artistic Director
1539 N. Bell
Chicago, IL 60622
773/489-0843
www.aardvarktheatre.com
Equity – CAT N – Itinerant – Ensemble Based
Send H/R attention **Ann Filmer.**

Founded in 1995. Starting pay is $10/performance. They call actors in from generals, files and past knowledge. Season auditions are in September.

The Aardvark is a collective of writers, designers, musicians and actors who believe in a theatre not only for the elite, but for the everyman/everywoman/ everychild.

Their 1998-1999 season included:
- The Spirits of Chicago
- Here's Buford
- Visit to a Small Planet

About Face Theatre
Eric Rosen & Kyle Hall - Artistic Directors
3212 N. Broadway
Chicago, IL 60657
773/549-7943 • 773/935-4483 - fax
www.aboutface.base.org
Equity – CAT N – Resident
Send H/R attention
Greg Copeland - Production Manager.

Founded in 1995. Starting non-Equity pay is $70/week. They call in actors from generals, files or past knowledge. The nearest eL stop is Belmont on the Red, Brown and Purple lines.

About Face is Chicago's award-winning, nationally recognized resident professional gay and lesbian theatre offering a host of acclaimed productions, an innovative youth theatre for gay and lesbian youth and a special program to develop new plays.

Their 1998-1999 season included:
- Dream Boy - Jeff Citations: Production, Director, Lighting, Sound
- The Santaland Diaries
- Cloud 9
- First Breath

American Theater Company
Brian Russell - Artistic Director
1909 W. Byron
Chicago, IL 60613
773/929-1031
www.ATCWEB.org
Equity – CAT N – Resident – Ensemble Based
Send H/R attention **Brian Russell.**

Founded in 1985. Starting non-Equity pay is $65/week. They call in actors from generals, files or past knowledge. The nearest eL stop is Irving Park on the Brown line. ATC believes theatre is for everyone, not just those who know the address.

Their 1998-1999 season included:
- The Three Penny Opera
- One Day Only
- Pledge of Allegiance - Jeff Recommended
- Below the Belt

Apollo Theater Center
Kolson Creative
916 S. Wabash #503
Chicago, IL 60605
773/935-9336
773/935-6100 - box office
312/461-1458 - fax
Equity – CAT VI – Resident

Send H/R attention **Nadine Heidinger - Account Executive.**

Founded in 1991. The nearest eL stop is Fullerton on the Red, Brown and Purple line.

Apollo Theater Center is a commercial theatre and music production company that also manages and produces the shows at the Apollo Theater.

Theatres

Apple Tree Theatre

Eileen Boevers & Gary Griffin - Artistic Directors
Alan Salzenstein - Managing Director
595 Elm Pl. #210
Highland Park, IL 60035
847/432-8223
847/432-4335 - box office
847/432-5214 - fax
www.appletreetheatre.com
Equity – CAT III – Resident
Send H/R attention **Tim Stadler - Production Manager.**

Founded in 1983. Starting non-Equity pay is $150/week. They hold open auditions for each show, and season auditions are in July.

Apple Tree Theatre is committed to producing a diverse and challenging selection of both dramas and musicals from new work to classics - all of which celebrate the tenacity of the human spirit, illuminate the human condiiton and expand the vision of artists and audiences alike– culturally, intellectually, emotionally and spiritually as they connect with one another.

Bailiwick Repertory

David Zak - Artistic Director
Debra Hatchett - Managing Director
1229 W. Belmont
Chicago, IL 60657
773/833-1090 • 773/525-3245 - fax
www.Bailiwick.org
Equity – CAT N – Resident
Send H/R attention **David Zak.**

Founded in 1982. Starting non-Equity pay varies. They hold open auditions for each show. The nearest eL stop is Belmont on the Red, Brown and Purple lines.

Bailiwick Repertory is dedicated to achieving the vision of gifted directors in works ranging from classics to world premieres. We strive to remain affordable, accessible and responsive to the diversities of our community.

Their 1998-1999 season included:

- DBA - Broken Spokes
- Snooty
- Mrs. Coney
- The Christmas Schooner
- The Cairn Stones
- Shopping & Fucking - Jeff Nominated
- A Month in the Country - Jeff Citation for Set Design

Black Ensemble Theatre

Jackie Taylor - Artistic Director
4520 N. Beacon
Chicago, IL 60640
773/769-4451 • 773/769-4533 - fax
Equity – CAT I – Resident
Send H/R to the **company address.**

Founded in 1976. Starting non-Equity pay varies with experience. They hold open auditions for each show. The nearest eL stop is Wilson on the Red line.

The Black Ensemble Theatre Company is a 23 year old non-profit theatre company who is providing theatre that serves as a cultural bridge, bringing people together of all colors and nationalities so that they may unite, celebrating the greatness of the human spirit.

Center Theater
1346 W. Devon
Chicago, IL 60660
773/508-0200
773/508-5422 - box office
773/508-9584 - fax
Equity – CAT I – Resident
Send H/R to **Dale Calandra - Creative Director.**

Founded in 1981. Starting non-Equity pay varies. They hold open auditions for each show. The nearest eL stop is Loyola on the Red line.

Center Theater is a professional Equity theatre providing quality theatrical productions on the cutting-edge of modern drama and training for actors, directors, playwrights and singers of all levels that inspires growth both personal and professionally.

Their 1998-1999 season included:
- Serengeti Plane - American Theater Critic Award Nominee
- Greater Tuna

Chicago Dramatists
Russ Tutterow - Artistic Director
1105 W. Chicago
Chicago, IL 60622-5702
312/633-0630 • 312/633-0610 - fax
Equity – CAT N – Resident
Send H/R attention **Russ Tutterow.**

Founded in 1979. Starting non-Equity pay was not released. They hold open auditions for each show. The nearest eL stop is Chicago on the Blue line.

Chicago Dramatists is dedicated to the development, advancement and production of playwrights and new plays.

Chicago Shakespeare Theater
Barbara Gaines - Artistic Director
800 E. Grand
Chicago, IL 60611
312/642-8394
www.chicagoshakes.com
Equity – CAT V – Resident
Send H/R attention **Rick Boynton - Casting Director.**

Founded in 1986. Starting non-Equity pay was not revealed. They call in actors from generals, files and past knowledge. Season auditions are held in spring and fall. The nearest eL stop is Grand on the Red line.

Chicago Theatre Company
Douglas Alan-Mann - Artistic Director
David Barr - Associate Artistic Director
Luther Goins - Managing Director
500 E. 67th
Chicago, IL 60637
773/493-0901
773/493-5360 - box office
773/493-0360 - fax
Equity – CAT N – Resident
Send H/R attention **Douglas Alan-Mann.**

Founded in 1984. Starting non-Equity pay is $75. They hold open auditions for each show. The nearest eL stop is 69th Street on the Red line.

Court Theatre
Charles Newell - Artistic Director
Diane Claussen - Managing Director
5535 S. Ellis
Chicago, IL 60637
773/702-7005
773/753-4472 - box office
773/834-1897 - fax
www.courttheatre.org
Equity – LORT D – Resident
Send H/R attention **Nick Bowling - Artistic Associate.**

Founded in 1955. Starting non-Equity pay is $150. They call in actors from generals, files and past knowledge. Season auditions are held in June and July. The nearest eL stop is 55th Street on the Red line.

Court Theatre creates theatre defined by classic themes, including works of enduring significance as well as newly discovered classics.

Drury Lane Oakbrook
Ray Frewen - Artistic Director
100 Drury Ln.
Oakbrook Terrace, IL 60181
630/530-8300
630/530-0111 - box office
630/530-4269 – fax
Equity – Dinner Theatre – Resident
Send H/R to the **company address.**

Founded in 1984. Starting non-Equity pay is $250/week. They hold open auditions for each show.

Their 1998-1999 season included:
- Jesus Christ Superstar
- Lend Me A Tenor
- Singin' in the Rain

Drury Lane Theatre - Evergreen Park
Marc Robbins - Artistic Director
2500 W. 95th St
Evergreen Park, IL 60805
708/422-8000
708/422-0404 - box office
708/422-8127 - fax
drurylane.com
Equity – Dinner Theatre – Resident
Send H/R to the **company address.**

Founded in 1988. Starting non-Equity pay was not revealed. They hold open auditions for each show. The nearest eL stop is 95th Street on the Red line.
Drury Lane Theatre - Evergreen Park is a theatre in-the-round featuring ice shows.

Their 1998-1999 season included:
- Perfect Wedding
- La Cage Aux Folles
- The All Night Strut

Theatres

Equity Library Theatre Chicago
4738 N. LaPorte
Chicago, IL 60630-3801
773/743-0266
Equity – ELT Showcase – Itinerant
Send H/R attention **Artistic Director.**

Founded in 1952. They don't use non-Equity actors. They hold open auditions for each show.

ELT is a not-for-profit theatre company showcasing Equity actors in showcase productions.

Their 1998-1999 season included:
- Strange Interlude
- A Midsummer Night's Dream
- As You Like It
- Vieux Carre

Famous Door Theatre
Karen Kessler - Artistic Director
Larry Neumann, Jr. - Managing Director
P.O. Box 57029
Chicago, IL 60657
773/404-8283 • 773/404-8292 - fax
famousdoortheatre.org
Equity – CAT N – Itinerant – Ensemble Based
Send H/R attention **Dan Rivkin.**

Founded in 1988. Starting non-Equity pay is $20/performance. They call in actors from generals, files or past knowledge. Season auditions are held in August.

Famous Door offers high quality productions of premiere or seldom produced plays.

First Folio Shakespeare Festival
Alison C. Vesely
146 Juliet Court
Clarendon Hills, IL 60514
630/986-8067
www.firstfolio.org
Equity – CAT III – Resident
Send H/R attention **Alison C. Vesely.**

Founded in 1996. Starting non-Equity pay is $100/week. They hold open auditions for each show, and season auditions are held in January or February.

First Folio Shakespeare is subtitled "The Nice Person's Theatre Company," as they not only hire people who are both talented and FUN TO WORK WITH, but also create an atmosphere which makes it fun to work--because if it's not fun, why are we all doing this?

First Stage Milwaukee
Rob Goodman - Artistic Director
Betsy Corry - Managing Director
929 N. Water St.
Milwaukee, WI 53211
414/273-2314
414/273-2314 x229 - box office
414/273-5595 - fax
www.firststage.org
Equity – TYA – Resident

Founded in 1987. Starting non-Equity pay is $301/week. They call in actors from generals, files or past knowledge. Generals are held in March.

First Stage Milwaukee, an Equity theatre for youth, provides exceptional, professional theatre experiences to young people and families and serves as an arts-in-education resource for area educators.

Their 1998-1999 season included:
- Charlotte's Web
- The Dream Thief
- The Homecoming, a Christmas Story
- Roll of Thunder, Hear My Cry
- Tom Sawyer
- Frog and Toad (Forever)
- The Irish Chord

Goodman Theatre
Robert Falls - Artistic Director
200 S. Columbus
Chicago, IL 60603
312/443-3811
312/443-3800 - box office
312/263-6004 - fax
www.goodman-theatre.org

Equity – LORT B/D – Resident
Send H/R attention **Tara Lonzo - Casting Director.**

Founded in 1925. Starting non-Equity pay was not revealed. They call in actors from generals, files and past knowledge. Season auditions are in the summer. The nearest eL stop is Monroe on the Red line.

---

greasy joan & company
P.O. Box 13077
Chicago, IL 60613
773/761-8284
www.greasyjoan.org
Equity – CAT N – Itinerant – Ensemble Based
Send H/R attention **McDonough.**

Founded in 1995. Starting non-Equity pay varies. They hold open auditions for each show.

greasy joan & co. is an ensemble of actors dedicated, but not limited to, producing theatre that is classical in scope.

Their 1998-1999 season included:
- Therese Raquin - Jeff Recommended
- The Mandrake - Jeff Recommended

Illinois Theatre Center
P.O. Box 397
Park Forest, IL 60466
708/481-3510 • 708/481-3693 - fax
Equity – CAT III – Resident
Send H/R attention **Etel Billig - Producing Director.**

Founded in 1976. Starting non-Equity pay is $200/week. They call actors in from generals, files and past knowledge. Season auditions are in July.

The Illinois Theatre Center is the only Equity theatre in the south suburbs.

Their 1998-1999 season included:
- The Value of Names
- Another Antigone
- 70, Girls, 70
- Playing with Fire
- Home
- Shadowlands
- Living the Dream

The Journeymen
Frank Pullen - Artistic Director
3915 N. Janssen
Chicago, IL 60613
773/529-5781
312/494-5720 - box office
www.TheJourneymen.org

Equity – CAT N – Itinerant
Send H/R attention **Frank Pullen.**

Founded in 1994. Starting non-Equity pay not revealed. They hold open auditions for each show.

The Journeymen draw upon humanities in a way that helps the general public understand a topic of public concern.

Lifeline Theatre
Dorothy Milne - Artistic Director
Melissa Bareford - Managing Director
6912 N. Glenwood
Chicago, IL 60626
773/761-4477
Equity – CAT N – Resident

Send H/R attention **Dorothy Milne.**

Founded in 1982.

Their 1998-1999 season included:
- Wrinkle in Time
- Stange Case: Jekyll & Hyde
- The Motherlode

Lookingglass Theatre Company
Heidi Stillman & David Kersner - Artistic Directors
Jacqueline Russell - Acting Managing Director
2936 N. Southport - 3rd floor
Chicago, IL 60657
773/477-9257 • 773/477-6932 - fax
Equity – CAT III – Itinerant – Ensemble Based
Send H/R to the **company address.**

Founded in 1988. Starting non-Equity pay is $200/week. They call in actors from generals, files and past knowledge.

Lookingglass creates adaptations of literature produced in a highly theatrical style.

Lyric Opera of Chicago
20 N. Wacker
Chicago, IL 60606
312/827-3537 • 312/332-2834 - fax
AGMA – Resident
Send H/R attention **Eric Eligator**.

Starting pay is $360/week. They hold open audtions for each show. The nearest eL stop is Washington on the Loop.

The Lyric Opera of Chicago is an internationally acclaimed opera house consistently offering its patrons world-class singers, directors and designers.

Madison Repertory
D. Scott Glasser - Artistic Director
Tony Forman - Managing Director
122 State St. #210
Madison, WI 53703-2500
608/256-0029
608/266-9055 – box office
608/256-7433 - fax
Equity – SPT – Resident
Send H/R attention **D. Scott Glasser.**

Founded in 1969. Starting non-Equity is $200. They call in actors from generals, files or past knowledge. Season auditions are in late April.

Madison's only professional theatre company, Madison Rep offers a rewarding playbill of 20th century classics and contemporary works in the Madison Civic Center's intimate Isthmus Playhouse.

Their 1998-1999 season included:
- Little Shop of Horrors
- Three Viewings
- How I Learned to Drive
- The Man Who Came to Dinner
- Lady Day at Emerson's Bar & Grill
- The Cripple of Inishmaan
- Sherlock's Last Case

Marriott Theatre
Dyanne Earley - Artistic Director
10 Marriott Dr.
Lincolnshire, IL 60069
847/634-0204
847/634-0200 - box office
847/634-7022 - fax
Equity – Dinner Theatre/TYA – Resident
Send H/R attention **Dyanne Earley.**

Founded in 1975. Starting non-Equity pay was not revealed. They call in actors from generals, files and past knowledge. Season auditions are held in December and May.

Their 1998-1999 season included:
- Do Black Patent Leather Shoes Really Reflect Up?
- Houdini
- Peggy Sue Got Married
- Victor Victoria

Mayfair Theatre
636 S. Michigan
Chicago, IL 60605
312/786-9317
312/786-9120 - box office
312/786-9177 - fax
www.shearmadness.com
Equity – Cabaret – Resident
Send H/R attention
Bruce Jordan or Tom Sellers.

Founded in 1982. Starting non-Equity pay was not revealed. They call in actors from generals, files and past knowledge. The nearest eL stop is Harrison on the Red line.

Mayfair Theatre contains Shear Madness, a comedy murder mystery with audience interaction that is continually changing with up-to-date humor.

New American Theatre
William Gregg - Artistic Director
118 N. Main St.
Rockford, IL 61101-1102
815/963-9343
815/964-6282 - box office
Equity – SPT – Resident
Send H/R attention **Bill Gregg.**

Founded in 1972. Starting non-Equity pay is $200-250/week. They hold season auditions in spring and fall.

New American Theater is a professional regional Equity theatre presenting quality productions of classic, modern and new works while providing education and cultural leadership in the communities they serve.

Their 1998-1999 season included:
- Triple Espresso
- Picasso at the Lapin Agile
- Peter Pan
- Murder by Misadventure
- The Importance of Being Earnest
- The Miracle Worker
- The Sunshine Boys

Next Theatre Company
Kate Buckley - Artistic Director
Allison Sciplin - Managing Director
927 Noyes St.
Evanston, IL 60201
847/475-6763
847/475-1875 - box office
847/475-6767 - fax
www.nexttheatre.org
Equity – CAT N – Resident
Send H/R attention **Sarah Tucker - Associate Artistic Director.**

Founded in 1982. Starting non-Equity pay is nothing. They call in actors from generals, files and past knowledge. Season auditions are in July. The nearest eL stop is Noyes on the Purple line.

Next Theatre Company says to expect the unexpected!

Their 1998-1999 season included:
- Are You Now or Have You Ever Been...? - Jeff Nominated
- The Adventures of Herculina - Jeff Nominated
- Between East & West - Jeff Nominated
- My Three Angels - Jeff Nominated
- HG Wells - Scientific Romances - Jeff Nominated

Theatres

Northlight Theatre

B.J. Jones - Artistic Director
Richard Friedman - Managing Director
9501 N. Skokie Blvd.
Skokie, IL 60076
847/679-9501
847/673-6300 – box office
847/679-1879 - fax
www.northlight.org
Equity – LORT – Resident
Send H/R attention **Janet Mullet - Company Manager.**

Starting non-Equity pay is $200. They call in actors from generals, files and past knowledge. Season auditions are in August. The nearest eL stop is Skokie on the Yellow line.

Northlight Theatre, dedicated to enhancing the cultural life of the North Shore and Chicago, presents life-affirming theatrical works which reflect and challenge the values and beliefs of the community it serves.

Their 1998-1999 season included:
- Master Class - Jeff Recommended
- Cowgirls
- How I Learned to Drive - Jeff Recommended
- The Old Neighborhood - Jeff Recommended
- The Cripple of Inishmaan - Jeff Recommended

Organic Theatre Company

Ina Marlowe - Artistic Director
Nina M. Jones - Managing Director
1420 Maple Ave.
Evanston, IL 60201
847/475-0600
847/475-2800 – box office
847/475-9200 - fax
www.organictheater.com
Equity – Resident
Send H/R attention **Ina Marlowe.**

Founded in 1972. Starting non-Equity pay is $100/week. They hold open auditions for each show. The nearest eL stop is Davis on the Purple line.

Organic Theater Company merged with Touchstone Theatre in 1996 and are now producing their first season in their new Evanston home.

Piven Theatre Workshop

Joyce Piven & Byrne Piven - Co-Artistic Directors
927 Noyes #102
Evanston, IL 60201
847/866-6597
847/866-8049 – box office
847/866-6614 - fax
Equity – Resident – Ensemble Based
Send H/R to the **company address.**

Founded in 1970. Starting non-Equity pay was not revealed. They cast from ensemble.

Red Hen Productions

Elayne LeTraunik - Artistic Director
2944 N. Broadway
Chicago, IL 60657
773/935-8950
312/409-8123 – box office
773/883-0618 - fax
Equity – CAT I – Itinerant

Founded in 1987. Starting non-Equity pay is $100/production. They hold open auditions for each show.

Red Hen produces rarely done, artistically worthy shows as well as new works.

Their 1998-1999 season included:
- Edward II
- Safe Harbor

Rivendell Theatre Ensemble
1711 W. Belle Plaine #3B
Chicago, IL 60613
773/472-1169
Equity – CAT N – Itinerant – Ensemble Based
Send H/R attention **Tara Mallen - Producing Director.**

Starting non-Equity pay was not revealed.

Rivendell is a professional Equity company whose mission is to create an intimate theatre experience which explores new voices and reinterprets classics in an engaging salon environment.

Roadworks
Debbie Bisno - Artistic Director
Phil M. Kohlmetz - Managing Director
1144 Fulton Market #105
Chicago, IL 60607
312/492-7150 • 312/492-7155 - fax
www.roadworks.org
Equity – CAT I – Itinerant – Ensemble Based
Send H/R attention **Shade Murray - Associate Artistic Director.**

Founded in 1992. Starting non-Equity pay is $75/week. They call in actors from generals, files and past knowledge. The nearest eL stop is Ashland on the Orange line.

Roadworks is committed to cultivating the next generation of theatre patrons by presenting high voltage, risky Midwest and world premiere works.

Their 1998-1999 season included:
Santaland Diaries
Disappeared - Jeff Recommended
Stupid Kids - Jeff Recommended

Seanachai Theatre Company
Michael Grant - Artistic Director
Tom Dunleavy - Managing Director
P.O. Box 8278
Chicago, IL 60640-8278
773/878-3727
www.seanachai.org
Equity – CAT N – Itinerant – Ensemble Based

Founded in 1995. Starting non-Equity pay is "not enough." They cast from ensemble and attend the Unifieds.

Seanachai Theatre is a group of theatre artists dedicated to bring beautiful stories to the stage.

Their 1998-1999 season included:
Translations

Second City
(See our ad on page 41)
Kelly Leonard
1616 N. Wells
Chicago, IL 60614
312/664-4032 • 312/664-9837 - fax
312/337-3992 – box office
www.secondcity.com
Equity – Special Agreement – Resident – Ensemble Based
Send H/R attention **Kelly Leonard.**

Founded in 1959. Starting non-Equity pay was not revealed. They cast from ensemble.

Second City is the most famous comedy theatre in the world.

Their 1998-1999 season included:
The Psychopath Not Taken
The Revelation Will Not Be Televised - Jeff Nominated

Shakespeare on the Green
Karla Koskinen - Artistic Director
Steve Carmichael - Managing Director
Barat College - 700 E. Westleigh Rd.
Lake Forest, IL 60045
847/604-6344 • 847/604-6342 - fax
www.sotg.pac.barat.edu
Equity – CAT N – Resident

Founded in 1992. Starting non-Equity pay is $400/production. They hold open auditions for each show, and season auditions are in April.

Shakespeare on the Green is a professional theatre company in residence at Barat College that offers one play by Shakespeare every summer. Shows are free to the public.

The Shakespeare Project of Chicago
Mara Polster - Artistic Director
2706 N. Albany
Chicago, IL 60647
773/252-5433
members.aol.com/TSPChicago
Equity – CAT N/Staged Reading – Resident
Sent H/R attention **Mara Polster.**

Founded in 1995. Starting non-Equity pay was not revealed. They call in actors from generals, files and past knowledge. Season auditions are held in autumn, winter and spring.

The Shakespeare Project exists to allow professional actors in Chicago to explore the complete works of William Shakespeare and other great dramatists while working in the company of other actors with like experience and interest levels.

Strawdog Theatre
Nic Dimond & Kirsten Kelly - Artistic Directors
Tim Zingelman - Managing Director
3829 N. Broadway
Chicago, IL 60622
773/528-9889
773/528-9696 – box office
773/528-7238 - fax
www.strawdog.org
Equity – CAT N – Resident – Ensemble Based

Send H/R attention **Richard Shavzin.**

Founded in 1988. Starting non-Equity pay is a $50 stipend. They call actors in from generals, files and past knowledge and attend the Unifieds. The nearest eL stop is Sheridan on the Red line.

Strawdog offers an edgier-than-average, darker perspective either through choice of material or the particular take on a piece that usually is done without exploration of the darker side.

Teatro Vista
Eddie Torres - Artistic Director
2114 W. Belmont
Chicago, IL 60618
773/568-7871
773/929-7140 – box office
773/924-0324 - fax
www.teatrovista.org

Equity – CAT I – Itinerant – Ensemble Based
Send H/R attention **Eddie Torres.**

Founded in 1989. Starting non-Equity pay is $75/week. They call in actors from generals, files and past knowledge.
Teotro Vista is a theatre company producing the works of Latino writers and plays about the Latino experience.

Terrapin Theatre
Brad Nelson Winters - Artistic Director
Pam Dickler - Managing Director
P.O. Box 138-356
Chicago, IL 60613
773/989-1006 • 312/738-1420 - fax
Equity – CAT N – Itinerant – Ensemble Based

Send H/R attention **Brad Nelson Winters.**

Founded in 1992. Starting non-Equity pay is $5/performance. They call in actors from generals, files and past knowledge.

Their 1998-1999 season included:
The Bathroom - French Cultural Services Theatre Grant

Theatre at the Center
Michael Weber - Artistic Director
John Mybeck - Managing Director
907 Ridge Rd.
Munster, IN 46321
219/836-0422
Equity – CAT III – Resident
Send H/R attention **Michael Weber.**

Founded in 1990. Starting non-Equity pay was not reveled. They call in actors from generals, files and past knowledge. Season auditions are in February. Theatre at the Center is an Equity theatre presenting Chicago area premieres and revivals of plays and musicals.

Thirteenth Tribe
Joanna Settle - Artistic Director
Katie Taber - Managing Director
1852 W. North
Chicago, IL 60622
773/252-2510
Equity – CAT N – Resident – Ensemble Based
Send H/R attention **Joanna Settle.**

Founded in 1995. Starting non-Equity pay is $150/production. They call in actors from generals, files and past knowledge.

Thirteenth Tribe's body of work includes the classics, new scripts, and premiere stage adaptations, and is distinctly driven by the sharply choreographed interplay of all theatrical elements: the language of the material, the actors' performances, the architecture of the performance space (as it interacts with the scenic design), light and color schemes, sound-scapes and tempo.

Their 1998-1999 season included:
- Bloodline: The Oedipus/Antigone Story
- The Enduring Legend of Marinka Pinka
- Tommy Atomic

Victory Gardens Theatre
Dennis Zacek - Artistic Director
Marcelle McVay - Managing Director
2257 N. Lincoln
Chicago, IL 60614
773/549-5788
773/871-3000 – box office
773/549-2779 - fax
www.victorygardens.org
Equity – CAT IV – Resident

Send H/R to the attention **Dennis Zacek.**

Founded in 1974. Starting non-equity pay is half Equity minimum. They call in actors from generals, files and past knowledge. The nearest eL stop is Fullerton on the Red, Brown and Purple lines.

Victory Gardens is dedicated to new work and to the Chicago playwright.

Writers' Theatre Chicago
Michael Halberstam - Artistic Director
Books on Vernon
664 Vernon Ave.
Glencoe, IL 60022
847/835-7366
847/835-5398 – box office
847/835-5332 - fax
www.illyria.com/writers.html
Equity – CAT III – Resident
Send H/R attention **Casting.**

Founded in 1992. Starting non-Equity pay is $150. They call in actors from generals, files and past knowledge and attend the Unifieds.

In the intimate 50 seat Nicholas Pennell Theatre located behind Books on Vernon, Writers' Theatre offers productions which bring their audience face to face with literature's greatest creators and creations, as realized by some of Chicago's finest theatrical practitioners.

Non-Equity Theatres

Albright Theatre
P.O. Box 61
Batavia, IL 60510
630/406-8838
Non-Equity – Resident
Send H/R attention **Jacquie Weirich.**

Founded in 1974. They hold open auditions for each show.

Albright is a great theatre in a small space - the historical Prairie Church - which is being rehabbed, little by little, as budget allows.

Alchymia Theatre
Scott Fielding & Kim Snyder-Vine - Artistic Co-Directors
4249 N. Lincoln
Chicago, IL 60618
773/755-6843

Non-Equity – Resident – Ensemble Based
Send H/R attention **Scott Fielding - Artistic Co-Director.**

Founded in 1999. Starting pay varies. They call in actors from generals, files and past knowledge. The nearest eL stop is Damen on the Brown line.

Alphabet Soup Productions
Susan Holm - Artistic Director
Mark Pence - Managing Director
P.O. Box 85
Lombard, IL 60148
630/932-1555
Non-Equity – Itinerant

Send H/R to the **company address.**

Founded in 1987. Starting pay is $20/performance. They hold open auditions for each show, and season auditions are held in September.

Alphabet Soup produces fractured fairytale versions of children's classics.

Attic Playhouse
Kimberly Loughlin - Artistic & Managing Director
410 Sheridan Rd.
Highwood, IL 60040
847/433-2660
www.atticplayhouse.com
Non-Equity – Resident
Send H/R attention **Kimberly Loughlin.**

Founded in 1998. Starting pay varies. They hold open auditions for each show.

Attic Playhouse strives to present a variety of plays and musicals showcasing the broad spectrum of theatre as an artform by producing classic straight plays, small musicals, one-acts, improvisational and skit comedies and theatre for young audiences.

Azusa Productions
Maggie Speer - Artistic Director
1639 W. Estes
Chicago, IL 60626
312/409-4207
Non-Equity – Itinerant
Send H/R attention **Maggie Speer.**
Only send H/R in response to specific audition notices.

Founded in 1996. Starting pay $0-100/production. They hold open auditions for each show. Azusa presents "everything from A to Z in the USA" and beyond.

Their 1998-1999 season included:
- Reservoir Dogs
- Jesse & The Bandit Queen
- La Turista
- Back Bog Beast Bait

Barrington Area Arts Council
Theatre in the Gallery
207 Park Ave.
Barrington, IL 60010
847/382-5626 • 847/382-3685 - fax
Non-Equity – Resident
Send H/R attention
Claudia Kirmse - Program Director.

Founded in 1977. Starting pay is nothing. They hold open auditions for each show. The Barrington Area Arts Council offers programs in the visual, literary and performing arts.

Their 1998-1999 season included:
Radio Theatre
Children's Theatre at the Gallery

Beverly Theatre Guild
9936 S. Harnew Rd.
Oak Lawn, IL 60453
312/409-2705
www.beverlytheatreguild.org
Non-Equity – Resident
Send H/R attention
Ed Fudacz - President.

Founded in 1962. Starting pay is nothing. They hold open auditions for each show.

Beverly Theatre Guild is an organization that promotes the development of theatrical talent and encourages community interest in theatre as well as encouraging fellowship among our members.

Their 1998-1999 season included:
Cinderella
E/R - Emergency Room
Do Patent Leather Shoes Really Reflect Up?

Bowen Park Theatre
Jack Benny Center for the Arts
39 Jack Benny Dr.
Waukegan, IL 60087
847/360-4741
847/360-4740 – box office
847/662-0592 - fax

Non-Equity – Resident
Send H/R attention **Rik Covalinski - Performance Supervisor.**

Founded in 1987. Starting pay is $250/production. They hold open auditions for each show.

Breadline Theatre Group
Paul Kampf - Artistic Director
Michael Oswalt - Managing Director
1802 W. Berenice
Chicago, IL 60613
773/275-4342
Non-Equity – Resident – Ensemble Based
Send H/R to the **company address.**

Founded in 1993. Starting pay is nothing. They call in actors from generals, files or past knowledge. The nearest eL stop is Irving Park on the Brown line. Breadline is a theatre collective dedicated to creating new, vibrant and highly theatrical works that speak to a contemporary audience.

Their 1998-1999 season included:
Elixir
Heart of a Dog

Brittany Productions, Inc.
Harlan & Haimes
975 Brittany Rd.
Highland Park, IL 60035
847/432-0048 • 847/432-8259 - fax
Non-Equity – Itinerant
Send H/R attention **Harlan & Haimes**

Founded in 1998. Starting pay was not revealed. They hold open auditions for each show. Brittany Productions is an independent producer of commercial theatre.

Their 1998-1999 season included:
Wrong For Each Other - Jeff Recommended

Theatres

Brook Players
Art Johnson - Managing Director
P.O. Box 1353
Bolingbrook, IL 60440
630/739-1335 • 630/530-3643 - fax
www.wmcProductions.com
Non-Equity – Resident
Send H/R to **Art Johnson.**

Founded in 1997. Starting pay is nothing. They hold open auditions for each show. Season auditions are in April or May. Brook Players is a not-for-profit community theatre company formed to produce high quality musical productions using amateur and semi-pro performers yet keep the ticket price low so the average family can afford to attend.

Chicago Kids Company
Jesus Perez - Artistic Director
Paige Coffman - Managing Director
3812 W. Montrose
Chicago, IL 60618
773/539-0455 • 773/539-0452 - fax
Non-Equity – Itinerant

Send H/R attention
Paige Coffman & Jesus Perez.

Founded in 1993. Starting pay is $20/show. They hold open auditions for each show. Chicago Kids Company produces professional live theatre for children and their families, presenting original adaptations– modernized musical versions of classic Fairy Tales.

Child's Play Touring Theatre
Janet Brooks - Artistic Director
June Podagrosi - Managing Director
2518 W. Armitage
Chicago, IL 60647
773/235-8911 • 773/235-5478 - fax
Non-Equity – Resident – Ensemble Based
Send H/R attention **Janet Brooks.**

Founded in 1978. Starting pay is $345/week. They call in actors from generals, files and past knowledge. Season auditions are in May. The nearest eL stop is Western on the Blue line.

Dedicated exclusively to performing literature written by children, Child's Play Touring Theatre tours locally and nationally providing educational performances, residencies and workshops that target elementary school students.

Their 1998-1999 season included:
Do the Write Thing
Animal Tales and Dinosaur Scales
One Monster After Another
The Christmas that Almost Wasn't

Fantasy Orchard Children's Theatre
Dana Low - Artistic Director
P.O. Box 25084
Chicago, IL 60625
773/539-4211 • 773/539-4200 - fax
www.kidtheater.com
Non-Equity – Resident
Send H/R attention **Dana Low.**

Founded in 1990. Starting pay is $20/performance. They hold open auditions for each show, and season auditions are held in September. The nearest eL stop is Wellington on the Brown line. Fantasy Orchard promotes arts, imagination, morals and belief in self through elaborate fairy tales.

Their 1998-1999 season included:
African Cinderella

Circle Theatre
Tony Vezner, Alena Murguia & Greg Kolack - Artistic Directors
7300 W. Madison St.
Forest Park, IL 60130
708/771-0700
Non-Equity – Resident – Ensemble Based
Send H/R to the **company address.**

Founded in 1985. Starting pay is $100-150/production. They hold open auditions, and they attend the Unifieds. The nearest eL stop is Harlem on the Blue line.

Unique in Chicago because we are a directing based company, Circle strives to produce a wide variety of excellent quality theatre including musicals, dramas and world premieres.

Their 1998-1999 season included:
- Cyrano
- Lips Together, Teeth Apart - Jeff Citation: Set Design
- Salome
- Inspecting Carol - Jeff Recommended
- Eating Raoul
- A Moon for the Misbegotten

Classics On Stage, Ltd.
Michele Vacca - Artistic Director
Bob Boburka - Managing Director
P.O. Box 25365
Chicago, IL 60625
773/989-0598
members.aol.com/classstage/classstage
Non-Equity – Resident
Send H/R attention **Michele Vacca.**

Founded in 1981. Starting pay is $45/performance and $8/hour for rehearsals. They call in actors from generals, files and past knowledge. Season auditions are in the fall.

Classics On Stage produces selected weekday and Saturday morning live theatre for young audiences during the school year in a LARGE former vaudeville performance space in Park Ridge.

Their 1998-1999 season included:
- Beauty and the Beast
- 'Twas the Night Before Christmas
- Pinocchio!

Cobalt Ensemble Theatre
Katherine Condit-Ladd - Artistic Director
Eric Danson - Managing Director
PMB 222
5315 N. Clark
Chicago, IL 60640
312/458-9182
Non-Equity – Itinerant
Send H/R attention **Katherine Condit-Ladd.**

Founded in 1998. Starting pay was not revealed. They hold open auditions for each show. Cobalt Ensemble Theatre is dedicated to producing theatrically compelling work, often for the first time in Chicago, that challenges our audience to advocate education, compassion and tolerance in their lives.

Their 1998-1999 season included:
- Dream of a Common Language

CollaborAction Theatre Company
1945 W. Henderson
Chicago, IL 60657
312/409-2741
Non-Equity – Itinerant
Send H/R attention **Kimberly Senior.**

Founded in 1997. Starting pay is nothing. They hold open auditions for each show, and generals are held in January.

CollaborAction works as an ensemble in all elements of production, and we look to create performance that challenges both actors and their audience.

Their 1998-1999 season included:
- No MSG Added 2-One Act Festival
- The dreamer examines his pillow
- When You Comin' Back Red Ryder? -Jeff Recommended
- Lone Star/Laundry and Bourbon

ComedySportz
Matt Kaye - Artistic Director
Stephanie DeWaegeneer - Managing Director
3210 N. Halsted - 3rd Floor
Chicago, IL 60657
773/549-8482
773/549-8080 - box office
Non-Equity – Resident – Ensemble Based
Send H/R attention **Matt Kaye.**

Founded in 1987. Starting pay was not revealed. They hold open auditions for each show. The nearest eL stop is Belmont on the Red, Brown and Purple lines.

ComedySportz provides Chicago's #1 comedy competition - fun, fast-paced, and completely audience-interactive.

Common Ground Theatre
Dawn Leader - Artistic Director
17022 S. Oak Park Ave.
Tinley Park, IL 60477
708/647-1319 • 708/647-1752 - fax
Non-Equity – Itinerant
Send H/R attention **Dawn Leader.**

Founded in 1993. Starting pay varies. They hold open auditions for each show.

Common Ground Theatre returns to their original "theatre with an attitude," presenting thought provoking theatre and giving young people an outlet for positively expressing their feelings while educating and impacting audiences.

Their 1998-1999 season included:
- The Outsiders
- Biloxi Blues
- Godspell
- Snow White

Corn Productions
Robert Bouman - Artistic Director
4210 N. Lincoln
Chicago, IL 60618
773/278-3274
312/409-6435 - box office
Non-Equity – Resident – Itinerant
Send H/R to the **company address.**

Founded in 1997. Starting pay is nothing. They hold open auditions for each show. The nearest eL stop is Western on the Brown line.

Corn Productions is not a theatre, they're a party!

Their 1998-1999 season included:
- Spin-Off
- Tales from Mom's Crypt II
- Tiff and Mom and the Cardio-plexoflex
- Fundraiser Freshman Formal
- The Passion Follies

CTM Productions
Nancy Thurow - Artistic Director
228 State St.
Madison, WI 53703
608/255-2080
608/266-9055 - box office
608/255-6760 - fax
www.theatreforall.com
Non-Equity – Itinerant – Ensemble Based

Founded in 1965. Starting pay varies. They hold open auditions for each show.

Defiant Theatre
Christopher Johnson - Artistic Director
Jennifer Gehr - Managing Director
3540 N. Southport #162
Chicago, IL 60657
312/409-0585
www.defianttheatre.org
Non-Equity – Itinerant
Send H/R attention **Christopher Johnson.**

Founded in 1993. Starting pay is nothing. The nearest eL stop is Addison on the Red line.

Defiant strives to subvert the social, moral, and aesthetic expectations of mainstream artistic expression by breaking down the barriers of conventional stagecraft and by tackling complicated, even taboo, issues without timidity but with a foundation of scholarship.

Their 1998-1999 season included:
- Bluebeard - Jeff Nominated: Martin McClendon - Scenic Design
- Action Movie: The Play - The Director's Cut

Dolphinback Theatre
Matt Wallace - Artistic Director
John Pieza - Managing Director
3500 N. Freemont #39
Chicago, IL 60657
312/409-7980
home.earthlink.net\~dback\
Non-Equity – Itinerant – Ensemble Based
Send H/R attention **Matt Wallace.**

Founded in 1993. Starting pay varies. They hold open auditions for each show.

Dolphinback Theatre Company is an ensemble dedicated to shattering American myths, exposing social issues, and provoking thought, discussion, and change.

Their 1998-1999 season included:
- Anna Weiss
- Dogs by Seven

Duncan YMCA
Chernin Center for the Arts
Ifa Bayeza - Artistic Director
Pam Dickler - Managing Director
1001 W. Roosevelt
Chicago, IL 60608
312/738-7980
312/798-5999 - box office
312/738-1420 - fax
Non-Equity – Resident
Send H/R attention **Pam Dickler.**

Founded in 1997. Starting pay is $10-25/performance. They hold open auditions for each show.

The Duncan YMCA Chernin's Center for the Arts is the first YMCA to be exclusively dedicated to the arts, with a 220-seat theatre, dance studio and rehearsal space.

Their 1998-1999 season included:
- Undesirable Elements - After Dark Award
- Little Shop of Horrors

Eclipse Theatre Company
Ken Puttbach - Managing Director
P.O. Box 578960
Chicago, IL 60657-8960
312/409-1687
www.mcs.net/~eclipse
Non-Equity – Itinerant – Ensemble Based
Send H/R to the **company address.**

Founded in 1991. Starting pay was not revealed. They call in actors from generals, files and past knowledge, and they attend the Unifieds.

Eclipse is the only theatrical ensemble in Chicago to focus on one playwright's works per season.

Their 1998-1999 season included:
- Confessional
- The Eccentricities of a Nightingale

Emerald City Theatre Company
Karen Cardarelli - Artistic & Managing Director
2936 N. Southport
Chicago, IL 60657
773/529-2690
773/525-3655 - box office
773/529-2693 - fax
www.emeraldcitytheatre.com
Non-Equity – Resident
Send H/R attention **Rita Vreeland - Company Manager.**

Founded in 1996. Starting pay is $10-20/performance. They call in actors from generals, files or past knowledge. Season auditions are September-November. The nearest eL stop is Armitage on the Brown line.

Emerald City is Chicago's only theatre company to exclusively produce family entertainment.

Their 1998-1999 season included:
Winnie the Pooh
Frosty Returns
Hercules Saves the World
The Last Dragon of Camelot

ETA Creative Arts
Runako Jahi - Artistic Director
7558 S. Chicago Ave.
Chicago, IL 60619
773/752-3955 • 773/752-8727 - fax
Non-Equity – Resident
Send H/R attention **Abena Joan Brown.**

Founded in 1971. Starting non-Equity pay is $30/performance. The nearest eL stop is 79th on the Red line.

ETA tells the African-American story in the first voice.

European Repertory
Yasen Peyankov - Artistic Director
P.O. Box 578220
Chicago, IL 60657-8220
773/248-0577 • 773/248-0523 - fax
Non-Equity – Itinerant – Ensemble Based

Founded in 1992. Starting non-Equity pay is nothing. They call in actors from generals, files and past knowledge, and they attend the Unifieds.

European Repertory presents exclusively European works, both classic and contemporary.

Their 1998-1999 season included:
Ivanov - Jeff Recommended
Happy End

Excaliber Shakespeare Company
Darryl Maximilian Robinson - Artistic Director
4200 W. Wilcox - 2nd floor
Chicago, IL 60624
773/533-0285
Non-Equity – Itinerant – Ensemble Based
Send H/R attention **Darryl Maximilian Robinson.**

Founded in 1987. Starting pay is $5-10/performance. They hold open auditions for each show.

Excaliber Shakespeare Company is a critically-praised, multicultural, professional chamber theatre for hire that is committed to giving theatre artists of all races, ages, financial situations and educational backgrounds an opportunity to perform and excel in quality, non-Equity productions of great plays in the genre of World Drama.

Their 1998-1999 season included:
The Blood Knot - Jeff Recommended

Fantod Theatre
Kristin Larson - Artistic Director
Kelly Cooper - Managing Director
P.O. Box 478016
Chicago, IL 60647
773/296-2805
Non-Equity – Itinerant – Ensemble Based
Send H/R attention **Guy Jackson.**

Founded in 1998. Starting pay was not revealed. They hold open auditions for each show.

Fantod produces solely new works and serves the purpose of giving intense up-and-comers a place to cut their teeth.

Firstborn Productions
Greg Gerhard - Artistic Director
1352 W. Bryn Mawr #1
Chicago, IL 60660
773/728-2814
www.firstborn.org
Non-Equity – Itinerant – Ensemble Based
Send H/R to the **company address.**

Founded in 1995. They call in actors from generals, files and past knowledge.

Firstborn Productions challenges themselves and their audience and maintain a strong sense of integrity.

Fleetwood-Jourdain Theatre
Phillip VanLear - Artistic Director
1655 Foster St.
Evanston, IL 60201
847/328-5703
847/328-5740 - box office
847/328-9093 - fax
Non-Equity – Resident
Send H/R attention **Phillip VanLear.**

Founded in 1979. Starting pay was not revealed. They hold open auditions for each show. The nearest eL stop is Foster on the Purple line.

Fleetwood-Jourdain Theatre is a 20 year old Evanston-based company dedicated to presenting theatre that makes a difference.

Their 1998-1999 season included:
- Blues for Mister Charlie - Black Theatre Alliance Nomination
- One Mo' Time - Best of the North Shore 1999 Season Nomination
- Mud, River, Stone - Black Theatre Alliance Nomination

Footsteps Theatre Company
Jean Adamak - Artistic Director
5377 N. Bowmanville
Chicago, IL 60625
630/633-1489
Non-Equity – Itinerant – Ensemble Based
Footsteps is not curently accepting H/R's.

Founded in 1987. Starting pay is a $50 stipend. They cast from the ensemble, and they attend the Unifieds.

Footsteps produces works for, by and about women: theatre from a woman's point of view.

Their 1998-1999 season included:
- Twelfth Night
- Babes With Blades
- The Wake of Jamie Foster

Theatres

Fourth Wall Productions
Stephen A. Donart
4300 N. Narragansett
Chicago, IL 60634
773/481-8535 • 773/481-8037 - fax
Non-Equity – Resident
Send H/R attention
Stephen A. Donart.

Founded in 1989. Starting pay is a stipend. They hold open auditions for each show.

Fourth Wall develops works that forge intellectual and emotional alliances with the audience, challenging them to hold a mirror to our common experiences and draw their own unique conclusions.

Their 1998-1999 season included:
Reckless - Jeff Recommended
A Loss of Roses
The Woolgatherer

Free Associates
Mark Gagne - Artistic Director
750 W. Wellington
Chicago, IL 60657
773/334-3255
773/975-7171 - box office
773/334-8060 - fax
home.earthlink.net/~free_assoc/
Non-Equity – Resident –
Ensemble Based
Send H/R attention **Mark Gagne.**

Founded in 1991. Starting pay varies. They hold open auditions for each show, and season auditions are held in November and May. The nearest eL stop is Wellington on the Brown line.

The Free Associates produces original works that celebrate the styles and standards of great literature, film and television through parody.

FreeStreet Theater
Ron Bieganski - Artistic Director
1419 W. Blackhawk
Chicago, IL 60622
773/772-7248
www.freestreet.org
Non-Equity – Resident
Send H/R attention **Anita Evans.**

Founded in 1969. Starting pay is $5.15/hour. They hold open auditions for each show, and season auditions are held in September. The nearest eL stop is Division on the Blue line.

FreeStreet creates original multi-arts performances within communities to better discover who we are and to challenge who we become. Free Street uses the performing arts to enhance the literacy, self-esteem, creativity and employability of populations consistently excluded from mainstream cultural programming. FreeStreet performances challenge assumptions on both sides of the stage.

Frump Tucker
Theatre Company
Vince Mahler - Artistic Director
Laura Wells - Managing Director
P.O. Box 118315
Chicago, IL 60611
312/409-2689
Non-Equity – Itinerant –
Ensemble Based
Send H/R attention **Vince Mahler.**

Founded in 1996. Starting pay depends on profits. They call in actors from generals, files and past knowledge. Season auditions are in the fall.

Frump Tucker works to honor plays and to provide audiences with entertaining, visceral theatre.

Their 1998-1999 season included:
Loose Knit
In Perpetuity Throughout the Universe
The Original Last Wish Baby
Fit to be Tied - Jeff Recommended

The Great Beast Theater

Michael Martin - Artistic Director
6651 N. Greenview #3
Chicago, IL 60626
773/465-5568 • 312/236-2834 - fax
312/409-2876 - box office
Non-Equity – Itinerant – Ensemble Based
Send H/R attention
Michael Martin - Artistic Director.

Founded in 1997. Starting pay is nothing. They call in actors from generals, files and past knowledge. Season auditions are in March.

Great Beast produces only work that promises direct, recognizable connection to its audiences lives: "Resonant Theatre."

Their 1998-1999 season included:
- Why We Have a Body
- Quentin T Do Amateur Night At De Apollo
- Ready for the River
- Beast Women
- Floaters

Green Highway Theatre

726 W. Addison #1
Chicago, IL 60613
773/334-6032
Non-Equity – Itinerant
Send H/R to the **company address.**

Founded in 1994. Starting pay is nothing. They hold open auditions for each show.

Green Highway is a feminist theatre which creates a safe place to be dangerous.

Grove Players

P.O. Box 92
Downers Grove, IL 60515
630/960-9327
630/964-6888 - box office
http://members.theglobe.com/groveplayers
Non-Equity – Itinerant
Send H/R attention
Kathryn Kellogg Frank - President.

Founded in 1935. Starting pay is nothing. They hold open auditions for each show.

Grove Players strives to produce high-quality theatre with a crew of talented, hard-working volunteers.

HealthWorks Theatre

Peter Reynolds - Artistic Director
Stephen Rader - Managing Director
3171 N. Halsted - 2nd floor
Chicago, IL 60657
773/929-4260 • 773/404-6815 - fax
www.healthworkstheatre.com
Non-Equity – Itinerant – Ensemble Based
Send H/R attention **Peter Reynolds.**

Founded in 1988. Starting pay is $40/performance. They call in actors from generals, files and past knowledge. Season auditions are in August and December.

HealthWorks Theatre is an educational theatre company committed to working with communities to address critical health and social issues.

Highland Park Players

West Ridge Center
Highland Park, IL 60035
847/604-4771 • 847/432-8259 - fax
Non-Equity – Itinerant
Send H/R attention **Susan Haimes.**

Founded in 1988. Starting pay was not revealed. They hold open auditions for each show.

Highland Park Players wants to provide a professional quality theatre for the community as well as an outlet for the talents of area residents.

Their 1998-1999 season included:
- Snow White and the Seven Dwarfs
- Oklahoma!
- Five Women Wearing the Same Dress.

Theatres

The Hypocrites
Sean Graney - Artistic Director
Mechelle Moe - Managing Director
P.O. Box 578542
Chicago, IL 60657-8542
312/409-5578
Non-Equity – Itinerant
Send H/R to the **company address.**

Founded in 1997. Starting pay was not revealed. They call in actors from generals, files and past knowledge. Season auditions are in December.

The Hypocrites produce affordable, unorthodox theatre that inspires and entertains.

ImprovOlympic
3541 N. Clark
Chicago, IL 60657
773/880-0199
773/880-9993 - box office
773/880-9979 - fax

Non-Equity – Resident –
Ensemble Based
Send H/R attention
Charna Halpern - Director.

Founded in 1981. Starting pay was not revealed. They cast from ensemble. The nearest eL stop is Addison on the Red line.

Inclusive Theatre
Nancy Sheeber - Artistic Director
640 North LaSalle #535
Chicago, IL 60610
312/295-2754 • 312/787-3234 - fax
www.stormin.com/inclusive
Non-Equity – Itinerant
Send H/R attention **Nancy Sheeber.**

Founded in 1996. Starting pay is gas or bus fare. They call in actors from generals, files or past knowledge.

Inclusive Theatre investigates (through writing, performance and teaching) our commonality.

Their 1998-1999 season included:
Macbeth
A Midsommer Night's Dreame

Shapeshifters Theatre Company
Josephine Craven - Artistic Director
Irish American Heritage Center
4626 N. Knox
Chicago, IL 60630
773/282-7035 x17
773/282-0380 - fax
www.irishamhc.com

Non-Equity – Resident
Send H/R to the **company address.**

Founded in 1985. Starting pay is food. They hold open auditions for each show. The nearest eL stop is Montrose on the Blue line.

The Irish American Heritage Center promotes Irish culture and arts through performance of theatre, music, dance, poetry and lecture.

J.A. Productions
Jeff Ahern - Artistic Director
1135 W. Grace #2N
Chicago, IL 60613
312/409-9793 • 773/528-8876 - fax
Non-Equity – Itinerant –
Ensemble Based

Send H/R attention **Jeff Ahern.**

Founded in 1997. Starting pay was not revealed. They call in actors from generals, files and past knowledge.

J.A. Productions produces funny, unique shows at an affordable price.

Kidworks Touring Theater Company
Andrea Salloum - Artistic Director
3510 N. Broadway #1
Chicago, IL 60657
773/883-9932 • 773/883-9080 - fax
Non-Equity – Itinerant – Ensemble Based
Send H/R attention **Andrea Salloum.**

Founded in 1987. Starting pay is $45/performance or $25/workshop. They call in actors from generals, files and past knowledge. They hold season auditions in September.

Kidworks is a touring theatre dedicated to opening the doors between education and imagination for pre-K to 8th graders.

Their 1998-1999 season included:
African-American History...Live
'Tis Shakespearish
Captain Oceanview's Adventures
Drama Residencies

Light Opera Works
Lara Teeter - Artistic Director
927 Noyes St.
Evanston, IL 60201
847/869-7930
847/869-6300 - box office
847/869-6388 - fax
www.light-opera-works.org
Non-Equity – Resident
Send H/R attention **Lara Teeter.**

Founded in 1980. Starting pay varies. They call in actors from generals, files and past knowledge. Season auditions are held in late January. The nearest eL stop is Foster or Davis on the Purple line.

Light Opera Works' mission is to produce and present various forms of music theatre from a variety of world traditions, engage the community through educational programs and to train artists in music theatre.

Their 1998-1999 season included:
Yeomen of the Guard
The Duchess of Chicago
The Fantastiks
The Desert Song

Low Sodium Entertainment
3737 N. Kenmore #3F
Chicago, IL 60613
773/549-3250
www.lowsodiumonline.com
Non-Equity – Itinerant – Ensemble Based

Founded in 1996. Starting pay is based on the box office. They hold open auditions for each show.

Low Sodium is a motivated, hungry, grass roots, no-holds barred theatre company that is very low in salt.

Marquee Theatre Company
Geoffrey Edwards - Artistic Director
P.O. Box 6364
Evanston, IL 60204
847/604-0535
www.phaseshift.com/marquee
Non-Equity – Resident
Send H/R to the **company address.**

Founded in 1992. Starting pay varies. They hold open auditions for each show. The nearest eL stop is Central on the Purple line.

Marquee Theatre Company is the only professional theatre group on the North Shore dedicated exclusively to bringing the Chicago area the finest in classic family entertainment.

MPAACT

P.O. Box 10039
Chicago, IL 60610
773/324-0757 • 773/262-0011 - fax
Non-Equity – Resident
Send H/R attention **Reginald Lawrence.**

Founded in 1991. Starting pay is $500/production. They hold open auditions for each show, and season auditions are in the fall or winter. The nearest eL stop is Morse on the Red line.

Focused exclusively upon new works and collaborative art, MPAACT produces, educates, and instructs, with the goal of bringing forth an understanding and appreciation of Afrikan Center Theatre and its interrelated disciplines.

Their 1998-1999 season included:
- The Abesha Conspiracy - Ira Aldridge Award: Best New Work
- Within the Dream
- Beneath A Dark Sky - New Voices Selection (Detroit, MI)
- Tales from an Urban Empire

Murder Mystery Players

Richard Bucchi - Artistic Director
945 N. Lombard
Oak Park, IL 60302
708/556-2495
630/543-5151 - box office
708/848-8177 - fax
www.mysteryplayers.com
Non-Equity – Resident – Ensemble Based
Send H/R attention **Richard Bucchi.**

Founded in 1995. Starting pay was not revealed.They call in actors from generals, files and past knowledge.

Murder Mystery Players performs interactive dinner theatre murder mysteries for public and private audiences, with a strong emphasis on comedy.

Murder Mystery Productions

Dave Kappas - Artistic Director
50 Burr Ridge Pkwy.
Burr Ridge, IL 60521
630/887-9988
630/887-9975 - fax
www.murderme.com
Non-Equity – Itinerant
Send H/R attention **Ron Rubin.**

Founded in 1986. Starting pay is $35/victim. They call in actors from generals, files and past knowledge.

Murder Mystery Productions produces three hour murder mystery dinner events that tests the imaginations and detective skills of our guests.

Music On Stage

P.O. Box 1786
Palatine, IL 60078
847/991-5990
Non-Equity – Resident
Send H/R in an envelope marked **Resumé.**

Founded in 1957. Starting pay is nothing. They hold open auditions for each show.

Music On Stage is a quality community theatre company presenting three musical plays per season, beginning in the fall of each year.

Their 1998-1999 season included:
- Company
- West Side Story - Boonie Award Nomination, Best Supporting Actress
- Rodgers & Hammerstein
- Cinderella - Boonie Award Nomination Best Actress, Best Actor, Best Supporting Actress

The Mystery Shop

551 Sundance Ct.
Carol Stream, IL 60188
630/690-1105 • 630/690-7928 - fax
www.TheMysteryShop.com
Non-Equity – Itinerant – Ensemble Based
Send H/R attention
Mary Heitert - Owner.

Founded in 1988. Starting pay is $30-40/performance. They call in actors from generals, files and past knowledge. Season auditions are in the spring.

They Mystery Shop is a traveling theatre company specializing in adult and children's participatory mysteries and programs.

NEIU Stage Center Theatre

5500 N. St. Louis
Chicago, IL 60625-4699
773/794-2938
773/794-6652 - box office
www.neiu.edu/~stagectr
Non-Equity – Resident
Send H/R attention
Anna Antaramion - Director of Theatre.

Founded in 1963. Starting pay is nothing. They hold open auditions for each show, and generals are held in September and January.

The Stage Center Theatre allows the artistic combination of professional and student actors performing classics and modern plays in a creative and experimental environment.

New Tuners Theatre

John Sparks - Artistic Director
1225 W. Belmont
Chicago, IL 60657
773/929-7367
773/327-5252 - box office
www.adamczyk.com/newtuners
Non-Equity – Resident – Ensemble Based
Send H/R attention **John Sparks.**

Founded in 1969. Starting pay is $25/production. They hold open auditions for each show, and season auditions are in the fall and spring. The nearest eL stop is Belmont on the Red, Brown and Purple lines.

New Tuners Theatre and Workshop is the only institution in the country (perhaps the world) where an ongoing workshop for writers of new musical theatre works is conducted by a theatre that regularly and exclusively produces new American musicals.

Their 1998-1999 season included:
Hans Brinker
Overland
Emma & Co.
10-Minute Tuners
Stages 99

The North Shore Theatre of Wilmette

Wilmette Park District
3000 Glenview Rd.
Wilmette, IL 60091
847/256-9694 • 847/251-4930 - fax
847/256-9787 - box office
Non-Equity – Resident
Send H/R attention **Robert E. Bierie.**

Starting pay was not revealed. They hold open auditions for each show.

Oak Park Village Players

Gigi Hudson - Artistic Director
John Kibler - Managing Director
1006 Madison St.
Oak Park, IL 60302
708/524-7892 • 708/524-9892 - fax
708/222-0369 - box office
www.angelfire.com/il/opvp
Non-Equity – Resident
Send H/R attention **Gigi Hudson.**

Founded in 1961. Starting pay was not revealed.

Paradise Productions
Jillann Gabriel - Artistic Director
7813-C W. North
River Forest, IL 60305
708/771-4904
847/674-1500 x3 - box office
773/237-0299 - fax
Non-Equity – Resident – Ensemble Based
Send H/R attention **Jillann Gabriel.**

Founded in 1994. Starting pay is $40/performance plus $100 for rehearsal. They call actors in from generals, files and past knowledge. The nearest eL stop is Skokie on the Yellow Line.

Paradise Productions is a theatrical ensemble subsidized by the Skokie Park District dedicated to producing great musical theatre works that are infrequently performed.

Park Ridge Gilbert & Sullivan Society
P.O. Box 339
Park Ridge, IL
60068-0339
847/604-4333
www.geocities.com/~parigass
Non-Equity – Resident
Send H/R to the **company address.**

Founded in 1973. Starting pay is nothing. They hold open auditions for each show.

PaRiGASS is a social group and community performing organization that produces professional quality Gilbert & Sullivan operettas, complete with full (25 piece) orchestra, that serves a growing northwestern suburban audience base.

Their 1998-1999 season included:
Princess Ida

Pegasus Players
John Econmos - Managing Director
1145 W. Wilson
Chicago, IL 60640
773/878-9761 • 773/271-8057 - fax
Non-Equity – Resident
Send H/R attention **Katie Klemme.**

Founded in 1979. Starting pay is a stipend plus $25/performance. They hold open auditions for each show. The nearest eL stop is Wilson on the Red line.

Pegasus Players' mission is two-fold: to produce the highest quality artistic work and to provide exemplary theatre, entertainment, and arts education at no charge to people who have little or no access to the arts.

Their 1998-1999 season included:
The Lynching of Leo Frank - Jeff Citation: Best New Work
The Thirteenth Young Playwrights Festival
The Magic Banjo
Saturday Night - Jeff Recommended

Pendragon Players
Peter Blatchford - Managing Director
4530 S. Avers
Chicago, IL 60632
773/890-1961
www.pendragonplayers.org
Non-Equity – Itinerant
Send H/R attention **Peter Blatchford.**

Founded in 1993. Starting pay is $25/hour. They hold open auditions for each show.

Pendragon Players is a touring readers theatre company, performing adaptations of classic books and stories in libraries and schools.

Their 1998-1999 season included:
The Count of Monte Cristo
Three In a Roe by Poe
The Adventures of Sherlock Holmes
The War of the Worlds
A Haunted Houseful

Pendulum Theatre Company
2936 N. Southport
Chicago, IL 60657
773/529-8692
www.manasota.com/pendulum/

Non-Equity – Itinerant
Send H/R attention **Bill Redding.**

Founded in 1996. Starting pay varies. They hold open auditions for each show and attend the Unifieds.

Their 1998-1999 season included:
The Insect Play

Pheasant Run Dinner Theatre
4051 E. Main St.
St. Charles, IL 60174
630/584-6300
630/584-6342 - box office
630/584-4693 - fax

www.pheasantrun.com
Non-Equity – Resident
Send H/R attention **Diana Martinez - Director of Entertainment.**

Founded in 1963. Starting pay is negotiable. They hold open auditions for each show.

Phoenix Ascending
Steve Roath - Artistic Director
4227 N. Lincoln
Chicago, IL 60618
773/327-2137
773/327-2134 - box office
phoenixascending.com
Non-Equity – Resident
Send H/R attention **Stephen Roath.**

Founded in 1998. Starting pay is $25-30/performance. They hold open auditions for each show. The nearest eL stop is Irving Park on the Brown line.

Phoenix Ascending is dedicated to forgotten musicals and dramas from the past.

Their 1998-1999 season included:
Charlie Brown
Vanities
The Gingham Dog
Torch Song Trilogy

Phoenix Rising Theatre
Maura Elizabeth Manning - Artistic Director
P.O. Box 4378
Wheaton, IL 60189-4378
312/409-2271 • 630/545-2087 - fax
www.enteract.com/~mmanning/Phoenix
Non-Equity – Itinerant – Ensemble Based
Send H/R attention **Maura Manning.**

Founded in 1998. Starting pay is a stipend. They hold open auditions for each show.

Phoenix Rising is dedicated to producing plays that offer interesting and non-traditional roles for women of all ages.

Their 1998-1999 season included:
The Loveliest Afternoon of the Year
Sometimes I Hear My Voice

Plasticene
Dexter Bullard - Artistic Director
2122 N. Winchester #1F
Chicago, IL 60614
312/409-0400
www.plasticene.com
Non-Equity – Itinerant – Ensemble Based
Send H/R to the **company address.**
Founded in 1995. Starting pay is variable.

They cast from ensemble, and they attend the Unifieds.

Plasticene is an award-winning and critically acclaimed physical theatre company dedicated to presenting original theatre developed by a unique creative process that emphasizes the most plastic elements of theatre creation - the objects, sound, and light.

Players Workshop's Children's Theatre
Stephen Roath - Artistic Director
2936 N. Southport
Chicago, IL 60657
773/929-6288 • 773/477-8022 - fax
playersworkshop.com
Non-Equity – Itinerant
Send H/R attention **Stephen Roath.**

Founded in 1970. Starting pay is nothing. They hold open auditions for each show.

Players Workshop's Children's Theatre is the oldest children's theatre in Chicago.

Porchlight Theatre
Walter Stearns - Artistic Director
Jeannie Lukow - Managing Director
2936 N. Southport
Chicago, IL 60657
773/325-9884 • 312/670-1578 - fax
www.porchlighttheatre.com
Non-Equity – Itinerant
Send H/R attention **Walter Stearns.**

Founded in 1995. Starting pay varies. They hold open auditions for each show.

Porchlight Theatre focuses on new musicals and relevant treatments of existing material that explore heightened realities and provides audiences with an extended theatre experience.

Their 1998-1999 season included:
- The Vanishing Point - After Dark Award: Original Musical Composition
- Ruthless!
- Falsettos - Jeff Recommended

Profiles Theatre
3761 N. Racine
Chicago, IL 60613
773/549-1815 • 312/944-4018 - fax
Non-Equity – Resident – Ensemble Based
Send H/R attention **Darrell W. Cox - Associate Artistic Director.**

Founded in 1988. Starting pay varies. They hold open auditions for each show, and season auditions are August. The nearest eL stop is Sheridan on the Red line.

Profiles' primary focus is bringing new plays to Chicago, generally works that illuminate the determination and resiliency of the human spirit.

Their 1998-1999 season included:
- Stray Dogs - Five Jeff Citations: Director, Principal Actress, Ensemble, Supporting Actor, Set Design

---

Prologue Theatre Productions
Anita Greenberg - Managing Director
c/o ArtsBridge - 2936 N. Southport #210
Chicago, IL 60657
847/681-0910 • 847/681-0449 - fax
Non-Equity – Itinerant
Send H/R to the **company address.**

Founded in 1987. Starting pay is $20/performance plus $100-200 for rehearsals. They hold open auditions for each show.

Prologue Theatre Productions does two to three small shows a year - mostly musicals.

Their 1998-1999 season included:
- Langston's Lab
- Cole: Songs of Cole Porter

Prop Thtr

Scott Vehill - Artistic Director
Jonathan Lavan - Managing Director
2621 N. Washtenaw
Chicago, IL 60647
773/486-7767
www.viprofix.com/proptheatre.html
Non-Equity – Itinerant
Send H/R attention **Jonathan Lavan.**

Founded in 1981. Starting pay is $200-350/production. They hold open auditions for each show.

Prop Thtr is the oldest surviving non-Equity new works company. Prop is known for their edgy adaptations of literary and counter-culture classics.

Their 1998-1999 season included:
- The Possessed
- New Play ë99
- Annie Sprinkle's Herstory of Porn: Reel to Real

Pyewacket

Linda LeVeque & Kate Harris - Associate Artistic Directors
2322 W. Wilson
Chicago, IL 60625
773/275-2201
Non-Equity – Itinerant – Ensemble Based
Send H/R attention **Kate Harris.**

Founded in 1997. Starting pay is 10% of the box office net. They call in actors from generals, files and past knowledge.

Pyewacket is committed to producing the highest quality theatrical productions of "middle tales." "Middle tales offer maps of the mid life passage." - Allen B. Chinen, M.D.

Their 1998-1999 season included:
- Belmont Avenue Social Club - Jeff Citation: Best Supporting Actor - Dan Fine
- Belle of Amherst
- The Turn of the Screw - Jeff Citation: Best Actor - Michael Nowak

Raven Theatre

Michael Menendian - Artistic Director
6931 N. Clark
Chicago, IL 60626
773/338-2177 • 773/338-4782 - fax
Non-Equity – Resident – Ensemble Based
Send H/R attention **Michael Menendian.**

Founded in 1983. Starting pay varies. They call in actors from generals, files and past knowledge. Season auditions are in the summer.

Raven Theatre focuses primarily on American masterpieces and other works which shed light on "The American Experience."

Their 1998-1999 season included:
- Glengarry Glen Ross - Jeff Nominated
- Six Degrees of Separation - Jeff Recommended

Realism Update Theatre

Christina Athanasiades
2957 N. Pulaski
Chicago, IL 60641
773/685-3077
Non-Equity
Send H/R attention **Christina Athanasiades.**

Founded in 1991. Starting pay is nothing.

Red Wolf Theater Company

Susan Block - Artistic Director
1609 W. Berteau
Chicago, IL 60613
312/409-6024
www.RedWolfTheatre.com
Non-Equity – Itinerant
Send H/R to the **company address.**

Founded in 1996. Starting pay is a stipend. They hold open auditions for each show.

Red Wolf produces theatre for the older actor.

Their 1998-1999 season included:
- Red Address - Jeff Recommended

Theatres

Runamuck Productions
Heath Corson - Artistic Director
4655 N. Campbell #3
Chicago, IL 60625
773/784-8100
Non-Equity – Itinerant
Founded in 1995. Starting pay is a share of 20% of a show's net. They hold open auditions for each show.
Runamuck Productions produces world premiere adaptations of children's literature in order to promote literacy.
Their 1998-1999 season included:
The Mysterious Cases of Mr. Pin
I Left My Sneakers in Dimension X

Saint Sebastian Players
c/o St. Bonaventure
1641 W. Diversey
Chicago, IL 60614
773/404-7922 • 773/525-3955 - fax
members.aol.com/stsebplyrs
Non-Equity – Resident – Ensemble Based
Send H/R to the **company address.**
Founded in 1981. Starting pay is nothing. They hold open auditions for each show. The nearest eL stop is Diversey on the Brown line.
SSP is an ensemble of actors, directors, designers and administrators approaching their 19th season of producing theatre that challenges them artistically and satisfies their audiences consistently.
Their 1998-1999 season included:
As You Like It
The Diviners

Schadenfreude
Sandy Marshall - Artistic Director
7016 N. Glenwood
Chicago, IL 60626
773/271-5318
773/293-0024 - box office
773/529-7688 - fax
www.schadenfreude.net
Non-Equity – Resident – Ensemble Based
Founded in 1997. Starting pay is nothing. They cast from ensemble. The nearest eL stop is Morse on the Red line.
Schadenfreude is dedicated to challenging overall perceptions of comedic and theatrical experiences, as well as maintaining the vision of establishing a new cultural institution.

Scrap Mettle SOUL
Richard O. Geer - Artistic Director
4753 N. Broadway #710
Chicago, IL 60640
773/275-3999
Non-Equity – Resident – Ensemble Based
Send H/R attention **Richard O. Geer.**
Founded in 1993. Starting pay is nothing. They hold open auditions for each show, and season auditions are in September and March. The nearest eL stop is Argyle on the Red line.
Scrap Mettle SOUL is a community performance ensemble based in oral history.
Their 1998-1999 season included:
Concerto for Two Dumpsters and a Neighborhood
Detours Home

Sense of Urgency
Edwin Wilson - Artistic Director
905 S. Grove - 1st floor
Oak Park, IL 60304
312/400-9298
Non-Equity – Itinerant – Ensemble Based
Send H/R attention **Edwin Wilson.**

Founded in 1995. Starting pay is $125/production. They hold open auditions for each show.

A Sense of Urgency strives to produce the highest quality theatre, while continuing to develop our audience and challenging our acting ensemble with provocative work.

Their 1998-1999 season included:
The Caretaker
Adapting To It

Setting the Stage
Alex DeTogne & Leslie Kuykendall - Co-Artistic Directors
402 E. Hawthorne
Arlington Heights, IL 60004
847/255-3010
847/818-1376 - box office
847/255-3010 - fax
Non-Equity – Resident
Send H/R to the **company address.**

Founded in 1996. Starting pay was not revealed.

Setting the Stage is a positive, educational and social way for creative children to work as a team, gain self-confidence and make friends.

Shakespeare's Motley Crew
Laura Jones Macknin - Artistic Director
Mark Myers - Managing Director
4926 N. Winchester
Chicago, IL 60640
773/878-3632 • 312/726-3726 - fax
Non-Equity – Itinerant – Ensemble Based
Send H/R attention
Laura Jones Macknin.

Founded in 1992. Starting pay was not revealed. They call in actors from generals, files and past knowledge.

SMC is committed to the works of William Shakespeare and his contemporaries - and to productions at once intimate and vibrant; contemporary and true and never subtle.

Their 1998-1999 season included:
Titus Andronicus - Jeff Recommended
Measure for Measure

Shattered Globe Theatre
Brian Pudil - Artistic Director
2856 N. Halsted
Chicago, IL 60657
773/404-1237
773/871-3000 - box office
312/621-1205 - fax
Non-Equity – Resident – Ensemble Based
Send H/R attention **Brian Pudil.**

Founded in 1981. Starting pay is $25/performance. They call in actors from generals, files and past knowledge. The nearest eL stop is Fullerton on the Red line.

Shattered Globe is centered around ensemble based acting, showcasing the unique dynamic created when a group of artists have worked together for 10 years mixing new works and American classics to follow the journey of everyman.

Skylab Theater

1420 W. Winnemac #2E
Chicago, IL 60640
773/784-3397
www.solarflare.org
Non-Equity – Itinerant
Send H/R attention
Fausto Fernos - Director.

Founded in 1969. Starting pay is $100-300/production. They hold open auditions for each show, and season auditions are in November.

Skylab Theater is a collaborative company of puppeteers, actors, designers, musicians, scientists, dancers, and off-the-wall types who put on musical productions of an interdisciplinary nature which incorporate elaborate costumes, puppets, dance, and ritual into shows that educate and inspire their audiences about issues concerning science.

Their 1998-1999 season included:
- Feast of Fools Cabaret

Stage Actors Ensemble

Stephan Turner - Artistic Director
656 W. Barry
Chicago, IL 60613
773/529-8337
Non-Equity – Resident – Ensemble Based

Founded in 1978. Starting pay was not revealed. They call in actors from generals, files and past knowledge. The nearest eL stop is Belmont on the Red, Brown and Purple lines.

Stage Actors Ensemble performs works that are strictly interracial or intercultural.

Their 1998-1999 season included:
- Three Ways Home
- The Bald Soprano - Jeff Recommended

Stage Left Theatre

Drew Martin - Artistic Director
Jacqueline Singleton - Managing Director
3408 N. Sheffield
Chicago, IL 60657
773/883-8830
members.aol.com/SLTChicago
Non-Equity – Resident – Ensemble Based
Send H/R to the **company address.**

Founded in 1982. Starting pay is 1% of the the gross receipts. They call in actors from generals, files and past knowledge, and they attend the Unifieds. The nearest eL stop is Addison on the Red line.

Stage Left is a not-for-profit corporation including an ensemble of 20 artists dedicated to producing works that raise the level of debate on political and social issues.

Their 1998-1999 season included:
- The Waiting Room - Jeff Citations: Actress, Supporting Actress
- Econo-Manic Depression
- Julius Caesar
- The Secret of the Old Queen
- Bocon
- We The People
- Amelia Earhart: First to Fly

Stage Right Dinner Theatre

Peter Verdica - Artistic Director
276 E. Irving Park Rd.
Wood Dale, IL 60191
630/595-2044
www.giorgiosbanq.com
Non-Equity – Resident
Send H/R attention **Peter Verdica.**

Founded in 1991. Starting pay is $20-60/performance. They hold open auditions for each show.

Stage Right Dinner Theatre produces quality musicals and plays and serves great food.

Stone Circle Theatre Ensemble

Jessica McCartney - Artistic Director
915 W. Fletcher
Chicago, IL 60657
773/525-9565
Non-Equity – Itinerant – Ensemble Based
Send H/R attention **Jessica McCartney.**

Founded in 1996. Starting pay was not revealed. They hold open auditions for each show.

The Stone Circle Theatre Ensemble is turning its focus to original and new works in the upcoming season.

Their 1998-1999 season included:
- The Winter's Tale
- The Collector

Summer Place Theatre

P.O. Box 128
Naperville, IL 60566
630/355-7969 • 630/416-3854 - fax
www.summerplacetheatre.com
Non-Equity – Resident
Send H/R attention **Judy DiVita.**

Founded in 1965. Starting pay is nothing. They hold open auditions for each show, and season auditions are in December, spring and August.

Summer Place produces high quality live plays and entertainment suitable for family audiences including drama, musicals and comedies for adults and 2-3 shows per year directed specifically at a younger audience.

Their 1998-1999 season included:
- Rainmaker
- Godspell
- Light Up The Sky
- Annie
- Charlie and the Chocolate Factory
- Ghost Stories in the Park in the Dark

Sweetback Productions

Kelly Anchors & Mike McKune - Artistic Directors
Steve Hickson - Managing Director
1517 W. Rosemont #3E
Chicago, IL 60660-1322
312/409-3925
Non-Equity – Resident
Send H/R attention **Steve Hickson.**

Founded in 1994. Starting pay is a split of audience donations. They hold open auditions for each show.

Sweetback is the camp headquarters for Chicago and the outlying area.

Their 1998-1999 season included:
- Scarrie! The Musical
- Rudolf the Red-Hosed Reindeer
- Joan Crawford Goes to Hell

Theatre of Western Springs

Tony Vezner - Artistic Director
Jeffrey P. Arena - Managing Director
4384 Hampton Ave.
Western Springs, IL 60558
708/246-4043
708-246-3380 - box office
708/246-4015 - fax
www.TheatreWesternSprings.com
Non-Equity – Itinerant – Ensemble Based
Send H/R attention **Jeffrey P. Arena.**

Founded in 1928. Starting pay is nothing. They cast from their ensemble.

Theatre of Western Springs is like a university drama department - focusing on artistic growth and community support - but without the university.

Theatre Q

P.O. Box 408733
Chicago, IL 60640-8733
773/271-9287 • 773/271-9291 - fax
members.aol.com/QtheatreQ/index.html
Non-Equity – Itinerant
Send H/R attention **John Koulias.**

Founded in 1996. Starting pay varies. They hold open auditions for each show.

Theatre Q is the only gay, lesbian, bisexual, transgender theatre company in Chicago.

TimeLine Theatre

P.J. Powers - Artistic Director
Pat Tiedemann - Managing Director
615 W. Wellington
Chicago, IL 60657
312/409-TIME
www.timelinetheatre.com
Non-Equity – Resident – Ensemble Based
Send H/R attention **P.J. Powers.**

Founded in 1997. Starting pay is nothing. They hold open auditions for each show, and they attend the Unifieds. The nearest eL stop is Belmont on the Red, Brown and Purple lines.

TimeLine Theatre Company is committed to bringing Chicago audiences exciting and provocative theatre that explores humanity through an historical perspective.

Their 1998-1999 season included:
No End of Blame

Timestep Players

Allen McCoy - Artistic Director
Tracy McCoy - Managing Director
P.O. Box 16442
Chicago, IL 60616
773/736-7077 • 773/736-6730 - fax
www.timestepplayers.com
Non-Equity – Itinerant
Send H/R attention **Allen McCoy.**

Founded in 1991. Starting pay is $300/week. They hold open auditions for each show, and season auditions are held in early March.

Timestep Players is a non-profit educational touring children's theatre company.

Their 1998-1999 season included:
Old Time Rock-n-Roll
Kites, Rockets and Boomerangs
The Incredible Time Machine
Trekkin' Through Time
Amazing Stories From Around the World
The Exploding Dino-mite Time Machine
Frizby's Circus
Sports Science
Don't Worry Be Healthy
The Adventures of Huckleberry Finn

TinFish Productions

Dejan Avramovich - Artistic Director
Laurie Kladis - Managing Director
4247 N. Lincoln
Chicago, IL 60618
773/549-1888
www.tinfish.org
Non-Equity – Itinerant – Ensemble Based
Send H/R attention **Dejan Avramovich.**

Founded in 1994. Starting pay is a stipend. They hold open auditions for each show.

Tinfish Productions produces plays by or about great European literary figures.

Tony 'n' Tina's Wedding

Joseph Tomaska - Artistic Director
Janice Dura - Managing Director
230 W. North
Chicago, IL 60610
312/664-6969
312/664-8844 - box office
312/664-7083 - fax
www.tonyntina.com
Non-Equity – Resident – Ensemble Based
Send H/R attention **John Lucas - Production Manager.**

Founded in 1993. Starting pay is negotiable. They call in actors from generals, files and past knowledge. Season auditions are held quarterly. The nearest eL stop is Sedgewick on the Brown line.

Tony 'n' Tina's is interactive improv.

Trap Door Theatre
Beata Pilch - Artistic Director
Michael Pieper - Managing Director
1655 W. Cortland
Chicago, IL 60647
773/384-0494 • 773/384-2874 - fax
Non-Equity – Resident – Ensemble Based
Send H/R to the **company address.**

Founded in 1994. Starting pay is based on tips. They hold open auditions for each show. The nearest eL stop is Damen on the Blue line.

Trap Door Theatre is committed to seeking out challenging yet obscure works and bringing them to life, whether it is the European classic rarely seen in the United States, an untarnished piece of American literature, or the playwright living next door.

Their 1998-1999 season included:
- Squat
- Orpheus Descending - Jeff Recommended
- Poona the Fuck Dog
- Polaroid Stories
- The Killing Game
- Feedlot
- Alien Hand - Jeff Recommended

Tripaway Theatre
Karin Shook - Artistic Director
Anita Evans - Managing Director
4615 N. Paulina #2B
Chicago, IL 60640
773/878-7785
www.tripaway.org
Non-Equity – Itinerant – Ensemble Based
Send H/R attention **Karin Shook.**

Founded in 1994. Starting pay is nothing. They hold open auditions for each show.

Tripaway Theare is known for its high-energy, inventive, off-kilter productions of Shakespeare and for its daring forays into the arena of original works.

Their 1998-1999 season included:
- A Midsummer Night's Dream
- Commedia Divino E Profano or Scourge of the Doom Pies!

Up & Coming Theatre Company
P.O. Box 473
Arlington Heights, IL 60006
847/706-6747
847/718-7700 - box office
www.uactheatre.com
Non-Equity – Resident
Send H/R attention **Jorge Bermudez.**

Founded in 1992. Starting pay is nothing. They hold open auditions for each show.

Up & Coming Theatre produces top quality musical theatre in the Northwest Suburbs with an emphasis on the character development and acting of a production.

Their 1998-1999 season included:
- Joseph and the Amazing Technicolor Dreamcoat
- Grease

Village Theatre Guild
P.O. Box 184
Glen Ellyn, IL 60137
630/469-8230
Non-Equity – Resident

Founded in 1963. Starting pay is nothing. They hold open auditions for each show.

Village Theatre Guild is a quality organization that is not afraid to take risks, stir up controversy, and do plays that are off the usual fare of community theatre.

Their 1998-1999 season included:
- Come Back to the Five and Dime, Jimmy Dean, Jimmy Dean
- A Delicate Balance
- Steambath
- Sylvia

Theatres

Voltaire Theatre
Lisa Dowda - Producing Director
4907 N. Glenwood #2B
Chicago, IL 60640
773/784-4752
www.voltairetheatre.org
Non-Equity – Resident
Send production proposals to:
Lisa Dowda - Producing Director.
Founded in 1990.

VORTEX
Gary Charles Metz - Artistic Director
c/o Community Park District -
920 Barnsdale Rd.
LaGrange Park, IL 60526
708/354-4580
Non-Equity – Resident – Ensemble Based
Send H/R attention **Gary Charles Metz.**

Founded in 1996. Starting pay is zero. They hold open auditions for each show.

VORTEX is committed to providing residents near LaGrange Park with original or little known family-oriented live theatre at affordable prices.

Their 1998-1999 season included:
- The Vampyre
- Christmas With Strangers
- Little League Baseball

Wing & Groove Theatre Company
Andrew Gall - Artistic Director
Rae Bucher - Managing Director
1935 1/2 W. North
Chicago, IL 60622
773/782-9416
www.wingandgroove.com
Non-Equity – Resident – Ensemble Based
Send H/R attention **Andrew Gall.**

Founded in 1997. Starting pay is a percentage of the gross revenues of an extended run. They call in actors from generals, files and past knowledge. Season auditions are in mid-summer. The nearest eL stop is Damen on the Blue line.

Wing & Groove is one of the fastest growing off-Loop companies in Chicago dedicated to producing provocative accessible theatre.

Winnetka Theatre
620 Lincoln Ave.
Winnetka, IL 60093
847/604-0275
Non-Equity – Resident
Send H/R attention **Stephanie Greene - President.**

Founded in 1973. Starting pay is nothing. They hold open auditions for each show.

Winnetka Theatre exists to provide an artistic outlet for non-professional performers, musicians, directors and technical staff which results in productions that entertain and enrich the lives of audience members and participants.

Their 1998-1999 season included:
- Secret Garden
- Lion in Winter
- The Goodbye Girl

WNEP Theater Foundation
Jen Ellison - Artistic Director
Mark Dahl - Managing Director
817 W. Lakeside #807
Chicago, IL 60640-6641
773/334-8661 x1
members.aol.com/WNEP
Non-Equity – Itinerant
Send H/R attention **Jen Ellison.**

Founded in 1993. Starting pay varies.

They hold open auditions for each show and attend the Unifieds.

WNEP Theater is committed to the creation of eccentric and often aggressively confrontational, original theatrical experiences.

Their 1998-1999 season included:
- Grotesque Lovesongs
- My Grandma's a Fat Whore in Jersey
- The Mysteries of Harris Burdick
- My Grandma's a Fat Whore in Jersey - Remounted

Women's Theatre Alliance
P.O. Box 64446
Chicago, IL 60664-0446
312/408-0095
www.wtac.org
Non-Equity – Itinerant

Send H/R attention
Marge Waterstreet - Office Manager.

Founded in 1992. Starting pay is nothing. They hold open auditions for each show.

The male and female members of the Women's Theatre Alliance encourage works by, for and/or about women.

Workshop Theatre
Michael Colucci - Artistic Director
1350 N. Wells #F521
Chicago, IL 60610
312/337-6602 • 312/337-6604 - fax
actorsworkshop.org
Non-Equity – Itinerant
Send H/R attention **Michael Colucci.**

Founded in 1994. Starting pay is nominal. They hold open auditions for each show and attend the Unifieds. The nearest eL stop is Sedgwick on the Brown line or Clark and Division on the Red line.

Workshop Theatre focuses on one playwright per season.

Their 1998-1999 season included:
The Monogamist

Audition? Help!

O pardon me, thou bleeding piece of earth,

That I am meek and gentle with these butchers!

By Michael Halberstam

This is a guideline, not a rigid series of rules to which you must strictly adhere. Also, it is likely that for every "do" list, you can almost certainly find someone who would put the same suggestions on a "don't" list. You should be fine if you use your common sense and trust your instincts.

Know your piece!

You'd be surprised how many actors audition with pieces from plays they have never read. Your choices can only be honest, specific and accurate if you are familiar with the context and source of your monologue. If the auditor has recently directed or seen the play from which you are performing, you may be asked questions. Rarely is it a good idea to perform a piece for the first time at an audition. Your nerves may inspire a new discovery with every breath of air that you take, and new discoveries have a way of obliterating recently memorized lines. Perform it for a few friends first.

If the audition is timed—time your piece. (Many do not, and then look cross or put out when the timer interrupts a glorious moment with an inglorious "TIME!") Avoid monologue books and try to do a little research to see if your piece is on the 10-most-popular-this-week list. If four other people do the same piece, it becomes a competition. (By the way, pulling a piece out of a production you have recently performed in is rarely a good idea. Auditions are a style unto themselves. Without the lights and the costumes and the other actors, the piece will lack foundation.)

Know the project or theatre for which you are auditioning!

Lack of research can insult the director or casting director and may inspire poor choices. If the theatre performs mostly the classics, then perform a classical piece. For contemporary or new works find a contemporary piece. If they are a movement based company then movement is a good thing to showcase, etc. If you are auditioning for a Shakespeare company or production, assume that the director has familiarity with the plays and resist the urge to tell them from which play your Romeo monologue comes.

As a general rule, always avoid setting up your piece with a plot preamble and never end the monologue with a vigorously yelled "Curtain!" or "Scene!"

Also, recognize the difference between a film audition and a theatre audition. If the production takes place in a 500-seat house, a tiny intimate performance with flashing eyes and a nostril flare or two is not going to inspire a callback.

In fact, while I'm on the subject of film…Film monologues from famous movies are only a good idea if you are doing something very different with them, or if you happen to be brilliant. (The film actor had 20 takes, a makeup artist, a close up and underscoring. You have work lights and new trousers.)

The audition begins when you enter the building and ends when you leave!

Your behavior throughout the audition is under scrutiny. Directors usually ask the monitor to mention actors who are difficult or rude. This is a small industry, and nothing travels faster than a bad reputation. Your director wants to know that you will be courteous, pleasant and professional to work with.

However, resist the urge to "put on a show" while waiting for your time. Part of being courteous is allowing others to prepare and concentrate. When you enter the room in which you will be auditioning, I encourage you to avoid attempting chitchat unless the auditor initiates. They have many people to see. (Trick: A simple slow inhalation of breath can help to draw focus as you enter. Try it!) Announce your piece clearly and simply, trippingly on the tongue. Don't wait too long to begin speaking. The longer you wait, the better you have to be when you start. Good preparation allows for a simple clean beginning.

Keep blocking simple and suit the action to the word. Finish, allowing a moment for the piece to settle, and then offer a thank you and leave. No need to wait around for conversation—the auditor will signal if they want you to stay. If you screw up, ask to start again. Most auditors will allow this. If you screw up again, leave! Very few moments in the theatre are more uncomfortable than watching an actor struggle to finish an unprepared or discombobulated piece.

They want you to be good!

The auditor is not the enemy (and by the way, avoid pieces which claim so—bitterness at auditions is tedious). He/she wants you to cast yourself in the show. Auditors are always thrilled when an actor walks in and nails an audition, especially when it is a surprise and even more so when it is against type.

Second guessing the auditor or projecting thoughts into his/her head, however, is always a mistake. That sour look they gave at the end of your piece may simply be indigestion. You are the best evaluator of your audition, and if you feel good about it, then it was probably a good audition.

Many good auditions do not get the job, and there are many reasons why. You could be too old, young, short, tall, large, small, bald, hairy, etc. You can never tell, and you should never try. Of course, it could be that you gave a lousy audition, but that's usually not the case. When I was auditioning, I used to take myself out and buy myself a new CD afterwards, and then forget about the audition. That way I was always surprised if I made a callback and never disappointed. Never vent your anger at a director for not casting you or calling you back. They will never call you in again.

Above all, to thine own self be true. If you feel you are being disrespected or harassed, leave. No job is worth compromising your self-worth. Finally, have fun. If theatre starts to become a grind, and the process wears you down…

Audition Checklist

The audition is the one constant of an actor's life. We're always looking for new work, and no one's come up with a better way to hire actors. It's unfair and inaccurate and a fact of life. All we can do is give the best audition we can at all times. Here's some advice on how.

1. Finding a Piece

Monologue Books

These have their ups and downs. On the up: The monologue is cut and ready to go. On the down: the monologue is convenient, so someone else has probably already used it.

Plays

Many fantastic writers have monologues to be found in their lesser-known works. That means you need to read those obscure works. Of course you should be reading plays all the time anyway, right? Right.

Other Sources

There are monologues to be found in literature, poetry, movies, biographies, soup cans, etc. Some directors prefer pieces from traditional sources, but, generally speaking, if it's a good piece it doesn't matter where it's from.

Write Your Own

This is a controversial possibility. Most directors seem to be opposed to this route because most actors aren't strong writers. If it's a good monologue, you might get away with it, but you probably shouldn't admit the pieces are original.

Cross-Gender Pieces

If you're going to do a piece intended for the opposite gender, make sure it's good. Auditors sometimes find these pieces distracting, so if you go for it, it had better be strong enough to overcome that possible reaction.

2. Preparing a Piece

Choosing a Piece

A good piece shows your strengths. If you're a physical actor, choose a piece that allows you to be physical. If you have great emotional range, find an emotionally charged piece.

Practice, Practice, Practice

Try the piece out for your friends; don't let your first performance of a piece count.

Over

3. What Should I Wear?!

Suggestions

You don't want to wear a costume. This would be bad. However, wearing a long skirt when you audition for a period piece can be worthwhile.

Don't Limit

Tight clothing, uncomfortable shoes or anything that limits your movement should be avoided.

4. Getting There

Leave Time

When you make the appointment, be sure you know how to get to the audition location. Be sure to leave more than enough time for travel. If you're late, the auditors won't care that the eL was running slowly or your car had a flat. They only care that you've upset their schedule, and they won't be sympathetic.

Call Ahead

If you can't make an audition, CALL. Nothing will anger an agent or director more than a missing actor. What's more, many of them have long memories.

5. On Site

Arrival

Be kind to everyone. The audition monitor isn't necessarily a mere peon for you to abuse. They can, and often do, let directors know about abusive or rude actors, and those people won't get work. Your audition begins the moment you enter the building.

The Walls Have Ears

Before and after your audition, be wary of voicing loud opinions. The walls are thin, and you never know who's listening.

Conflicts

Be honest in listing your conflicts. If you try to introduce them after being cast, you'll only anger the director/producer/whomever. If you have to be out of town for a wedding, let them know. If a conflict is negotiable, let them know that. Keep communicating though, or you'll alienate someone.

6. The Audition

Choose a Focal Point

Be sure you're going to be performing at least three-quarters front. No profiles. Most auditors seem to prefer you not act to furniture. Above all, don't focus on the person for whom you're auditioning. They want to watch your piece, not be a part of it.

Make Strong Choices

Strong choices are key—both in monologues and cold readings. The auditors see dozens of auditions; don't let yours blend in with the rest.

Take Direction

If the director asks for a new take on a piece, do it. This is a good thing. It means the director is interested and wants to see if you can take direction. Take it.

Get In, Get Out

Enter with confidence, perform with confidence, leave with confidence.

Don't Apologize!

Never, ever, ever. The audition you feel was poor may have seemed fine to the director. Let them decide how you did.

7. Musical Auditions

Make Your Music Friendly

Put it in a three-ring binder on sturdy paper that's easy to handle. The accompanist is sight reading and turning pages, so make seeing and handling the music easy.

Keep It Playable

Don't expect your accompanist to transpose for you. You'll just piss them off. Also, choose songs with easy accompaniments. You don't want your audition destroyed because the accompanist can't play your song.

Set a Tempo

Let them know how you like it.

Don't Shoot the Piano Player

Your accompanist is doing his/her best. Don't blame the accompanist when they screw up. Even if it's awful, keep the beat, keep singing and let the accompanist follow you. The auditors know when the accompaniment is a mess, but they won't appreciate you pointing it out in word or gesture. Keep a smile on your face.

8. Afterwards

Send a Card

Particularly after a call back or after being called in from a general, send a postcard saying thanks. Don't ask about the decision, just say "Hi."

Don't Be Rude

If you're offered a part you don't want or can't take, call back and let them know. Someone else is waiting on your decision, so make it and make the call.

Improv

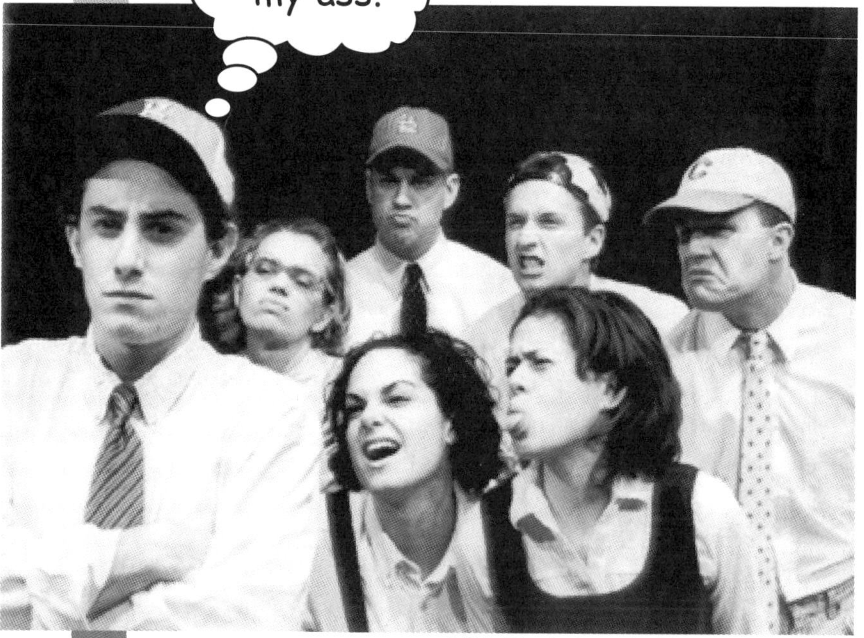

Griffin's "There's a Boy in the Girls' Bathroom"

Improv and the Actor

There was more foolery yet, if I could remember it.

By Jason Chin

Welcome to Chicago, without a doubt the greatest city in the world for learning and performing improvisation. Within these city limits you will find more outlets, training centers, teams, and theatres devoted to improvisation than in any other city in the world.

An improv show is different from any other kind of theatre; it is a one-of-a-kind experience that will never be repeated. Based on audience suggestions, an improvised show will be funnier or more dramatic depending on the night and cast involved.

Even though improv is first and foremost fun to perform, it also takes months of training and experience to learn how to improvise well. While it is true that just about any "funny" person could take to a stage, get suggestions and do a show, that may not be a show you wish to watch (or be in). Just like any person with a glass of water could be firefighter, that's not necessarily the person you want putting out your blazing house.

A professional (any group that charges money to see their show should be held to these standards) improv troupe will rely on their training to help them make interesting choices and support their fellow players instead of relying on breaking up on stage or flaunting their own lines for a laugh.

Years of training, work and even rehearsal go into the best improv shows. A great improviser is a very good actor because they both rely on the same tools: commitment, relationship, listening and reacting, and a dedication to the craft. An improviser uses not only his/her own instincts and abilities, but also his/her teammates' abilities and skills to create a full show.

Improv is a group effort to create a specific set of scenes or games. While most improvisers could be excellent stand-up comedians, the reverse usually does not hold true. An improviser's first job is to support the other players on stage by elaborating and heightening what others do and say. It takes time to learn how to do all this.

Yes and....What's the point?

Improvisers are actors by nature; it's just that their training is different. The skills taught by improv schools are invaluable to an actor: listening and reacting, staying in the moment, making choices that heighten and elaborate the scene, and supporting your fellow players. Improv also allows you to become several different people/characters in one show, which can be an tremendous asset to an actor. The actor trained in improvisation has an advantage over others not so "blessed." Perhaps the most important ability of an improviser is the ability to adapt. Things are constantly flowing in any improv show, and it's the job of an improviser to not only go with that flow but to add to it and make it flow either better or faster. This ability makes script or set changes easier to deal with; a missed cue or line flub becomes part of the show instead of a flaw in a show.

Even though there are no scripts involved, improv can help a writer in many different ways. Many playwrights have said that they become their characters as they write them, or that the characters write themselves. An improviser will play several different characters in one show and sometimes may even do a scene playing several people at the same time. The ability to adapt quickly also comes into play when writing. When script changes are needed fast, an improv-trained writer can handle it. There's a reason why almost all of the writers on "Saturday Night Live" and the "Conan O'Brian Show" are improvisers.

The play's the thing

The first thing is to have fun. Improvisers constantly use the word "play" when discussing their performance. "Do you want to play with us?" "Did you play tonight?" "When are you playing next?" This is because improvisation, though set by some general rules, is done in that magical land of make-believe where we spent a great deal of our childhood. It takes an child's imagination to play with a cardboard box; it takes an improviser's imagination to play with a box that isn't there.

Improv, at its worst, is the worst kind of theater to see. That's why it's improv; there is no sure guarantee that everything will work perfectly. That's why there are classes, to help minimize the chances of sucking. When improv works, it's a wonder to behold. An audience gives more to an improv show and gets more as well. There is a spirit of co-operation, of "Well, we're all in this together" that bonds an audience with a improv team. That's why improvisers sometimes get applause or laughter from their mistakes as well as their successes.

Once you begin and discover that you love improvisation, you may find it addictive. That's why there are so many improvisers in Chicago and beyond. That's why improvisers that have gone on to high-paying TV gigs come back and play. Isn't that something we all wish we could do? Go back to the old neighborhood and play with the kids that live there now?

A level field

Most of the schools of improvisation here in Chicago are based on levels. Each class meets once a week for eight weeks and generally costs about $200 for each eight-week session. Since everyone usually begins at level one, even if you have never taken a improv class before you will be with people at the same level. There are several schools of improvisation in Chicago and, like all the different martial arts schools (kung fu, karate, tae kwon do) have the goal of making the other guy go down, the improv schools all have the same goal as well: to make the audience laugh. Though there are great differences in the teaching styles of each school, they all agree on the fundamental basics of agreement and support. This base knowledge set will help you should you decide to go to several improv schools (as many people do).

Let's take a look at some of the most popular schools and what they aim for.

Second City teaches improv as a means of creating scripted material. This craft of creating scripts from improv has served Second City well for 40 years and is a great ability to have. Students put up shows in the Skybox theater at the end of several levels.

ImprovOlympic teaches improvisation as an artform and performance piece in itself. Created by Del Close and called "long-form improv," or their signature long-form "The Harold," their shows are usually 25-40 minutes of uninterrupted, interweaving scenes relating to a single audience suggestion. Students may be chosen to be on one of their performing teams, and students put on an improvised show at the end of their course study. The Annoyance Theater teaches fast, fun improv centering on personal growth and development and provides personal attention that may be lacking at the other two major schools. Students put on a show at the end of their course study.

Short-form improv games (à la Whose Line Is It Anyway?) are taught by the Chicago branch of the nation-wide franchise ComedySportz. Short-form games are sure audience pleasers and rely on the same basic tenets that the other schools teach as well.

The Players Workshop of the Second City has nothing to do with The Second City theater, but also teaches both sketch and improv.

There are several other improv-based theatres like The Free Associates, the Factory Theater, and the Neo-Futurists that offer classes from time to time as well. If there is a particular show you enjoy or even a particular performer, ask if there are classes or if he/she are currently teaching somewhere.

The best way to discover what school you should attend is to go to one of their shows. Even on a tight budget most of these theaters offer either 2-for-1's or even free nights. Go see a show and decide whether or not that show is something you would like to perform in. It's really that simple.

A quickie before we go

A fast way to experience all of above mentioned theatres' shows and teaching styles is the Chicago Improv Fest (www.cif.com), now in its third year. The fest not only hosts groups from around the nation, but they provide workshops with some of Chicago's best teachers in one weekend. Most of Chicago's improv theatres perform at some point during the fest as well. It's a great way to take a glance at what Chicago improv has to offer.

Have fun.

Improv Training

Annoyance Theater
3747 N. Clark
Chicago, IL 60613
773/929-6200
www.annoyance.com
Beginning, Intermediate and Advanced Improv

ComedySportz
3210 N. Halsted - 3rd Floor
Chicago, IL 60657
773/549-8482
A - First level of training consisting of fundamentals and games.
AA - Advanced scenework techniques and more games.
AAA - Intensive work on styles, music, characters, dialects and advanced scene work.
Minor League Performance Level- Students workshop and perform an eight-week run of their own ComedySportz style show.
Our Minor League Workshops are ideal for actors and improvisers alike. Using the teachings of Viola Spolin, ComedySportz offers its students the opportunity to make instant, strong, and exciting choices, a skill invaluable for the auditioning actor as well as the performing improviser. Cultivate skills, gain confidence, and HAVE FUN.

ImprovOlympic
3541 N. Clark
Chicago, IL 60657
773/880-0199 • 773/880-9979 - fax
Long-Form Improv - Six levels, geared towards performance; classes run eight weeks.

Low Sodium Entertainment
3737 N. Kenmore #3F
Chicago, IL 60613
773/549-3250
www.lowsodiumonline.com

Old Town School of Folk Music
4544 N. Lincoln
Chicago, IL 60625
773/728-6000
www.oldtownschool.org

Players Workshop of Second City
(See our ad on page 213)
2936 N. Southport
Chicago, IL 60657
773/929-6288 • 773/477-8022 - fax
www.intelli.com/pw
Improvisational Program
Sketch Writing
Musical Improv
Physical Improv
Character Study
Advanced Acting

Second City
(See our ad on page 41)
1616 N. Wells
Chicago, IL 60614
312/664-3959 • 312/664-9837 - fax
www.secondcity.com
Conservatory - The art of improv, Second City revue style.
Improv for Actors - For experienced performers with little improv training or as a brush-up course.
Writing - Techniques of comedy writing for beginning and advanced writers.
Beginning - Foundations of improv for students with limited theatre or improv experience.

Improv-Friendly Theatres

These theatres either offer improvised shows or are known for using improv as a major force in creating new works.

Annoyance Theater
3747 N. Clark
Chicago, IL 60613
773/929-6200
www.annoyance.com

ComedySportz
3210 N. Halsted - 3rd Floor
Chicago, IL 60657
773/549-8482

Free Associates
Mark Gagne - Artistic Director
750 W. Wellington
Chicago, IL 60657
773/334-3255
773/975-7171 – box office
773/334-8060 - fax
home.earthlink.net/~free_assoc/

ImprovOlympic
3541 N. Clark
Chicago, IL 60657
773/880-0199 • 773/880-9979 - fax

Low Sodium Entertainment
3737 N. Kenmore #3F
Chicago, IL 60613
773/549-3250
www.lowsodiumonline.com

Players Workshop's Children's Theatre
Stephen Roath - Artistic Director
2936 N. Southport
Chicago, IL 60657
773/929-6288 • 773/477-8022 - fax
www.playersworkshop.com

WNEP Theater Foundation
Jen Ellison - Artistic Director
Mark Dahl - Managing Director
817 W. Lakeside #807
Chicago, IL 60640-6641
773/334-8661 x1
members.aol.com/WNEP

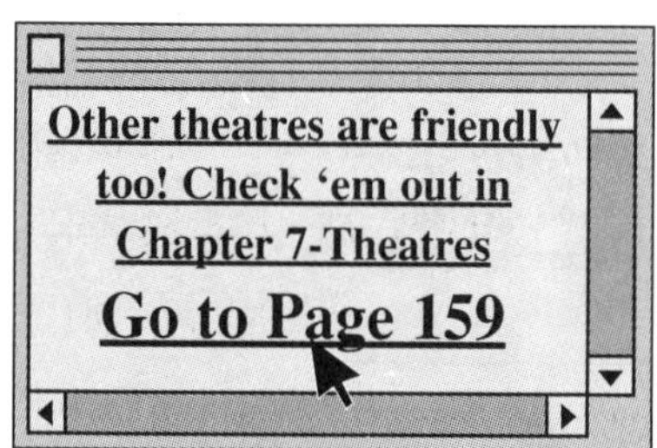
Other theatres are friendly
too! Check 'em out in
Chapter 7-Theatres
Go to Page 159

Improv Groups

Improv groups emerge and vanish in Chicago with startling frequency. Most groups form around a class, last for a while, and then the members go their separate ways. Following are a few groups that have shown above-average permanence.

Baby Wants Candy
773/880-9993

Broken Pilgrims in Gothic Sneakers
1925 W. Newport #F
Chicago, IL 60657-1025
312/974-2110

Detonate Productions
1410 W. Belle Plaine #1
Chicago, IL 60613
773/549-8190

Oui Be Negroes
1432 W. Lunt #208
Chicago, IL 60626
773/274-4563
www.ouibenegroes.com

Sheila Theater Group
4835 N. Kenmore #3
Chicago, IL 60640
773/275-3625

Sirens
Jacqueline Stone
3638 N. Pine Grove #1
Chicago, IL 60613
773/222-7053

Improv

Running a Small Theatre Company

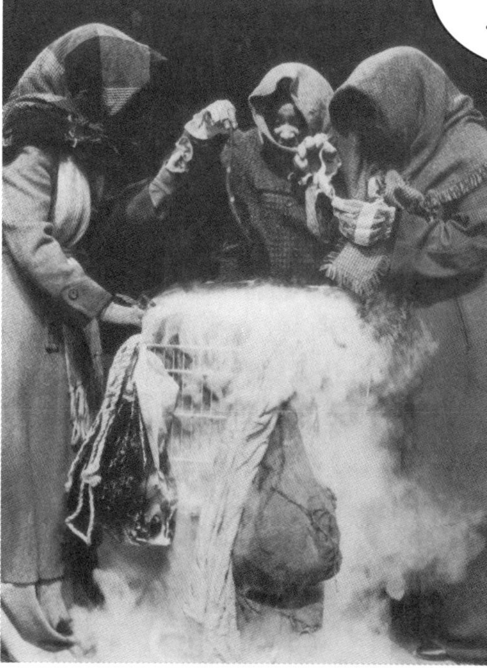

You're sure this'll get us the grant?

Shakespeare Repertory's "Macbeth"

Theatres for Rent

About Face Theatre
3212 N. Broadway
Chicago, IL 60657
773/549-7943 • 773/935-4483 - fax
Mainstage: 100 - Thrust

American Theater Company
1909 W. Byron
Chicago, IL 60613
773/929-1031 • 773/929-5171 - fax
www.ATCWEB.org
Mainstage: 137 - Thrust

Apollo Theater Center
916 S. Wabash #503
Chicago, IL 60605
773/935-9336
773/935-6100
312/461-1458 - fax
Mainstage: 440 - Thrust

Arts Center at College of DuPage
425 22nd St.
Glen Ellyn, IL 60137
630/942-3950 • 630/942-3995 - fax
www.cod.edu

Athenaeum
2936 N. Southport
Chicago, IL 60657
773/935-6860
Mainstage: 976
Studio: 55
Stage 3: 80

Attic Playhouse
410 Sheridan Rd.
Highwood, IL 60040
847/433-2660
www.atticplayhouse.com
Mainstage: 94 - Black Box

Bailiwick Repertory
(See our ad on page 163)
1229 W. Belmont
Chicago, IL 60657
773/833-1090 • 773/525-3245 - fax
www.bailiwick.org
Mainstage: 150
Studio: 90
Loft (in development): 25

Breadline Theatre Group
1802 W. Berenice
Chicago, IL 60613-2720
773/275-4342
www.Breadline.org
Mainstage: 40 - Black Box

Center Theatre
1346 W. Devon
Chicago, IL 60660
773/508-0200 • 773/508-9584 - fax
Mainstage: 60 - Black Box
Studio: 25

Chicago Actors Studio
1567 N. Milwaukee
Chicago, IL 60622
773/645-0222 • 773/645-0040 - fax
www.actors-studio.net
Mainstage: 80+ - Thrust

Chicago Cultural Center
78 E. Washington
Chicago, IL 60602
312/744-3094
www.ci.chi.il.us/culturalaffairs/

Chicago Dramatists
1105 W. Chicago
Chicago, IL 60622
312/633-0630 • 312/633-0610 - fax
Mainstage: 77 - Proscenium

Chicago Shakespeare Theater
800 E. Grand
Chicago, IL 60611
312/595-5656 • 312/595-5607 - fax
www.chicagoshakes.com
Studio: 200 - Proscenium

Chopin Theatre
1543 W. Division
Chicago, IL 60622
773/278-1500
Mainstage: 220 - Black Box
Studio: 100 - Black Box

Corn Productions
4210 N. Lincoln
Chicago, IL 60618
773/278-3274
Mainstage: 60 - Thrust

Court Theatre
5535 S. Ellis
Chicago, IL 60637
773/702-7005 • 773/834-1897 - fax
www.courttheatre.org
Mainstage: 251 - Thrust

Duncan YMCA Chernin Center for the Arts
1001 W. Roosevelt
Chicago, IL 60608
312/738-7980 • 312/738-1420 - fax
Mainstage: 220 - Proscenium
Studio: 125

Griffin Theatre
5404 N. Clark
Chicago, IL 60640
773/769-2228
Mainstage: 125 - Thrust

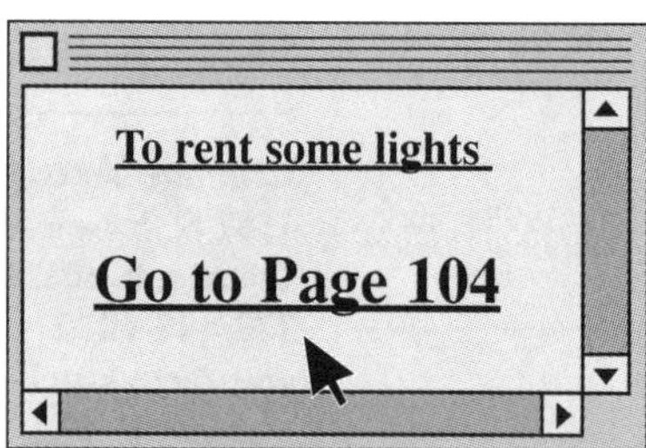
To rent some lights
Go to Page 104

ImprovOlympic
3541 N. Clark
Chicago, IL 60657
773/880-0199 • 773/880-9979 - fax
Mainstage: 100 - Proscenium

Irish American Heritage Center
4626 N. Knox
Chicago, IL 60630
773/282-7035 x17
773/282-0380 - fax
www.irishamhc.com
Mainstage: 600 - Proscenium

Links Hall
3435 N. Sheffield
Chicago, IL 60657
773/281-0824
Mainstage: 75 - Black Box

Marriott Theatre
10 Marriott Dr.
Lincolnshire, IL 60069
847/634-0204 • 847/634-7022 - fax
Mainstage: 882 - In-the-Round

The Neo-Futurists
5153 N. Ashland
Chicago, IL 60640
773/275-5255
www.neofuturists.org
Mainstage: 149 - Thrust

New American Theatre
118 N. Main St.
Rockford, IL 61101-1102
815/963-9343
Mainstage: 282 - Thrust
Studio: 90

North Island Center
8 E. Galena Blvd. #230
Aurora, IL 60506
630/264-7202 • 630/892-1084 - fax
www.paramountarts.com
Paramount Arts Centre: 1888
Copley Theatre: 216
In-house tech staff. Computerized ticketing available. Great for live performances and meetings. Easily accessible location for 1,000,000+ in primary market area. Lodging within walking distance.

Pheasant Run Dinner Theatre
4051 E. Main St.
St. Charles, IL 60174
630/584-6300 • 630/584-4693 - fax
www.pheasantrun.com
Mainstage: 272 - Proscenium

Phoenix Ascending
4227 N. Lincoln
Chicago, IL 60618
773/549-9647
Mainstage: 80 - Proscenium

Profiles Theatre
3761 N. Racine
Chicago, IL 60613
773/549-1815
Mainstage: 52 - Proscenium

Raven Theatre
6931 N. Clark
Chicago, IL 60626
773/338-2177 • 773/338-4782 - fax
Mainstage: 70 - Black Box

Schadenfreude
7016 N. Glenwood
Chicago, IL 60626
773/271-5318 • 773/529-7688 - fax
www.schadenfreude.net

Second City
(See our ad on page 41)
1616 N. Wells
Chicago, IL 60614
312/664-3959 • 312/664-9837 - fax
www.secondcity.com

Stage Actors Ensemble
656 W. Barry
Chicago, IL 60657
773/252-5433
Mainstage: 75 - Black Box

Stage Left Theatre
3408 N. Sheffield
Chicago, IL 60657
773/883-8830
members.aol.com/SLTChicago
Mainstage: 50 - Black Box

Strawdog Theatre
3829 N. Broadway
Chicago, IL 60622
773/528-9889 • 773/528-7238 - fax
www.StrawDog.org
Mainstage: 74 - Black Box

The Theatre Building/New Tuners Theatre
(See our ad on page 216)
1225 W. Belmont
Chicago, IL 60657
773/929-7367 • 773/327-1404 - fax
North - 148 - Black Box
South - 148 - Proscenium
West - 148 - Black Box

Theatre of Western Springs
4384 Hampton
Western Springs, IL 60558
708/246-4043 • 708/246-4015 - fax
members.aol.com/twsctws
Mainstage: 415 - Proscenium
Studio: 130

TimeLine Theatre
615 W. Wellington
Chicago, IL 60657
773/409-TIME
www.timelinetheatre.com
Mainstage: 90

TinFish Productions
4247 N. Lincoln
Chicago, IL 60618
773/549-1888
www.Tinfish.org
Mainstage: 80 - Black Box

Trap Door Theatre
1655 W. Cortland
Chicago, IL 60647
773/384-0494 • 773/384-2874 - fax
Mainstage: 35 - Proscenium

Victory Gardens Theatre
2257 N. Lincoln
Chicago, IL 60614
773/549-5788 • 773/549-2779 - fax
www.victorygardens.org
Mainstage: 195 - Thrust
Studio: 60

Wellington Avenue United Church of Christ
615 W. Wellington
Chicago, IL 60657
773/935-0642 • 773/935-0690 - fax

Wing & Groove Theatre Company
1935 1/2 W. North
Chicago, IL 60622
773/782-9416
Mainstage: 50-55 - Black Box

Women in the Director's Chair
941 W. Lawrence #500
Chicago, IL 60640
773/907-0610 • 773/907-0381 - fax
www.widc.org

Rehearsal Space for Rent

Act One Studios, Inc.
(See our ad on page 34)
640 N. LaSalle #535
Chicago, IL 60610
312/787-9384 • 312/787-3234 - fax
www.actone.com

Belle Plaine Studio
2014 W. Belle Plaine
Chicago, IL 60618
773/935-1890 • 773/935-1909 - fax

Chase Park
4701 N. Ashland
Chicago, IL 60640
312/742-7518

Chicago Actors Studio
1567 N. Milwaukee
Chicago, IL 60622
773/645-0222 • 773/645-0040 - fax
www.actors-studio.net

Chicago Federation of Musicians
Local 10 208 AFM
175 W. Washington
Chicago, IL 60602
312/782-0063 • 312/782-7880 - fax
www.livemusichicago.com

Defiant Theatre
3540 N. Southport #162
Chicago, IL 60657
312/409-0585
www.art-wpage.com/defiant

Noyes Cultural Arts Center
927 Noyes
Evanston, IL 60201
847/491-0266 • 847/328-1340 - fax

Roadworks
1144 Fulton Market #105
Chicago, IL 60607
312/492-7150 • 312/492-7155 - fax
www.roadworks.org

Sheil Park
3505 N. Southport
Chicago, IL 60657
312/742-7826

The Theatre Building/New Tuners Theatre
(See our ad on page 216)
1225 W. Belmont
Chicago, IL 60657
773/929-7367 • 773/327-1404 – fax

Under the Ginkgo Tree (Bed & Breakfast)
Gloria Onischuk
300 N. Kenilworth
Oak Park, IL 60302
708/524-2327 • 708/524-2729 - fax
A spacious home ideally used for filming, photo shoots, etc.

Wellington Avenue United Church of Christ
615 W. Wellington
Chicago, IL 60657
773/935-0642 • 773/935-0690 - fax

So You Want to Be a Non-Profit?

Therefore, let our alliance be combin'd,

Our best friends made, our means stretch'd;

And let us presently go sit in council.

By Greg Mermel

American business is supposed to be about making a profit, or at least trying to make a profit. And in the right circumstances, the arts can be profitable indeed. But for many, the art comes first, and they merely hope to eke out an adult income from the work. As a result, the performing arts—particularly live performance—occupy a curious place in our society: Some are organized for profit and some not-for-profit. Except for medicine, I can think of no other field in which such a blend occurs.

Budding theatre companies are often surprised to learn that there is much more to being a non-profit than recognizing they will never make money at what they are doing. Think for a minute about some of the big, established non-profit arts companies: Steppenwolf, Lyric Opera, Chicago Shakespeare Theater. Who owns them? The answer is: nobody. Their boards of directors are, technically, trustees for the people of the state of Illinois, holding and handling these assets for the public good.

That's only the first difference, but it is symbolically important: These organizations exist to serve a Higher Good, and not to make money for their owners. This is not to say that people can't be paid fairly for their work. They can be, and should be, and often are if the organization can afford it. This also means that the company's operations and finances are open to much more public scrutiny. Financial information must be made available to anybody who asks, and anyone can ask the IRS to examine a copy of the tax return of a non-profit organization. The IRS is even working on a pilot program to make the tax returns of the country's largest charities available on the IRS's website.

For most arts organizations, the critical reason to become a non-profit is the tax-exemption. Not paying income taxes if the company actually makes money (and generally being exempt from sales tax) is nice, but more important is the ability to accept contributions and for those who make the contributions to receive a tax deduction. Without that, the flow of non-earned money to the arts in America would wither to a slow drip.

Obtaining tax-exempt status requires more than just incorporating under the Illinois Not-for-Profit Corporations Act. These companies apply to the Internal Revenue Service for recognition of tax-exempt status, and it is not a simple application. The application is lengthy, full of potentially tricky questions designed to ferret out certain potentially improper situations. They also charge a fee of several hundred dollars.

Let me digress for a moment. We are speaking here of organizations the Internal Revenue Service gracefully describes as being organized for "religious, charitable, scientific, literary and educational organizations." These are sometimes 501(c)(3) organizations, after that section of the Internal Revenue Code. There are actually many types of non-profit organizations, including labor unions, political parties and the National Football League, all of which operate under different rules.

Art may be your god, but it took no little effort to put theatre on the same legal footing as the Red Cross and the Second Presbyterian Church. Originally, the idea of non-profit organizations was limited to charity and religion, and only later broadened. This is where doing art matters, because art is educational.

You do remember that from college, don't you, the part about uplifting and enlightening, holding up a mirror to ourselves and society, and a few other bits of rhetoric?

Even with the symphony orchestras and art museums having led the way, obtaining tax-exempt status for a theatre was often difficult—until 1964. That year, the IRS issued a public ruling that any organization which "develops the interest of the American public in the dramatic arts and which operates a permanent repertory theatre in furtherance thereof" is entitled to tax-exempt status. Probably not by coincidence, this was about the time when most states created arts councils, the National Endowment for the Arts was established, and the idea of government subsidy for the arts first obtained widespread acceptance in the United States.

Be aware that obtaining tax-exempt status for an organization is not a do-it-yourself project. The laws are complex, designed to prevent charitable scams and the use of foundations to evade estate taxes. If you have good advice (and a meritorious cause), it can be easy; otherwise, it can be hell, or impossible.

The Whys and Wherefores of Boards of Directors

Let me have men about me that are fat,

Sleek headed men, and such as sleep a-nights.

By *Joan Gunzberg,* *— Executive Director, Arts & Business Council of Chicago*

For non-profit art groups to thrive, they need strong artistic and management leadership, as well as strong boards. When everyone is in sync, a beautiful partnership can develop with everyone clearly understanding their roles and responsibilities. Boards of directors are a required and crucial part of all non-profit organizations, although they are often misunderstood as to the whys and wherefores. Over the past few years, the functions of governing boards have received attention as never before, and there is a growing acceptance of the notion that effective governance determines organizational effectiveness.

While many arts groups focus on where to find and how to attract new board members with fundraising potential, they frequently overlook or are unfamiliar with the breadth and depth of the boards' full range of responsibilities. By fully understanding the function of a board, you are helping to equip board members to be successful partners.

All organizations undergo a metamorphosis over time that calls for periodic review, fine-tuning, renewal and sometimes major overhaul of their governance structures. As arts groups travel through various stages of development, the makeup and functions of the board typically require adjustments and growth. This summary will help to clarify and distinguish the responsibilities of the board as a collective entity as well as those of individual board members.

Ensure the organization's mission and purposes

Board members need to ensure that a mission statement exists and that it articulates goals, directions, constituents, distinctiveness. The mission statement should be compelling and should help with priorities and fund-raising. The board assesses the group's activities against the mission and should serve as a guide to organizational planning, board and staff decision-making, volunteer initiatives, marketing strategies and priority setting.

However, **the central artistic mission of the organization is the driving and defining element in all its relationships**. This artistic center is a unique combination of the philosophy, aesthetic/programmatic framework, the person(s) at the center, and the unique culture of an organization.

Supervise and evaluate the organization's performance

The board hires, monitors and periodically reviews the performance of the executive director (who manages the organization's day-to-day business operations) and the artistic director (who is responsible for artistic decisions). Note that the duties of the E.D. and the A.D. may be vested in one person, especially in smaller organizations. The board is responsible for making sure that personnel policies are in place and are clear, and that they define the board's roles vs. directors' roles. Working with the arts group to create a succession plan can avoid major setbacks when key staff changes occur. The board is there to provide feedback and support.

Ensure adequate resources

The board needs to make sure that a game plan for fundraising exists. While fundraising is an essential responsibility for board members, it is only a part of their job as partner and advocate of the organization. Board members monitor, support and guide fundraising and open doors to increase resources. Each board member usually makes an annual personal donation to demonstrate board giving commitment and expand individual giving.

In addition to their commitment to help raise contributed dollars, board members can be instrumental in helping arts groups think practically and creatively about ways to develop earned income to support their work. Additionally, providing access to ongoing in-kind donations, such as professional services and expertise, office equipment, etc. can also be an important way for board members to make a contribution to their organization.

Ensure effective financial and legal management

The board helps develop and then approves the annual budget. Therefore, board members need to have an understanding of the budgeting process. They ensure timely, intelligible, accurate financial reports, and regular monitoring of performance against budget. The board oversees and advises on wise investment strategies (should the organization be so financially solid as to have a reserve) and assures an annual audit, if the organization's budget size requires an audit. The board ensures compliance with local, state and federal laws, regulations, and tax reporting requirements that apply to non-profit organizations.

Develop strong board leadership

Ongoing board development linked to the mission and vision of the organization is a key board member responsibility. The board needs to strategically recruit new members, mentor and develop leadership, become actively engaged on committees, support staff and ensure alignment of programs with mission and with needs of constituents. The board should provide the oversight to ensure that resources are focused on appropriate priorities.

Enhance the public image and advocate on behalf of the organization

The board needs to ensure that regular communications promote the organization's image effectively and that there is an effective public relations program in place with clarity about who speaks for the organization. Individual board members should expand the organization's sphere of influence and should advocate as a representative of the organization to its broader constituents. To do so, board members need to become knowledgeable and conversant about what is unique about the organization and the challenges it is facing. They should actively promote attendance and build enthusiasm for performances, exhibitions, programs, events, etc. sponsored by the organization.

Assess its own performance

Periodically, the board should review its effectiveness in meeting its responsibilities, including membership composition, board structure, committees, roles, and performance of individual board members. Various assessment tools are available to facilitate this process.

Board-related resources

The Arts & Business Council of Chicago's On BOARD program offers a variety of resources to help non-profit arts organizations develop their boards. **(312/372-1876)**

There are a vast number of publications related to Boards of Directors. The National Center for Non-profit Boards (NCNB) stands out as being a key resource and publishes a wide range of excellent board related materials. **(800/883-6262)**

A sample of useful publications include:

Nonprofit Board Answer Book: Practical Guidelines for Board Members and Chief Executives by Robert C. Andringa and Ted W. Engstrom (NCNB)

The Chief Executive's Role in Developing the Nonprofit Board by Nancy Axelrod (NCNB)

The Art of Serving on a Performing Arts Board by Sabrina Klein (NCNB)

How to Build a More Effective Board by Thomas Holland (NCNB)

Successful Fundraising for Arts and Cultural Organizations The Oryx Press

Articles:

"Navigating the Tightrope between Mission and Money: Changing the Face of Funding" by Jerr Boschee. *Board Member,* Volume 8, Number 1, NCNB.

"The New Work of the Nonprofit Board" by Barbara Taylor, Richard Chaitt and Thomas P. Holland. *Harvard Business Review,* September/October 1996. (800/274-3214)

Websites:

Board Café: **www.supportcenter.org/sf/boardcage.html** (free monthly online newsletter)

Drucker Foundation for Nonprofit Management: **www.pfdf.org**

National Center for Nonprofit Boards: **www.ncnb.org**

National Endowment for the Arts Lessons Learned Toolsite: **www.arts.endow.gov/pub/lessons/index.html** for planning advice from arts consultants

Nonprofit Managers Library: **www.mapnp.org**

Grant Writing

I did send to you

For certain sums of gold,
which you denied me;

by Robert Ayres

For a variety of reasons, grantwriting can be an intimidating undertaking. Artists frequently get annoyed that they need to justify themselves and their work in a process relying less on art than on administrative discourse and bureaucratic forms. Many artists eventually give up on grants because they find grantwriting too odious to justify taking time away from their art to compete for miniscule funding amounts in a reductive and demeaning evaluation process.

With a sufficiently calculating attitude and a handful of simple guidelines, however, grantwriting can become a useful skill which can help you cultivate at least a portion of the support you need to do your work. The following suggestions may be of use to grantwriters who are either starting out or who have run into difficulties competing for funding in the past.

You and your art are not being evaluated – Your application is

Artists are so used to putting themselves and their work on the line that they immediately (and understandably) feel vulnerable and defensive — attitudes which can lead to a variety of problems. For example, artists sometimes try to cram every experience and aspiration into an application hoping to overwhelm a panel with their energetic scope of activities. Unfortunately, in trying so desperately to show the panel their worth as artists, they end up submitting convoluted and confusing applications which communicate the quality of their work poorly and reflect badly on the quality of the applicant's thinking. Less expansive but more explanatory narratives work better.

One's best art, as well as one's experiences and aspirations, are important to the process only as the raw materials from which you will craft your case for support. The key here is to shift the emphasis of a grant application from the applicant to the evaluator. The evaluators neither know you nor have time to unbury evidence of your good work hidden in an unclear application. If you don't speak so as to be heard, what you say will fall on deaf ears; so don't focus on expressing why you deserve support — focus on communicating why the granter should support you. It's a subtle shift, but once accomplished everything else will fall into place.

Understand, follow, and use the evaluation process

Thoroughly read all application guidelines until every detail is clear. Such guidelines are often the maddeningly confusing product of a committee process, but you can't afford to let the confusion or madness get in your way. Sort through the verbiage as carefully as you can, and ask questions until you get answers.

Once you understand the guidelines, follow them. If you're not supposed to staple your application, don't; all it does is create useless work for the people who then must remove your staple. If you don't fill out a form correctly, either you or someone else will have to do it again. Every guideline is there for a reason, and a failure to comply only annoys the people running the process — people you want and need as allies.

At best, try to read the guidelines' subtext. Every process has certain goals and biases, and if you look for the patterns and recurring themes in a review process, you may gain an appreciation for its aims. For example, if detailed financial statements are requested and administrative specialists are going to be on the review panel, you can be sure that the quality of your financial management will be scrutinized. If eligibility guidelines contain a substantial residency requirement and outreach is included as a review criterion, your track record of community service will be an important factor in the evaluation. Understanding the tilt of the field can help you craft your application accordingly.

Think like a panelist

Most strategic questions can be answered by thinking like a panelist. Find out who the panelists are if you can, and if you can't, find out who's been on the panel in the past. Seek to understand how panelists are selected. Ask about the process from the panelist's point of view. How are the program's goals described to them? Just what information do they receive, when, and in what order? What instructions are provided to help them evaluate the applications? If it's possible to sit in on a panel meeting, make it a strict priority to do so. If you know people who have served as panelists in the past, take them to lunch and pepper them with questions. If a past panel book is available for you to review, review the entire book like a panelist. Go application by application and rate each one according to the review criteria. Once you know how a panelist thinks, it will be that much easier to give them what they want.

Neatness counts

In general, panelists get inadequate time to review a relatively large amount of information. Panel books are thick with xeroxed copies of applications, and reading them can be tedious and taxing. Make your application easy on panelists' eyes! Provide good-sized margins and an easy to read font, check your spelling and arithmetic, and use simple, clear and concise grammar. Never encourage panelists to pause or strain as they read your application; rather, give them every reason to smile at your work as they make their way through their stack of paper.

Get proofreaders

Because grantwriters are generally quite close to both the applications and the work represented therein, their work is susceptible to narrative gaps and mistaken emphases. The best way to check your work is to secure a range of proofreaders with varying abilities and levels of familiarity with your work. For example, an artist who has worked with you can help you develop accurate and thorough descriptions of the work, while administrators less familiar with you can perhaps identify holes in your projected budgets; the greater the variety, the more likely you'll catch mistakes.

Respond directly to review criteria

The only tool panelists have to cut through their books is the list of review criteria. Find out what these criteria are and use them to organize your narrative. Use the criteria — in sequence — as paragraph headings, then respond directly to each one with your case for support. Set the criteria up like a series of hoops, then jump through them with precision and grace.

If review criteria aren't explicitly used or available, you need to speak to the people who will be running the panel meeting. Ask them how they will respond to the questions panelists will ask when guidance is needed. For example, if "artistic quality" is a consideration in your application's evaluation, ask the meeting coordinator, "When panelists ask you how you define artistic quality, how will you respond?" The answer to this question must then guide your description of your group's artistic quality, whether or not you share the given definition of "artistic quality."

One additional consideration to explore is the relative weighting of review criteria. Find out if, for example, your rating for artistic quality will count for 30% of your overall score, community outreach 20%, and management 50%. If so, calibrate your application accordingly, ensuring that you expand upon your excellent administrative technique — perhaps at the expense of your outreach descriptions.

Use all your application components in concert

Every application will enable you to use a variety of components as you make your case for support. For example, you may need to submit a narrative description of your group or your proposed project, a budget, support materials (videotapes, slides, etc.), and resumés. Consider the case you want to make and how each of the application components can best be used to make that case. Don't needlessly reiterate the points you make in different parts of your application, but rather try to have the different components complement one another, with each element making the points it best can make.

Strike a balance between ambition and practicality

Every panel, by virtue of panel dynamics, will provoke one panelist to serve as the conservative defender of quality and another panelist to serve as the liberal advocate of artists. Hoping to ensure that every grant will prove to be a sound investment, the conservative will look for evidence of solid management and achievable goals. The liberal will test your application for inspired creativity and a commitment to artists and innovation.

You need to satisfy both poles. Even if you harbor wild ambitions, your stated plans need to be clearly appropriate to your means. Simultaneously, if your group has been cruising along producing the same successful programming for years, you need to make it clear that something besides sheer momentum is driving you to do next year's program.

Understand the procedures used during panel meetings

In general, a panel meeting has three components: an orientation, a step-by-step review of the applications in sequence, and a final ranking procedure. You need to know exactly what happens and how during each of these steps.

The orientation is important because it sets the context for review. Find out what is covered during this introductory period and consider how it might influence the panel. For example, if panelists are given a brief history of the granting organization, and the organization has just begun to rebound from a period of instability, the panel will probably review the applications more conservatively.

The step-by-step review is when the panel actually evaluates your application. Who speaks first? Can you get this person to be an advocate for you? In what order are the application's elements considered? Obviously, the first component considered will be the most important. When and for how long are the support materials reviewed? If a panel may only be looking at the first 30 seconds of your video, make sure the tape is cued to the 30 seconds you most want them to see. Most importantly, in what order are applications reviewed? If your application is going to be reviewed towards the end of a meeting, you'll probably get less time than applications reviewed at the beginning; clarity and energy will be even more important in this case. Will you be considered in alphabetical order? In order of budget size? How will the order of review affect the evaluation of your application? How might the panelists be feeling at that point, and how can you use that context to your benefit? Seek advantage wherever you can find it.

The last stage in the process is generally a formality during which the panel confirms its previous evaluations by voting on a ranked list of the applicants, but it's worthwhile to explore the details of this procedure to see if it has any negotiable ramifications for your application's review.

Find out about the award process

Between a panel's favorable review and the cutting of a check, an award amount needs to be determined. At this point, granting organizations sometimes give themselves the chance to push and pull on the results of the panel process. If so, you need to know who translates panel scores into award amounts, and the guidelines and priorities (both stated and unstated) they use to determine the awards. If, as is often the case, the administrators who run the panel meeting are charged with this task, you may wish to familiarize them with you and your work as directly as possible. You might want to find out something about their background and proclivities. It may even be useful to find out who among your various artistic colleagues has the administrators' ear. Because this is the stage in the process when the quiet hand of the bureaucrat is at its most powerful, it may be difficult to get detailed answers about just who does what and why, but for the exact same reason it's a point in the process with which you definitely need to familiarize yourself.

Consistent success in grantwriting obviously requires a big investment of time and energy. However, with a bit of legwork and know-how, it's a process that can help your theatre thrive. Courses on grantwriting are frequently offered; check with the Useful Organizations list in this chapter. Don't let this potentially forbidding process keep you from getting the money you need to do your work.

The Press and You

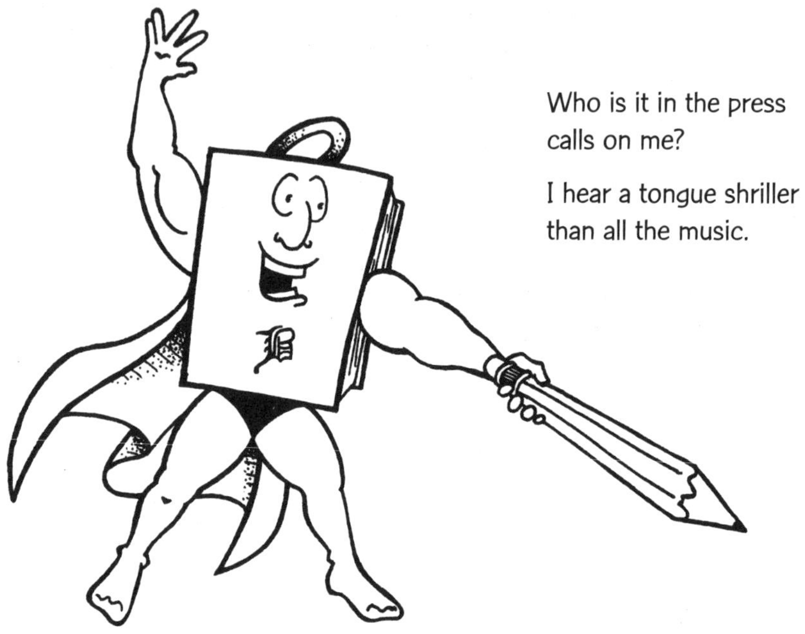

Who is it in the press calls on me?

I hear a tongue shriller than all the music.

By Lucia Mauro

In a theatre market as saturated as Chicago's Off-Loop scene, producers face an overwhelming task: claiming a share of the theatregoing public. The press, both in listings and criticisms, provide a major avenue of communication to that public, so cultivating a strong relationship with the press should be a top priority. More than anything else, companies should strive for consistency, promptness and clear communication.

The press release: What should be on it?

Put all the essentials in the first two paragraphs. Don't assume the press reads the entire press release. It's a sad but true fact. Editors have deadlines, lots of them, and there are also lots of theatres, dance troupes, performance collectives and multimedia clown poets in the city. Needless to say, having the essentials presented in a clear form increases your chances of getting coverage, as well as reducing our chances of making mistakes. Make sure that your previews are included in your run dates; putting them in increases your coverage time.

Tell us to think about it, not what to think about it. Let us know what is interesting about the show—if it's a world premiere, a new collaboration or your own great creation. Tell us why you're excited about it. Above all, include a concise plot summery of the play. The fact that your show is a stunning indictment of man's inhumanity to man is fine, but what we'll remember is that it's about five people trapped in a diner during a snowstorm. A plot summary also helps an editor assign a critic who's suited to your show.

Proofread the release—and that means more than running spell check. Misspellings make you look unprofessional, which will make editors less likely to give you time and space. Also, check your dates. Don't have your show opening on Thursday, June 28 if June 28 is really a Friday. People on deadline may not be able to check if it opens on Thursday or on June 28. They shouldn't have to anyway.

Also, be sure to send papers corrections and updates. We'll assume your open run show is running forever until you tell us otherwise (Two words: Shear Madness). Conversely, if you don't tell us you've extended your run, we'll stop running your listing.

Understand the difference between wrong information (which we like to be corrected on) and a difference in style (which we really hate to be corrected on). A paper's listing belongs to the paper. As long as it gives accurate information about a show, then how long or short it is, or exactly what information is in it, or what order the information is in, depends entirely on who is writing it.

Where should it go?

Keep your contact list updated and find out when deadlines are. Nothing is more irritating than a warm and personal pitch letter to the person whom the editor replaced three years ago. Not only will correct names make editors feel important, they'll also save some time. Correct names cut down on misrouted mail, which gives your show a greater chance of getting listed on time.

Additionally, keep a list of freelance writers and the publications to which they regularly contribute, together with the areas they most frequently cover. Some writers don't mind receiving press releases directly. As you develop relationships with individual critics, inquire about adding them to your press list if they're not there already.

Photos: When (and where) to send them

It's amazing how many theatres cut corners when it comes to photos. Following a few basic guidelines will get your photos published.

Get them to the papers. Find out your deadlines. Papers need the photos well in advance of the production opening, so have them ready and get them there. Whatever you do, don't trust the post office for this. Drop them off, FedEX, messenger, whatever. Just be sure they get where they're supposed to go.

Make them publishable. Most papers prefer shots of a scene over headshots. Make them interesting. Make them tell a story. The better the quality of the photo, the more likely they are to be in the paper. Most papers prefer 8x10's although many will accept 5x7's. Black and white is better than color. Keep the lighting bright; photos with too many shadows don't reproduce as well.

Label them clearly. Every photo should have the company, play, people in the photo and photographer responsible for the shot (the photo credit). A caption explaining the action can also be helpful.

Know who wants them. Some papers don't take photos. Some don't need them in the press packet; they need them sent in directly. Find out the photo practices of all the publications on your list.

The Press Kit: What to include?

On the subject of press kits, include only basic, but important, information. A fact sheet with the press opening date and time in bold capital letters should be displayed at the top. The fact sheet should also include all performance dates and times, ticket prices and the number to call for reservations, as well as a press contact.

Besides the fact sheet, a more detailed news release discussing the play, production and artistic team is helpful. Avoid including positive local reviews that have already come out. Critics want to make up their own minds.

After the Review: Who Said That?

When you're working up all that post-review publicity, be careful how you quote the critics. Taking them drastically out of context will only embitter that critic towards your company. No one likes to be misrepresented, especially if that misrepresentation is used for advertising.

When to Call: Use Your Telephone Wisely

Like an actor calling an agent, calling reporters, editors and other press representatives should be handled in a polite and considerate manner. Ask if they're busy or under deadline and, if they are, be brief or call at another time. If there's an error in a listing, calmly point it out (be aware of the difference between an error and a style difference). The last thing you want is to create a confrontational relationship with the press.

Finally, do your best to keep critics attending your show happy. In times of crisis call them, particularly if canceling or delaying a show. Reserve their seats, and be sure that those seats are good ones. If possible, hold a parking spot for them.

Ideally, your relationship with the press is one that will benefit both you and the paper. You get publicity; the paper gets story ideas. If those lines of communication are open, clear and complete, the press can be a great asset.

Additional material contributed by Nicole Bernardi-Reis and Kevin Heckman.

Five Steps for Audience Development

Then follow me and give
me audience, friends.

by Julie L. Franz

There's nothing more exciting than striking out on your own and building your own theatre company. It's tempting to think that if we throw all of our efforts into what goes on the stage, people will magically recognize superiority and show up in droves. But like any small business, there are thousands of details to tend to outside of artistic excellence that can make or break your business, especially when it comes to attracting, and keeping, audiences.

Much of that has to do with thinking longer term than the next show. It's hard when you're starting, since you're literally financing things from show to show, so this article will focus on things that, hopefully, are easy and inexpensive, but will help set the stage for long-term success.

There are as many wrong definitions of marketing as there are stars in the sky. Marketing is not just promotions, and it's not sales. It's not posters or a good review or a direct mail piece. It's developing a deep understanding of your customer and how they relate to your artistic product. It's customer-focused, and it includes thinking though issues regarding product, price, place and promotion, and understanding the relationship between your artistic product and the customer. Here are five basic audience development issues to think through as you consider starting your own theatre company.

First, make absolutely sure your theatre company really is unique. Chicago is full of actors and theatre companies. To Joe Consumer perusing the CHICAGO TRIBUNE Friday Arts Section in search of something to do, you're just one of hundreds of arts listings. People buy on uniqueness and trust. You can communicate uniqueness in your marketing materials; you build trust with artistic excellence.

In making sure you're really unique, ask yourself why you couldn't have just joined another theatre company. Why, artistically, did you have to strike out on your own? What do you do that no other theatre company does? And answer the question as if you're explaining it to your mom and her friends. (Most ticket buyers and arts decision makers are women.) In other words, use consumer language, or language the common man can understand.

"Ensemble theatre" is one of my favorite phrases, since no one but us theatre professionals has any understanding what it means; it only describes how you're organized, and it's a fact, not a consumer benefit. Tell your mom how and why what she sees on the stage will be different from something out there already. Focus your communications pieces, posters and fliers on benefits, not just facts. It's a fact that you're presenting a certain play on a certain night at a certain time and location. But how will that benefit the customer? Most consumers are unfamiliar with the standard repertory. Tell them what the show is about. Is it a comedy, drama, mystery or musical? Which specific emotions will it stir?

Second, now that you can describe your uniqueness, spend money to have a logo designed by a professional. Having a single, distinct visual image is paramount in the consumer's ability to recognize you in an instant. And it stays with you forever. With a few minor revisions and updates, the Hubbard Street Dance Chicago logo hasn't changed dramatically since their inception. Neither has Steppenwolf's or Victory Gardens'.

Third, budget for marketing and promotions. Again, it's tempting to put all your money and effort into the artistic product, then leave nothing for promotion. It's like throwing the most elaborate birthday party in the world, but forgetting to budget for invitations. Typically, when first starting out, you'll need about 25% of your budget devoted to audience development.

Fourth, take advantage of free promotional opportunities. This means developing a strong press relations program and habitually updating newspaper and website entertainment listings. Deborah Popely of Deborah Popely & Company in Des Plaines touts the following as the "Seven Secrets of Highly Successful Publicists:"

1. Have a smart media strategy that targets publications that reach your audience, includes a unique story angle, looks beyond the usual media, and puts you at the right place at the right time.
2. Pitch a creative story angle, not just the fact that you're mounting a new production.
3. Provide a well-written presentation of that creative story.
4. Provide strong visuals to help make the story come alive.
5. Be fearless and persistent in pitching story ideas.
6. Have a well-researched, up-to-date media list.
7. Have a service orientation toward the media. (You're solving their need for fresh ideas, they're not solving your need for publicity.)

And, don't overlook free listings. The TRIBUNE and SUN-TIMES are great, but focus too on your neighborhood newspaper and newsletters from neighborhood associations and religious organizations. Most of your initial audience will come from a 5-10 minute walk or drive. Make the time to consistently send update listings to the TRIBUNE, state tourism and city tourism websites. They're seen by millions during the year, many of whom are locals.

Fifth, and finally, capture the name, address and phone number of every audience member. It's easier and less expensive to retain a current customer than to get a new one. Why start at ground zero for each show when you can, for less time and effort, invite past audience members, then build a larger audience from there? Use personal letters, newsletter, press releases, etc. to keep your audience informed. Treat them like one of the family, since your most loyal audiences will actually believe they "belong" to your theatre. Hold special receptions or "meet the director" nights to break down the fourth wall and help them become more intimately involved with you and your group.

Time and again, The Arts Marketing Center works with arts groups to help develop new audiences. More times than not, we end up having to go back and"fix" these five areas of marketing and audience development. But if you're contemplating founding your own company, now is the time to get it right from the start.

PR Firms

Carol Fox & Associates
1412 W. Belmont
Chicago, IL 60657
773/327-3830 • 773/327-3834 - fax

GSA Advertising
211 E. Ontario #1750
Chicago, IL 60611
312/664-1999 • 312/664-9017 - fax

K.D.-P.R.
K.D. Kweskin
2732 N. Clark
Chicago, IL 60614
773/248-7680 • 773/883-1323 - fax

Jay Kelly
2254 W. Grand
Chicago, IL 60612
312/633-1992 • 312/633-1994 - fax

Margie Korshak, Inc.
875 N. Michigan #2750
Chicago, IL 60611
312/751-2121 • 312/751-1422 - fax

MMPR
Michelle Madden
1636 W. Summerdale #1
Chicago, IL 60640
773/784-8347 • 773/784-8599 - fax

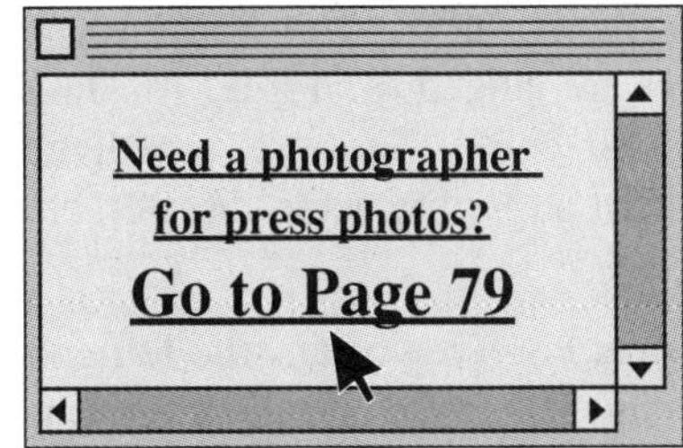

Need a photographer
for press photos?
Go to Page 79

The Joseph Jefferson Awards

I do believe that these applauses are

For some new honours that are heap'd on Caesar.

By Carrie L. Kaufman

The Jeffs

The Joseph Jefferson Awards, or Jeffs as they're commonly called, started in 1967 when four actors got together to honor the best and brightest actors in Chicago. Six awards from seven theatres were given out at the first ceremony in 1968. Thirty years later, the Jeffs are split into three different sections which give out almost 100 awards a year.

Equity awards

The Equity wing of the Joseph Jefferson Awards judges theatres that have contracts with Actors Equity Association.

Local Equity theatres are judged from Aug. 1 to July. 31, with an awards ceremony in November. They are formally called the Joseph Jefferson Awards. What an Equity actor, director, etc. wins that night is a Jeff Award.

And they only win one. For a few years, the Jeff committee tried giving multiple awards in each category, which is what they do for the Non-Equity Citations. But a consultant the committee hired told them that the community overwhelmingly preferred to be singled out.

"At the end of the day, they still really thought the value of the award was more significant if it were for single winners," said current Jeff committee chair Joan Kaloustian.

Some of those single winners can be for lower tier Equity theatres. Since Equity instituted its new tier system in the mid-90's, a CAT N theatre, which produced a show with only one Equity actor at a very low pay scale, can compete with a major LORT or CAT V theatre that has a budget in the millions and actually come out on top. This has done much to obliterate the distinctions between Equity and non-Equity theatre and also to showcase the remarkable work by people and theatre companies that are non-union—something which is unique to Chicago.

Non-Equity citations

The Citations wing of the Joseph Jefferson Awards, instituted in 1973, is for non-Equity theatres. Citations are judged from April 1 to March 31, with a ceremony in early June. That ceremony is called the Joseph Jefferson Citations. The Jeff committee is very careful to keep the word "award" as far away from non-Equity theatre as possible. They structure the non-Equity ceremony to be completely non-competitive. There are "honorees," who may be called "winners," but there are absolutely no "losers." Of course, with the multiple recipients structure, there have been instances in which four out of the five people nominated have been "honored" with Citations, leaving a very clear "loser."

Non-Resident productions

About four years ago, the Jeff committee began giving awards for touring productions, such as Show Boat, Ragtime and Aida. Frankly, these awards have little credibility in the theatre community and are often looked upon—rightly or wrongly—as opportunities for the Jeff committee to get free tickets to the hot post- or pre-Broadway shows.

That may be a bit unfair, and it may be more of a reflection on the gripers than the committee. The Jeff committee argues that they support the theatre community and that the bigger shows—especially now that they seem to be taking up long-term residence—are part of that community. That sentiment sticks in the craw of many small, struggling artists.

There's also the argument that many of these non-resident shows cast out of Chicago and a good deal of the actors may be local. In fact, some of the producers may be too. Shouldn't they be honored? Have they somehow given up their community status by taking or producing a big show?

Even if it's true that the committee only wants the free tickets to the bigger shows, who cares? The Jeff committee members go to an awful lot of theatre, and they deserve to see the big budget stuff. Frankly, if people are going to gripe about the Jeff committee going to touring shows, they should gripe about critics going too. Neither make any difference to whether or not a show that size is a hit.

Eligibility

The Jeff committee rules for eligibility are Byzantine. Barely anyone in Chicago theatre outside the committee understands them, and I dare say there are some people on the committee who would have trouble reciting every single rule. But if you work through the complexities, a remarkably fair, and strangely beautiful, system emerges.

There are two sets of rules. One qualifies theatres and shows to be judged. The other details exactly how a show is recommended—or not.

For a show to be Jeff eligible, it must be produced at a theatre within a 30 mile radius of the corner of State and Madison and in the state of Illinois. Some theatres, such as Marriott Theatre in Lincolnshire, were Jeff eligible before this rule was in place and have been grandfathered in.

For non-Equity theatres, the producing theatre must have been in existence for at least two years and produced at least four productions during those two years, with at least two productions in the preceding year. Equity theatres are automatically eligible.

For an individual production to be Jeff eligible, it must have a minimum of 18 performances. In addition, it must have at least two consecutive weekend performances, with at least one weekend night performance per week available to Jeff members.

The Jeff committee does not judge children's theatre, nor does it judge performance art. Late night shows—which are quite standard in Chicago—are also not eligible. Curtain for an eligible show must be no later than 9:30 p.m. This is not because the Jeff committee does not like these things (many of them go to ineligible shows just for fun); it's that they have to draw the line somewhere.

For judges to come to a theatre's opening night (or opening weekend) performance, the theatre must put in its request a minimum of three weeks before opening night or the 25th of the preceding month. They would prefer you get them in before the 25th, when the assignments are made. All requests must be in writing.

If the theatre is doing a co-production with another theatre, both theatres must be Jeff eligible. It doesn't matter how long the first theatre has been in existence—or how many Jeff Citations or Awards it has won in the past—if it hooks up with a brand new theatre company, the Jeff committee won't come.

These rules were instituted as a sort of filter. While there is much good theatre in Chicago, there is a lot of bad theatre here too and, frankly, the Jeff members don't want to waste their time. They figure that if a company has been able to attract audiences and stay afloat for two years, it must be doing some good stuff. Similarly, they feel that if a company is willing to take the risk of putting up an Equity bond and pay its actors, they probably aren't fly-by-night.

Of course, this means that some really good theatre can't be nominated for a Jeff. But it doesn't mean a new theatre isn't on the Jeff's radar screen. Many members show up to good shows by new theatre companies that aren't yet Jeff eligible.

Nominating process

Once the theatre has called the Jeff committee and is deemed eligible, five committee members are assigned to attend opening night of an Equity or non-Equity show. If those Jeff committee members like the show or categories within the show, then the show is Recommended. (This is true whether the show is Equity or non-Equity. They used to refer to Equity shows as "nominated" at this point in the process. But it was confusing, and they changed their nomenclature.)

Those recommendations come out the day after opening night. Judges must call in their votes by 11 a.m. and theatres are notified by 2 p.m.

The term "recommended," however, does not mean that the Jeff committee is giving an unqualified endorsement of the show. A show that was particularly awful in all but one area could be recommended because the opening night judges thought that one area was so outstanding—maybe even because it was good despite the rest of the piece—that it deserves to be recognized.

How a show is deemed to be recommended is the most complicated part of the Jeff committee's rules. There are now three ways a show can get recommended.

If three judges vote positively in any one category and a fourth judge votes positively in any category, then the show is recommended or nominated. For instance, if three judges loved and voted for the lead actress and a fourth judge loved and voted for the lead actor, even if the fifth judge hated the show entirely, the production is nominated. They don't have to like anything more about the show, though frequently if they like a show, they like it in multiple categories.

That last fact, and a few incidents in which judges have picked lots of categories but no three matched, prompted the committee to add a second way shows can be recommended or nominated. If at least 10 positive votes—scattered across any of the categories—are cast by all five judges, and each one of the five casts at least one positive vote, then the production is recommended or nominated.

Now those tinkerers on the committee have come up with a third way, to make up for a judge who just might be having a bad day. If four of the five judges cast a total of 15 or more positive votes, even if the fifth judge didn't cast any positive votes at all, then the show is recommended.

Once the show is recommended, the rest of the Jeff committee is informed and must see the show within 60 days of opening night. They are not told which categories were the ones that garnered the positive votes. They fax, e-mail or mail in their votes in each category after they've seen each show. Those votes are tabulated. The recipients of the most votes in each category are put onto a final ballot, which is sent out to each of the members at the end of the Aug. 31 (for Equity) or March 31 (for non-Equity) judging season. Those final ballots are the nominations for each category.

After those Award and Citation nominations are made, the committee sends in those final ballots for the winners or recipients. The results of that vote are announced at either the November Awards or the June Citations.

Structure

The Jeff committee is made up of 45 people dedicated to the theatre industry in Chicago. Quite simply, they love theatre. They see upwards of 125 shows a year and in the busy seasons—around September/October and February/March—they see around six shows a week. Many even see two shows a day on weekends when it's busy.

"This is a labor of love for people. You've got to love it if you're doing it for 125 nights a year with no compensation," says chairwoman Kaloustian.

As with any awards, there are people who don't like the Jeffs or who discount them. Funny though, Jeff Awards and Citations always seem to show up on peoples' resumes and in ads for shows or theatres. Some people have pointed to the Jeff committee and said that there are few working theatre artists among its members. The committee has countered with the fact that it has tried to recruit working theatre artists who balk at the idea of going to see someone else's show 4-6 nights a week. And while many committee members aren't currently theatre professionals, almost half of the membership have been professionally involved in theatre, according to Kaloustian.

The Jeff committee, no matter what their formal training, is always trying to learn more about theatre and the crafts that come together to make a show. Each meeting they have a speaker or program designed to help them learn more about stage crafts. Designers have taught them about the elements that are not supposed to be noticed. They have talked with directors and dramaturgs. And one cannot discount the point that no matter what one knows about theatre before joining the committee, they learn a hell of a lot after seeing 125—often bad—shows. I wonder if many theatre artists have that kind of education.

To contact the Jeff committee, call 773/388-0073

Helpful Organizations

Arts and Business Council of Chicago
70 E. Lake #500
Chicago, IL 60601
312/372-1876 • 312/372-1102 - fax
www.artsbiz-chicago.org

Arts Bridge
Suellen Burns - Executive Director
2936 N. Southport
Chicago, IL 60657
773/296-0948 • 773/296-0968 - fax
www.artsbridge.org

Arts Marketing Center
70 E. Lake #500
Chicago, IL 60601
312/372-1876 • 312/372-1102 - fax
www.artsbiz-chicago.org

Association of Consultants to Nonprofits
P.O. Box 4852
Chicago, IL 60680
312/580-1875
www.ACNconsult.org

Center for Communication Resources
Nalani McClendon
1419 W. Blackhawk
Chicago, IL 60622
773/862-6868 • 773/862-0707 - fax
www.bham.net/soe/ccr

Community Media Workshop at Columbia College
600 S. Michigan
Chicago, IL 60605
312/344-6400 • 312/344-6404 - fax
www.newstips.org

CPAs for Public Interest
222 S. Riverside Plaza - 16th floor
Chicago, IL 60606
312/993-0393 • 312/993-9432 - fax
www.icpas.org/cpaspi.htm

Cultural Facilities Fund
78 E. Washington #250
Chicago, IL 60602
312/372-1710 • 312/372-1765 - fax

Chicago Department of Cultural Affairs
Richard Vaughn -
Director of Legal Affairs
312/742-1175
www.ci.chi.il.us/CulturalAffairs

Department of Revenue
Gladys Alcazar-Anselmo
312/744-6398
www.ci.chi.il.us/Revenue

Donors Forum of Chicago
208 S. LaSalle #735
Chicago, IL 60604
312/578-0175 • 312/578-0158 - fax
www.donorsforum.org

Executive Service Corps of Chicago
30 W. Monroe #600
Chicago, IL 60603
312/580-1840 • 312/580-0042 - fax
www.esc-chicago.org

Illinois Alliance for Arts Education
200 N. Michigan #404
Chicago, IL 60601
312/750-0589
800/808-ARTS
312/750-9113 - fax
www.artsmart.org

Illinois Arts Alliance
200 N. Michigan #404
Chicago, IL 60601
312/855-3105 • 312/855-1565 - fax
www.artsalliance.org

Illinois Arts Council
100 W. Randolph #10-500
Chicago, IL 60601
312/814-6750 • 312/814-1471 - fax
www.state.il.us/agency/iac

IT Resource Center
Sarah Oaks - Marketing Director
6 N. Michigan #1405
Chicago, IL 60602
312/372-4872 • 312/372-7962 - fax
www.npo.net/itrc

Lawyers for the Creative Arts
213 W. Institute #401
Chicago, IL 60610
312/944-2787
800/525-ARTS
312/944-2195 - fax
www.cityofchicago.org/culturalaffairs/CulturalProgramming/Lawyers.html

League of Chicago Theatres
228 S. Wabash #300
Chicago, IL 60604
312/554-9800 • 312/922-7202 - fax
www.theaterchicago.org

Nonprofit Financial Center
111 W. Washington #1221
Chicago, IL 60602
312/606-8250 • 312/606-0241 - fax
www.nonprofitfinancial.org

Pre-Paid Legal Services, Inc.
9242 W. National Ave.
West Ellis, WI 53227
414/329-3047

Season of Concern
(See our ad on page 161)
203 N. Wabash #2104
Chicago, IL 60601
312/332-0518 • 312/372-0272 - fax
members.aol.com/sochicago/

The Support Center
3811 N. Lawndale #100
Chicago, IL 60618
773/539-4741 • 773/539-4751 - fax
www.supportcenter.org/sf/

Living

You really need to take care of yourself!

Northlight Theatre's "The Cripple of Inishmaan" – pictured: Ann Noble Massey, Martin McClendon – photo: Michael Brosilow

Legal, Tax and Insurance

Accountants and Tax Preparers

American Express Tax and Business Services
Craig Minnick
30 S. Wacker #2600
Chicago, IL 60606
312/499-1649 • 312/207-2954 - fax

Bob Behr
Resumés by Mac
4738 N. LaPorte
Chicago, IL 60630
773/685-7721 • 773/283-9839 - fax

Checkers, Simon & Rosner
1 S. Wacker
Chicago, IL 60606
312/917-0649

David P. Cudnowski, Ltd.
70 W. Madison #5330
Chicago, IL 60602
312/759-1040 • 312/759-1042 - fax
www.lawyers.com/talentlaw

David Turrentine, E.A. Income Tax Service
3907 N. Sacramento
Chicago, IL 60618
773/509-1798 • 773/509-1806 - fax

Gerald Bauman & Company
75 E. Wacker #2100
Chicago, IL 60601
312/726-6868 • 312/726-3683 - fax

H&R Block
179 W. Washington
Chicago, IL 60602
312/424-0268 • 312/424-0278 - fax
www.hrblock.com

H&R Block
246 Janata Blvd. #320
Lombard, IL 60148
630/792-1063 • 630/792-1066 - fax
www.hrblock.com

Jay-EMM Acct./Tax/Consulting
735 S. Victoria
Des Plaines, IL 60016
847/679-8270

Joel N. Goldblatt, Ltd.
100 N. LaSalle #1910
Chicago, IL 60602
312/372-9322 • 312/372-2905 - fax

Katten, Muchin & Zavis
525 W. Monroe #1600
Chicago, IL 60661
312/902-5200 • 312/902-1061 - fax

H. Gregory Mermel
(See our ad on the previous page)
2835 N. Sheffield #311
Chicago, IL 60657
773/525-1778 • 773/525-3209 - fax

Mangum, Smietanka & Johnson, L.L.C.
35 E. Wacker #2130
Chicago, IL 60601
312/368-8500

Weiner & Lahn, P.C.
900 Ridge Rd. #F
Munster, IN 46321
708/849-6800 • 219/836-1515

Attorneys

Chicago Bar Association Lawyer Referral
321 S. Plymouth
Chicago, IL 60604
312/554-2001
www.chicagobar.org

David P. Cudnowski, Ltd.
70 W. Madison #5330
Chicago, IL 60602
312/759-1040 • 312/759-1042 - fax
www.lawyers.com/talentlaw

Tom Feezy
310 S. County Farm Rd. #J
Wheaton, IL 60187-2409
630/561-7676 • 630/839-1923 - fax

Joel N. Goldblatt, Ltd.
100 N. LaSalle #1910
Chicago, IL 60602
312/372-9322 • 312/372-2905 - fax

JoAnne Guillemette
311 S. Wacker #4550
Chicago, IL 60606
312/697-4788 • 312/697-4799 - fax
800/616-5964 - pgr.

Jay B. Ross & Associates, P.C.
838 W. Grand #2W
Chicago, IL 60622-6565
312/633-9000 • 312/633-9090 - fax
www.jaybross.com

Katten, Muchin & Zavis
525 W. Monroe #1600
Chicago, IL 60661
312/902-5200 • 312/902-1061 - fax

Lawyers for the Creative Arts
213 W. Institute #401
Chicago, IL 60610
312/944-2787 • 800/525-ARTS
312/944-2195 - fax
www.cityofchicago.org/culturalaffairs/CulturalProgramming/Lawyers.html

Mangum, Smietanka & Johnson, L.L.C.
35 E. Wacker #2130
Chicago, IL 60601
312/368-8500

Pre-Paid Legal Services, Inc.
9242 W. National Ave.
West Ellis, WI 53227
414/329-3047

Fred Wellisch
1021 W. Adams #102
Chicago, IL 60607
312/829-2300 • 312/829-3729 - fax

William Borah and Associates
2024 Hickory Rd. #105
Homewood, IL 60430
708/799-0066 • 708/799-0122 - fax

Insurance

Myers-Briggs and Company, Inc.
125 S. Wacker #1800
Chicago, IL 60606
312/263-3215 • 312/263-0979 - fax

Paczolt Financial Group
913 Hillgrove
LaGrange, IL 60525
708/579-3128 • 708/579-0236 - fax
www.paczolt.com

Ronald Shapero Insurance Associates
Health Insurance Specialists
260 E. Chestnut #3406
Chicago, IL 60611
312/337-7133

Movie Theatres *(Cool and Cheap Ones)*

Biograph Theatre
2433 N. Lincoln
Chicago, IL 60614
773/348-4123

Davis Theatre
4614 N. Lincoln
Chicago, IL 60625
773/784-0893

Esquire Theater
58 E. Oak
Chicago, IL 60611
312/280-0101

Facets Multimedia
1517 W. Fullerton
Chicago, IL 60614
773/281-9075
773/929-5437 - fax
www.facets.org

Fine Arts Theatres Cineplex-Odeon
418 S. Michigan
Chicago, IL 60611
312/939-3700

Logan Theatre
2646 N. Milwaukee
Chicago, IL 60647
773/252-0627

Music Box
3733 N. Southport
Chicago, IL 60613
773/871-6604
www.musicboxtheatre.com

Three Penny Theatre
2424 N. Lincoln
Chicago, IL 60614
773/935-5744

The Vic Theatre (Brew & View)
3145 N. Sheffield
Chicago, IL 60657
312/618-VIEW
773/472-0449
www.victheatre.com

Village North
6746 N. Sheridan
Chicago, IL 60626
773/764-9100
www.villagetheatres.com

Village Theater
1548 N. Clark
Chicago, IL 60622
312/642-2403
www.villagetheatres.com

Health & Fitness

Health Clubs - Personal Training

Bally Total Fitness
2828 N. Clark
Chicago, IL 60657
773/929-6900
800-FITNESS
www.ballytotalfitness.com

Chicago Fitness Center
3131 N. Lincoln
Chicago, IL 60657
773/549-8181 • 773/549-4622 - fax
www.chicagofitnesscenter.com

Gorilla Sports
2727 N. Lincoln
Chicago, IL 60614
773/477-8400 • 773/477-8476 - fax

Gold Coast Multiplex
1030 N. Clark
Chicago, IL 60610
312/944-1030 • 312/944-6180 - fax
www.gcmultiplex.com

Know No Limits
5121 N. Clark
Chicago, IL 60640
773/334-4728

Know No Limits
3530 N. Lincoln
Chicago, IL 60657
773/404-1950

Lake Shore Athletic Club
441 N. Wabash
Chicago, IL 60611
312/644-4880 • 312/644-4870 - fax

Lake Shore Athletic Club
1320 W. Fullerton
Chicago, IL 60614
773/477-9888

Lehmann Sports Club
2700 N. Lehmann
Chicago, IL 60614
773/871-8300 • 773/871-3506 - fax
www.lehmannsportsclub.com

One on One Fitness Personal Training Service, Inc.
Michael Sokol
312/642-4235 • 312/642-7686 - fax

Webster Fitness Club
957 W. Webster
Chicago, IL 60614
773/248-2006 • 773/248-3195 - fax
www.websterfitness.com

Women's Workout World
1031 N. Clark
Chicago, IL 60610
312/664-2106

World Gym
909 W. Montrose
Chicago, IL 60613
773/348-1212
www.worldgymchi.com

World Gym
150 S. Wacker
Chicago, IL 60606
312/357-9753 • 312/357-0577 - fax
www.worldgymchi.com

World Gym - Hyde Park
1451 E. 53rd St.
Chicago, IL 60615
773/363-1212 • 773/363-2010 - fax
www.worldgymchi.com

YMCA
801 N. Dearborn
Chicago, IL 60610
800/935-9622

Health Food Stores

Advance Nutrition Center
55 E. Washington - Lobby
Chicago, IL 60602
312/419-1940

Life Spring
3178 N. Clark
Chicago, IL 60657
773/327-1023 • 773/327-1030 - fax

Sherwyn's
645 W. Diversey
Chicago, IL 60614
773/477-1934

Whole Foods Market
1000 W. North
Chicago, IL 60622
312/587-0648
www.wholefoods.com

Whole Foods Market
3300 N. Ashland
Chicago, IL 60657
773/244-4200
www.wholefoods.com

Nutritionists

Lake Shore Naprapathic Center
3166 N. Lincoln #410
Chicago, IL 60657
773/327-0844

Rose Quest Nutrition Center
200 N. Michigan #404A
Chicago, IL 60602
312/444-9234

Weight Control

A Creative Change
Honora Simon, Ph.D.
541 W. Diversey #208
Chicago, IL 60614
773/528-6313
www.reducestress.com

Professional Weight Clinic
200 E. Ohio #501
Chicago, IL 60611
312/664-2255

Weight Watchers
800/651-6000

Women's Workout World
1031 N. Clark
Chicago, IL 60610
312/664-2106

Counselors

A Creative Change
Honora Simon, Ph.D.
541 W. Diversey #208
Chicago, IL 60614
773/528-6313
www.reducestress.com

Abraham Lincoln Center Screening & Support
(specialize in children)
1950 W. 87th
Chicago, IL 60620
773/239-7960 • 773/239-0272 - fax

Associated Psychologists and Therapists
77 W. Washington #1519
Chicago, IL 60602
312/630-1001 • 312/630-1342 - fax
www.psychologists.org

Community Counseling Centers of Chicago
Mental Health Center
4740 N. Clark
Chicago, IL 60640
773/769-0205 • 773/769-0344 - fax

Community Counseling Centers of Chicago
5710 N. Broadway
Chicago, IL 60660
773/728-1000 • 773/728-6517 - fax

Dance Therapy Center
Fine Arts Building
410 S. Michigan
Chicago, IL 60605
312/461-9826 • 312/461-9843 - fax

Great Lakes Psychological Providers
111 N. Wabash #1408
Chicago, IL 60602
312/443-1400 • 312/443-1307 - fax

Ann L. Hammon, M.D.
550 W. Surf #101C
Chicago, IL 60657
773/296-2195

Harambee Wellness Center
1515 E. 52nd - 2nd floor
Chicago, IL 60615
773/752-7867

Hartgrove Hospital
520 N. Ridgeway
Chicago, IL 60624
773/722-3113 • 773/722-6361 - fax

Howard Brown Health Center
4025 N. Sheridan
Chicago, IL 60613
773/388-1600

Institute for Psychoanalysis
122 S. Michigan #1300
Chicago, IL 60603
312/922-7474 • 312/922-5656 - fax
www.chianalysis.org

Panic Anxiety Recovery Center
680 N. Lake Shore #1325
Chicago, IL 60611
312/642-7954 • 312/642-7951 - fax

Jason Simpson and Group Solutions
888/415-1530
mirconnect.com/doc/simpson.html

Hypnotists

Associated Psychologists and Therapists
77 W. Washington #1519
Chicago, IL 60602
312/630-1001
312/630-1342 - fax
www.psychologists.org

Gerald Greene, Ph.D.
500 N. Michigan #542
Chicago, IL 60611
312/266-1456

World Hypnosis Organization, Inc.
2521 W. Montrose
Chicago, IL 60618
773/267-6677

Meditation

Peace School
3121 N. Lincoln
Chicago, IL 60657
773/248-7959
773/248-7963 - fax

Vajrayana Buddhist Center
827 W. Roscoe #1
Chicago, IL 60657
773/529-1862
www.geocities.com/athens/academy/6362

Zen Buddhist Temple (Chinese Culture Academy)
608 Dempster St.
Evanston, IL 60202
847/869-0554

Religious Groups

AGLOChicago
Archdiocesan Gay & Lesbian Outreach
711 W. Belmont #106
Chicago, IL 60657
773/525-3872

Chicago Genesis
A Creative Christian Collective
773/275-3490

Congregation Or Chadash
656 W. Barry
Chicago, IL 60657
773/248-9456

Dignity Chicago
(Roman Catholic)
3023 N. Clark - Box 237
Chicago, IL 60657
773/296-0780
www.dignitychicago.org

The Ethical Humanist Society of Greater Chicago
7574 N. Lincoln Ave.
Skokie, IL 60077
847/677-3334
www.ethicalhuman.org

Grace Baptist Church
1307 W. Granville
Chicago, IL 60660
773/262-8700

HAVURA
Jewish Community Group
7316 N. Tripp
Lincolnwood, IL 60712
847/679-8760

Holy Trinity Lutheran Church
1218 W. Addison
Chicago, IL 60613
773/248-1233
www.holytrinitychicago.org

More Light Presbyterians
600 W. Fullerton
Chicago, IL 60614
773/784-2635
www.mlp.org

Second Unitarian Church/Unitarian Universalist
656 W. Barry
Chicago, IL 60657
773/549-0260 - office
773/549-3933 - minister
www.2uchicago.org

Vajrayana Buddhist Center
827 W. Roscoe #1
Chicago, IL 60657
773/529-1862
www.geocities.com/athens/academy/6362

Wellington Avenue United Church of Christ
615 W. Wellington
Chicago, IL 60657
773/935-0642
773/935-0690 - fax

Chiropractors

Advance Center
Dr. Michael Luban
55 E. Washington #1310
Chicago, IL 60602
312/553-2020 • 312/553-5128 - fax

Belmont Health Care
Lena Granlund
2110 W. Belmont
Chicago, IL 60618
773/404-0909

Chicago Chiropractic Center
18 S. Michigan #400
Chicago, IL 60603
312/726-1353 • 312/726-5238 - fax

Chicago Neck and Back Institute
5700 W. Fullerton #1
Chicago, IL 60639
773/237-8660 • 773/237-3159 - fax

Chiropractic Chicago
Dr. Ellisa J. Grossman
407 W. North
Chicago, IL 60610
312/255-9500

Graham Chiropractic
Dr. Betty E. Graham
5344 N. Lincoln
Chicago, IL 60625
773/769-6666 • 773/334-1696 - fax

Greater Chicago Chiropractic
Dr. Dale Zuehlke
561 W. Diversey #221
Chicago, IL 60614
773/871-7766 • 773/871-0781 - fax

Franklin D. Ing
2451 N. Lincoln
Chicago, IL 60614
773/525-2444 • 773/525-9989 - fax

Progressive Chiropractic
Rehabilitation & Wellness Center
2816 N. Sheffield
Chicago, IL 60657
773/525-WELL • 773/525-9397 - fax
www.progressivechiro.net

Dr. Kevin Regan
Holistic Practitioner
55 E. Washington #1630
Chicago, IL 60602
312/578-1624 • 312/578-8717 - fax
www.doctorkev.com

Seaman Chiropractic Center
4941 W. Foster
Chicago, IL 60630
773/545-2233 • 773/545-8383 - fax

Dr. Briana S. Skarbek
513 Waukegan Rd.
Northbrook, IL 60062
847/509-0005

Stiles Chiropractic Offices
48 E. Chicago
Chicago, IL 60611
312/642-1138

Naprapaths

Belmont Health Care
Lena Granlund
2110 W. Belmont
Chicago, IL 60618
773/404-0909

Karen L. Bruneel
4770 N. Lincoln #6
Chicago, IL 60625
773/769-1133
773/769-1134 - fax

Chicago National College of Naprapathy
3330 N. Milwaukee
Chicago, IL 60641
773/282-2686 • 773/282-2688 - fax
www.naprapathy.edu

Lake Shore Naprapathic Center
3166 N. Lincoln #410
Chicago, IL 60657
773/327-0844

Acupuncture

Advance Center
Dr. Michael Luban
55 E. Washington #1310
Chicago, IL 60602
312/553-2020 • 312/553-5128 - fax

American Acupuncture Association
65 E. Wacker
Chicago, IL 60601
312/853-3732

Beth Braun, Ph.D.,C.M.T.
Miro Center for Integrated Medicine
1639 Orrington Ave.
Evanston, IL 60201
847/733-9900 • 847/733-0105 - fax
www.mirocenter.org

Chicago Acupuncture Clinic
Dan Plovanich, Dipl. Ac.
3723 N. Southport
Chicago, IL 60613
773/871-0342 • 773/871-0348 - fax

Chiropractic Chicago
Dr. Ellisa J. Grossman
407 W. North
Chicago, IL 60610
312/255-9500

East Point Associates, Ltd.
Mary Rogel & Unsoo Kim
1525 E. 53rd #705
Chicago, IL 60615
773/955-9643 • 773/955-9953 - fax

Graham Chiropractic
Dr. Betty E. Graham
5344 N. Lincoln
Chicago, IL 60625
773/769-6666 • 773/334-1696 - fax

Franklin D. Ing
2451 N. Lincoln
Chicago, IL 60614
773/525-2444 • 773/525-9989 - fax

Know No Limits
3530 N. Lincoln
Chicago, IL 60657
773/404-1950

Progressive Chiropractic
Rehabilitation & Wellness Center
2816 N. Sheffield
Chicago, IL 60657
773/525-WELL
773/525-9397 - fax
www.progressivechiro.net

Dr. Kevin Regan
Holistic Practitioner
55 E. Washington #1630
Chicago, IL 60602
312/578-1624
312/578-8717 - fax
www.doctorkev.com

Seaman Chiropractic Center
4941 W. Foster
Chicago, IL 60630
773/545-2233
773/545-8383 - fax

Dr. Briana S. Skarbek
513 Waukegan Rd.
Northbrook, IL 60062
847/509-0005

Massage

American Massage Therapy Association
Illinois Chapter
708/484-9282 • 708/484-8601 - fax

Anna Sas European Facials
Barbara's Skin Care
645 N. Michigan #420
Chicago, IL 60611
312/943-4728

Back to One
5342 N. Winthrop
Chicago, IL 60640
773/561-5893

Beth Braun Ph.D.,C.M.T.
Miro Center for Integrated Medicine
1639 Orrington Ave.
Evanston, IL 60201
847/733-9900
847/733-0105 - fax
www.mirocenter.org

Karen L. Bruneel
4770 N. Lincoln #6
Chicago, IL 60625
773/769-1133
773/769-1134 - fax

Chiropractic Chicago
Dr. Ellisa J. Grossman
407 W. North
Chicago, IL 60610
312/255-9500

Diamond Beauty Clinic
151 N. Michigan #1018
Chicago, IL 60601
312/240-1042

Greater Chicago Chiropractic
Dr. Dale Zuehlke
561 W. Diversey #221
Chicago, IL 60614
773/871-7766
773/871-0781 - fax

Hair Loft
14 E. Pearson
Chicago, IL 60611
312/943-5435

Heidi's Salon
110 E. Delaware
Chicago, IL 60611
312/337-6411
312/337-7174 - fax

Leslie Kahn
Licensed Massage Therapist
1243 N. Damen
Chicago, IL 60622
773/276-4665

Know No Limits
3530 N. Lincoln
Chicago, IL 60657
773/404-1950

Know No Limits
5121 N. Clark
Chicago, IL 60640
773/334-4728

Mario Tricoci
Hair Salon & Day Spa
277 E. Ontario
Chicago, IL 60611
312/915-0960
312/943-3138 - fax

Massage Therapy Professionals
3047 N. Lincoln #400
Chicago, IL 60657
773/472-9484
773/472-8590 - fax

Massage Works
4039 N. Lavergne
Chicago, IL 60641
773/777-2396

Progressive Chiropractic
Rehabilitation & Wellness Center
2816 N. Sheffield
Chicago, IL 60657
773/525-WELL
773/525-9397 - fax
www.progressivechiro.net

Rodica European Skin & Body Care Center
Water Tower Place - Professional Side
845 N. Michigan #944E
Chicago, IL 60611
312/527-1459
www.facialandbodybyrodica.com

Seaman Chiropractic Center
4941 W. Foster
Chicago, IL 60630
773/545-2233
773/545-8383 - fax

Sun Center
1816 N. Wells - 3rd floor
Chicago, IL 60614
312/280-1070
www.home.earthlink.net/~suncenter

Alexander Technique

Chicago Center for the Alexander Technique
Ed Bouchard
2216 W. Palmer #2R
Chicago, IL 60647
773/862-3320 • 773/235-9534 - fax

Yoga

Art Linkletter's Young World
1263 S. Main St.
Lombard, IL 60148
630/495-4940

Belle Plaine Studio
2014 W. Belle Plaine
Chicago, IL 60618
773/935-1890 • 773/935-1909 - fax

Dance Center of Columbia College
4730 N. Sheridan
Chicago, IL 60640
773/989-3310 • 773/271-7046 - fax
www.colum.edu

Global Yoga and Wellness Center
1823 W. North
Chicago, IL 60622
773/489-1510

Hedwig Dances
Administrative Offices
2936 N. Southport #210
Chicago, IL 60657
773/871-0872 • 773/296-0968 - fax
www.enteract.com\~hedwig

North Shore School of Dance
107 Highwood
Highwood, IL 60040
847/432-2060 • 847/432-4037 - fax
www.northshoredance.com

NU Yoga Center
3047 N. Lincoln - 3rd floor
Chicago, IL 60657
773/327-3650
www.yogamind.com

Peace School
3121 N. Lincoln
Chicago, IL 60657
773/248-7959
773/248-7963 - fax

Sivananda Yoga Center
1246 W. Bryn Mawr
Chicago, IL 60660
773/878-7771
www.sivananda.org/chicago

Temple of Kriya Yoga
2414 N. Kedzie
Chicago, IL 60647
773/342-4600
773/342-4608 - fax

Yoga Circle
Gabriel Halpern - Director
401 W. Ontario - 2nd floor
Chicago, IL 60610
312/915-0750
www.yogacircle.com

Tai Chi

Dance Center of Columbia College
4730 N. Sheridan
Chicago, IL 60640
773/989-3310
773/271-7046 - fax
www.colum.edu

Physicians

ARR/Alternative Reproductive
2000 N. Racine
Chicago, IL 60614
773/327-7315 • 773/477-0287 - fax

Beth Braun, Ph.D.,C.M.T.
Miro Center for Integrated Medicine
1639 Orrington Ave.
Evanston, IL 60201
847/733-9900 • 847/733-0105 - fax
www.mirocenter.org

Center for Human Reproduction
750 N. Orleans
Chicago, IL 60610
312/397-8200 • 312/397-8338
312/397-8394 - fax

Harambee Wellness Center
1515 E. 52nd - 2nd floor
Chicago, IL 60615
773/752-7867

Howard Brown Health Center
4025 N. Sheridan
Chicago, IL 60613
773/388-1600

University Family Physicians
1953C N. Clybourn
Chicago, IL 60614
773/348-1414
773/348-1477 - fax

University of Chicago Physicians Group
4640 N. Marine
Chicago, IL 60640
773/564-5333
773/564-5334 - fax

Women's Health Resources
3000 N. Halsted #309
Chicago, IL 60657
773/296-3500

AIDS Resources

Harambee Wellness Center
1515 E. 52nd - 2nd floor
Chicago, IL 60615
773/752-7867

Horizons Anti-Violence Hotline
773/871-2273

Horizons Community Service
Gay and Lesbian Hotline (6-10pm)
773/929-4357

Howard Brown Health Center
4025 N. Sheridan
Chicago, IL 60613
773/388-1600

IL AIDS Hotline
800/451-6651

Stop AIDS
3651 N. Halsted
Chicago, IL 60613
773/871-3300 • 773/871-2528 - fax
www.howardbrown.org

Test Positive Aware Network
1258 W. Belmont
Chicago, IL 60657
773/404-8726 • 773/404-1040 - fax
www.tpan.com

Grooming & Appearance

Salons

Alfaro Hair Design
3454 N. Southport
Chicago, IL 60657
773/935-0202

Alpha Wave Hair Design Studio
2652 N. Halsted
Chicago, IL 60657
773/327-2200

Nancy Angelair Salon
1003 N. Rush
Chicago, IL 60611
312/943-3011

Curl Up and Dye
2837 N. Clark
Chicago, IL 60657
773/348-1000
773/348-2802 - fax

Diamond Beauty Clinic
151 N. Michigan #1018
Chicago, IL 60601
312/240-1042

Femline Hair Designs, Inc.
3500 Midwest Rd.
Oak Brook, IL 60522
630/655-2212

Hair Loft
14 E. Pearson
Chicago, IL 60611
312/943-5435

Heidi's Salon
110 E. Delaware
Chicago, IL 60611
312/337-6411 • 312/337-7174 - fax

J. Gordon Designs, Ltd.
2326 N. Clark
Chicago, IL 60614
773/871-0770 • 773/871-2514 - fax

Marianne Strokirk Salon
361 W. Chestnut
Chicago, IL 60610
312/944-4428 • 312/944-4429 - fax
www.mariannestrokirk.com

Mario Tricoci
Hair Salon & Day Spa
277 E. Ontario
Chicago, IL 60611
312/915-0960 • 312/943-3138 - fax

Media Hair & Makeup Group
Maureen Kalagian
708/848-8400

Molina Molina
19 E. Chestnut - 2nd floor
Chicago, IL 60611
312/664-2386

Niko's Day Spa
3200 N. Lake Shore
Chicago, IL 60657
773/472-0883

Paul Rehder Salon
939 N. Rush
Chicago, IL 60611
312/943-7404

Salon Absolu
1216 W. Belmont
Chicago, IL 60657
773/525-2396

Southport Hair Studio
3430 N. Southport
Chicago, IL 60657
773/477-9319

Timothy Paul Salon
200 E. Delaware
Chicago, IL 60611
312/944-5454 • 312/944-5460 - fax

Trio Salon, Ltd.
11 E. Walton
Chicago, IL 60611-1412
312/944-6999
877/944-6999
312/944-9572 - fax
www.triosalon.com

Trio Salon, Ltd.
1913 Central St.
Evanston, IL 60201-2227
847/491-6999
www.triosalon.com
"Chicago models turn to TRIO...for many of the shortest, coolest looks seen on the hottest new faces in town...(TRIO) has been recognized nationally for its creative and technical works...(the) name (being) synonymous with flattering, precision cuts and picture perfect stylings." MODERN SALON. Open Seven Days A Week.

Cosmetic Surgery

Associated Plastic Surgeons
Dr. Otto J. Placik
680 N. Lake Shore #930
Chicago, IL 60611
312/787-5313 • **800/232-0767**
847/398-1784 - fax

Dr. Diane L. Gerber
680 N. Lake Shore #930
Chicago, IL 60611
312/654-8700

Wafik A. Hanna, M.D.
12 Salt Creek Ln. #225
Hinsdale, IL 60521
630/887-8180 • 630/887-8188 - fax

Raymond Konior, M.D.
1 S. 224 Summit #310
Oakbrook Terrace, IL 60181
630/932-9690 • 630/932-8125 - fax
www.thenewyoudoc.com

Liposuction Institute of America
Dr. Leon Tcheupdjian
1700 W. Central Rd.
Arlington Heights, IL 60005
847/259-0100 • 847/398-3855 - fax
www.lipodoc.com

New Dimensions Centre for Cosmetic Surgery
60 E. Delaware - 15th floor
Chicago, IL 60611
312/440-5050 • 312/440-5064 - fax
www.nd-plasticsurgery.com

Skin Care

Anna Sas European Facials
Barbara's Skin Care
645 N. Michigan #420
Chicago, IL 60611
312/943-4728

Cheryl Channings
54 E. Oak - 2nd floor
Chicago, IL 60611
312/280-1994 • 312/280-1929 - fax
www.channings.com

Femline Hair Designs, Inc.
3500 Midwest Rd.
Oak Brook, IL 60522
630/655-2212

Hair Loft
14 E. Pearson
Chicago, IL 60611
312/943-5435

Heidi's Salon
110 E. Delaware
Chicago, IL 60611
312/337-6411 • 312/337-7174 - fax

Marilyn Miglin Institute
112 E. Oak
Chicago, IL 60611
800/662-1120
312/943-1184 - fax
www.marilyn-miglin.com

Mario Tricoci Hair Salon & Day Spa
277 E. Ontario
Chicago, IL 60611
312/915-0960
312/943-3138 - fax

Nouvelle Femme
1157 Wilmette Ave.
Wilmette, IL 60091
847/251-6698

Rodica European Skin & Body Care Center
Water Tower Place - Professional Side
845 N. Michigan #944E
Chicago, IL 60611
312/527-1459
www.facialandbodybyrodica.com

Salon Absolu
1216 W. Belmont
Chicago, IL 60657
773/525-2396

Syd Simons Cosmetics, Inc.
6601 W. North Ave.
Oak Park, IL 60302
877/943-2333
708/660-0266
www.sydsimons.com

Electrolysis

Amber Electrolysis
3734 N. Southport
Chicago, IL 60613
773/549-3800

Carol Block, Ltd.
Permanent Hair Removal
166 E. Superior #301
Chicago, IL 60611
312/266-1350
www.cyberconnect.com/carolblock/home.htm

Water Tower Hair Removal
845 N. Michigan #972W
Chicago, IL 60611
312/787-4028
312/787-4092 - fax
www.purelazer.com

Dentists

Belmont Dental Care
3344 N. Lincoln
Chicago, IL 60657
773/549-7971 • 773/348-7544 - fax

Dr. David B. Drake
739 W. Belmont
Chicago, IL 60657
773/248-8813 • 773/248-8898 - fax

Dr. Jeffrey Gaule
3120 N. Ashland
Chicago, IL 60657
773/281-7550 • 773/281-0808 - fax

Gold Coast Dental Associates
Dr. Jeffrey Weller
1050 N. State - Mezzanine
Chicago, IL 60610
312/654-0606 • 312/654-1606 - fax

Dr. Martin Lieberman & Dr. William T. Tetford
5419 N. Sheridan #105
Chicago, IL 60640
773/728-9200

Lincoln Park Cosmetic and General Dentistry
424 W. Fullerton
Chicago, IL 60614
773/404-0101

Dr. Craig Millard, D.D.S., P.C.
30 N. Michigan #920
Chicago, IL 60602
312/726-5830
312/726-7290 - fax

Michelle Rappeport, D.D.S.
3056 N. Southport
Chicago, IL 60657
773/935-4960

Ravenswood Dental Group
1945 W. Wilson
Chicago, IL 60640
773/334-3555
773/334-5771 - fax

Dr. Marianne W. Schaefer
4801 W. Peterson
Chicago, IL 60646
773/777-8300
www.the-toothfairy.com

Dr. Joseph S. Toups
25 E. Washington #1325
Chicago, IL 60602
312/263-6894

Dr. Glenn Ulffers, D.D.S.
1001 N. Clark
Chicago, IL 60610
312/337-1318 • 312/642-5166 - fax
All phases of general dentistry emphasizing cosmetics including bleaching, porcelain veneers, and crowns. All done in a friendly environment in order to make the apprehensive patient comfortable. Nitrous oxide analgesia is available for those who are most fearful.

Dr. Gray Vogelmann
155 N. Michigan #325
Chicago, IL 60601
312/819-1104

Dr. Roger M. Wills
30 N. Michigan #1414
Chicago, IL 60602
312/332-7010
312/332-1812 - fax

Dr. Ieva Wright
333 N. Michigan #2900
Chicago, IL 60601
312/236-3226
312/236-9629 - fax

Wrigleyville Dental Group
1353 W. Cornelia
Chicago, IL 60657
773/975-6666

Public Service Phone Numbers

ArtLaw Hotline
312/944-ARTS

Attorney General
312/814-3000

CTA/PACE Information
836-7000 (All area codes)

Equal Employment Opportunity Commission
Chicago, IL
312/353-2713

League of Chicago Theatres Hotline
900/225-2225

IRS Taxpayer Information
Chicago, IL
800/829-1040

Movie Phone
312/444-FILM

Chicago Park District
Chicago, IL
312/747-2200

Police (Non-Emergency)
Chicago, IL
312/746-6000

Post Office Information
312/654-3895

Ticket Master
312/559-1950

Women's Bureau
U.S. Department of Labor
230 S. Dearborn
Chicago, IL 60604
312/353-6985
312/353-6986 - fax

February 2000

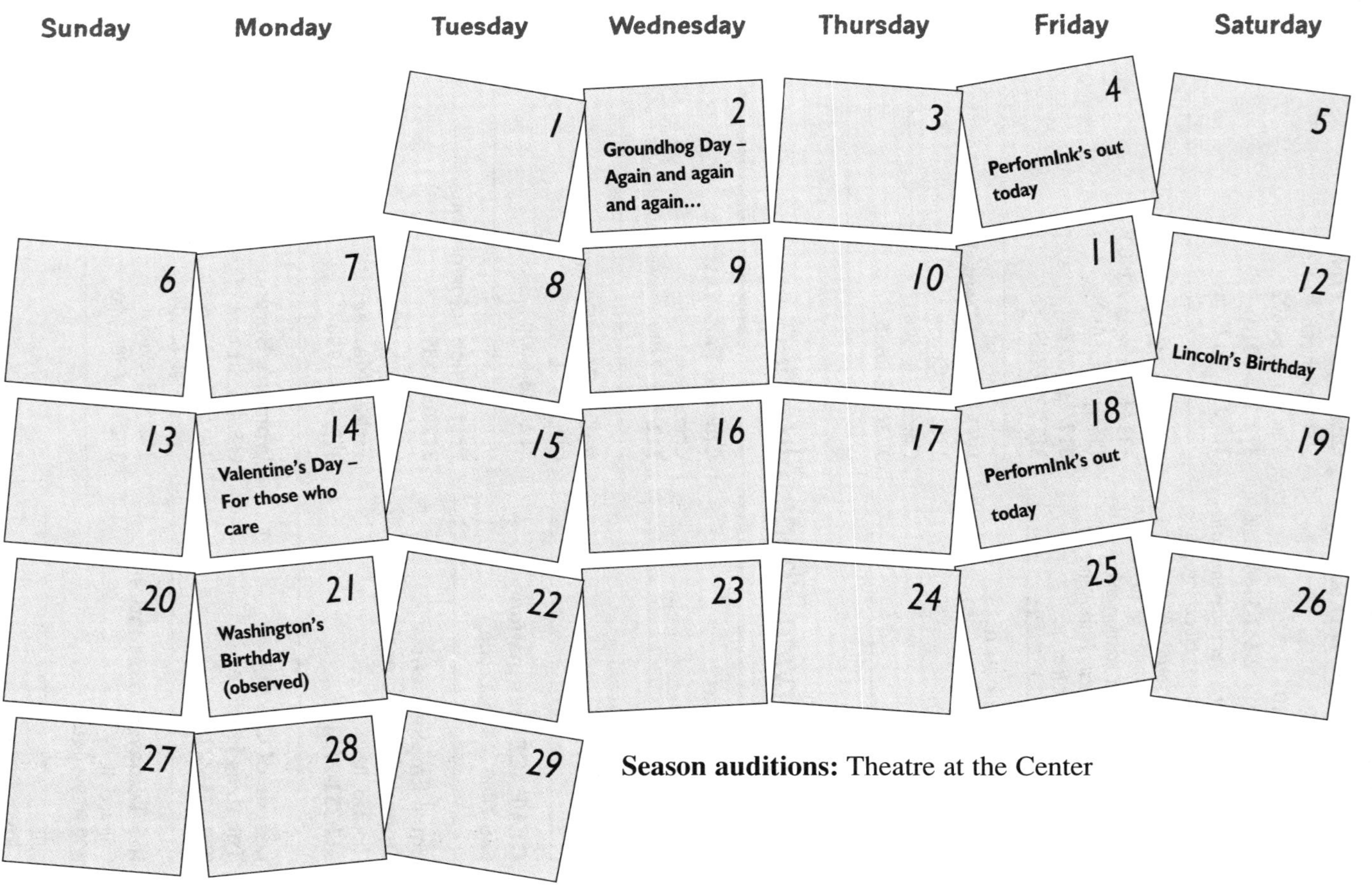

Sunday
Monday
Tuesday
Wednesday
Thursday
Friday
Saturday
1
2
Groundhog Day – Again and again and again…
3
4
PerformInk's out today
5
6
7
8
9
10
11
12
Lincoln's Birthday
13
14
Valentine's Day – For those who care
15
16
17
18
PerformInk's out today
19
20
21
Washington's Birthday (observed)
22
23
24
25
26
27
28
29
Season auditions: Theatre at the Center

March 2000

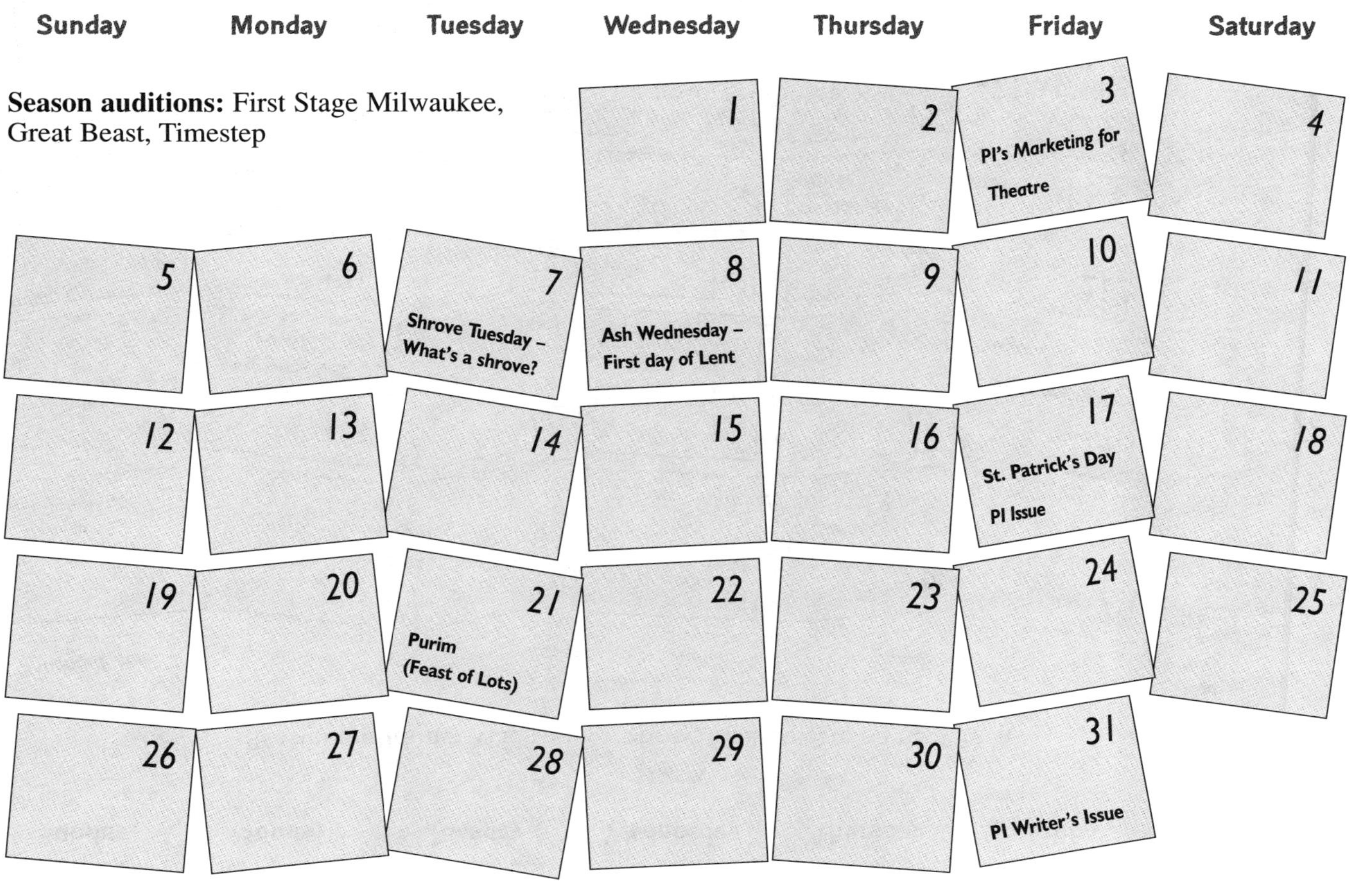
Sunday
Monday
Tuesday
Wednesday
Thursday
Friday
Saturday
Season auditions: First Stage Milwaukee, Great Beast, Timestep
1
2
3
PI's Marketing for Theatre
4
5
6
7
Shrove Tuesday – What's a shrove?
8
Ash Wednesday – First day of Lent
9
10
11
12
13
14
15
16
17
St. Patrick's Day
PI Issue
18
19
20
21
Purim (Feast of Lots)
22
23
24
25
26
27
28
29
30
31
PI Writer's Issue

April 2000

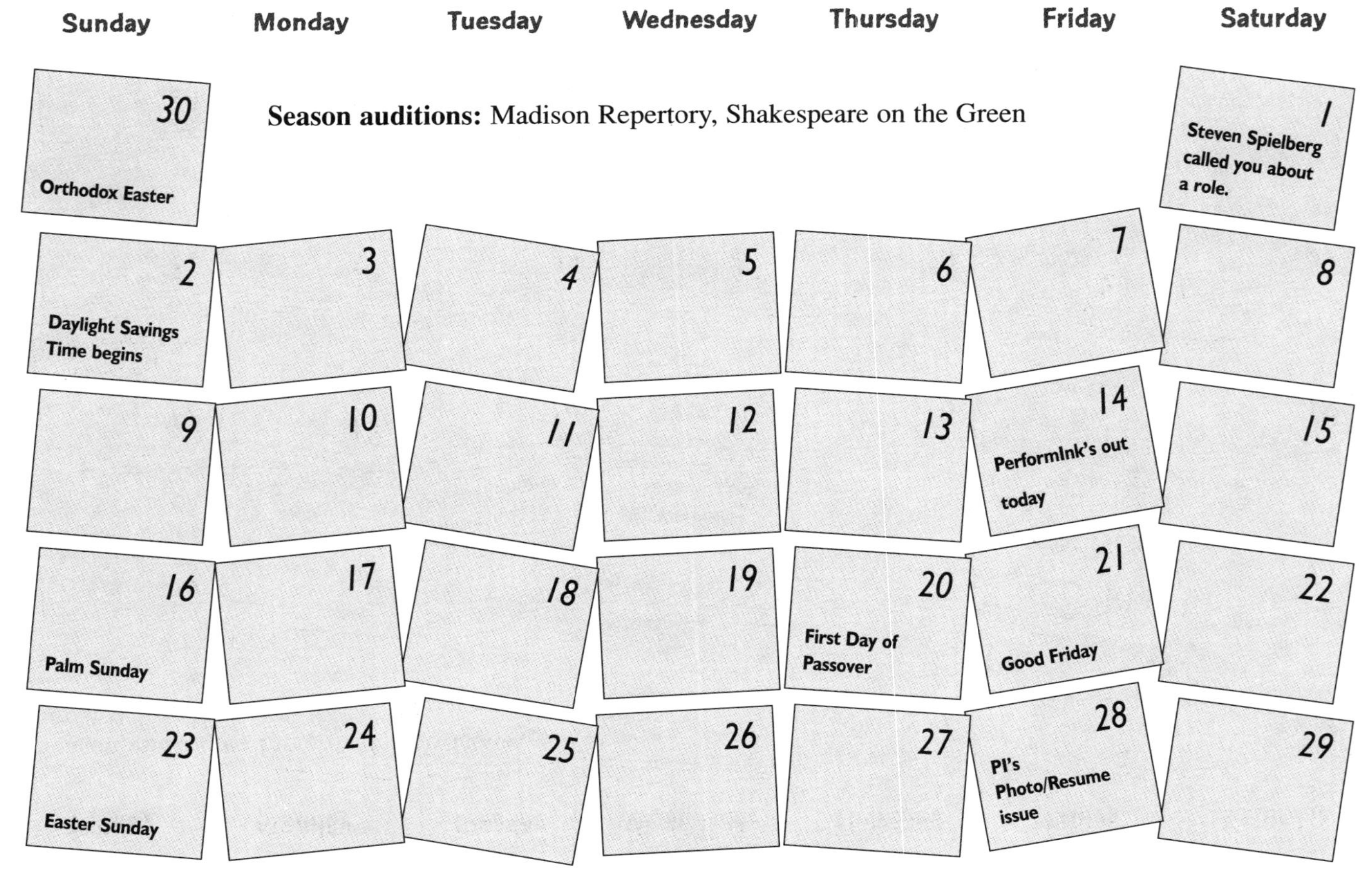

Sunday
Monday
Tuesday
Wednesday
Thursday
Friday
Saturday
30
Orthodox Easter
Season auditions: Madison Repertory, Shakespeare on the Green
1
Steven Spielberg called you about a role.
2
Daylight Savings Time begins
3
4
5
6
7
8
9
10
11
12
13
14
PerformInk's out today
15
16
Palm Sunday
17
18
19
20
First Day of Passover
21
Good Friday
22
23
Easter Sunday
24
25
26
27
28
PI's Photo/Resume issue
29

May 2000

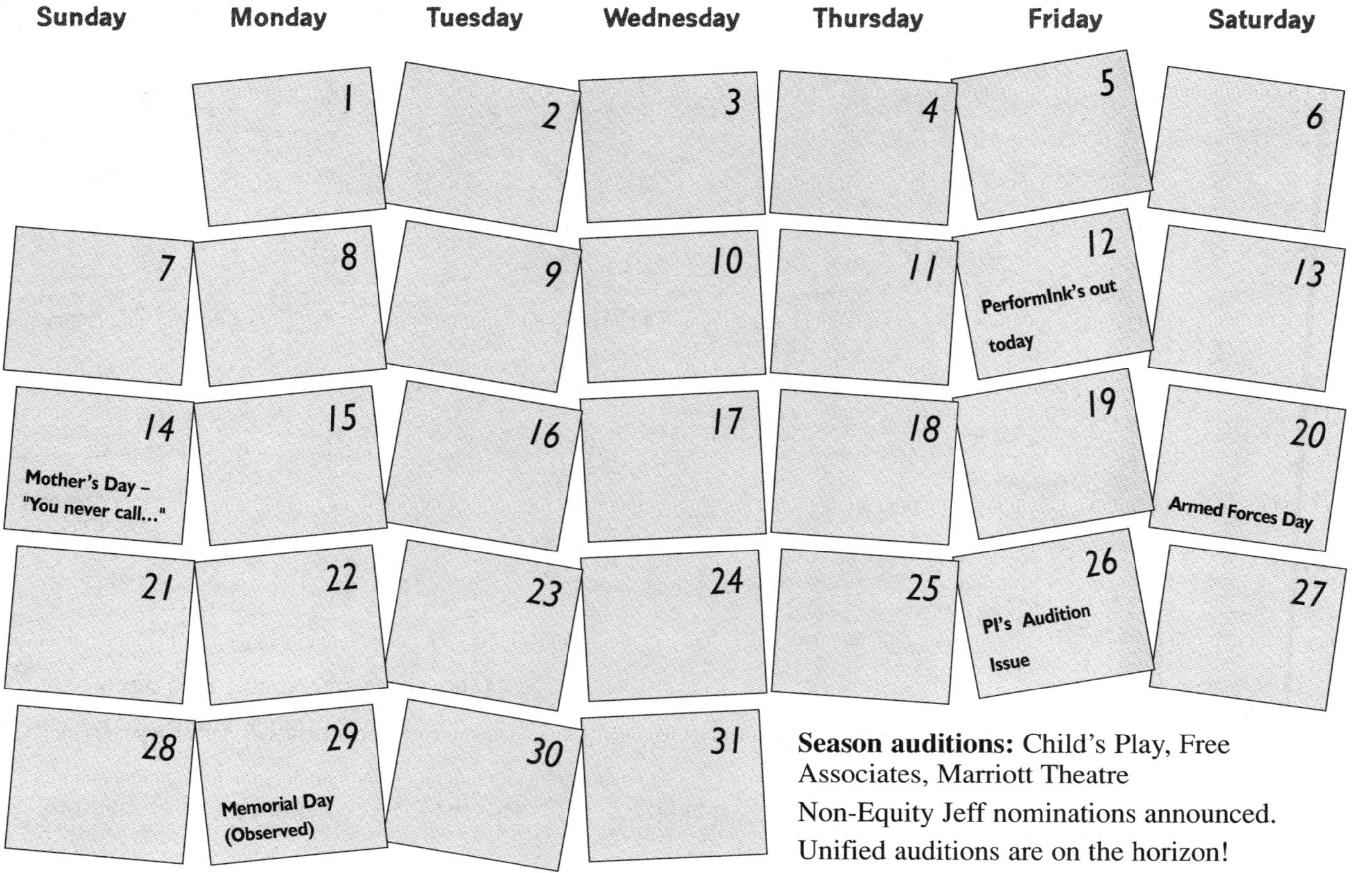

Sunday	Monday	Tuesday	Wednesday	Thursday	Friday	Saturday
	1	2	3	4	5	6
7	8	9	10	11	12 PerformInk's out today	13
14 Mother's Day – "You never call..."	15	16	17	18	19	20 Armed Forces Day
21	22	23	24	25	26 PI's Audition Issue	27
28	29 Memorial Day (Observed)	30	31			

Season auditions: Child's Play, Free Associates, Marriott Theatre

Non-Equity Jeff nominations announced.

Unified auditions are on the horizon!

June 2000

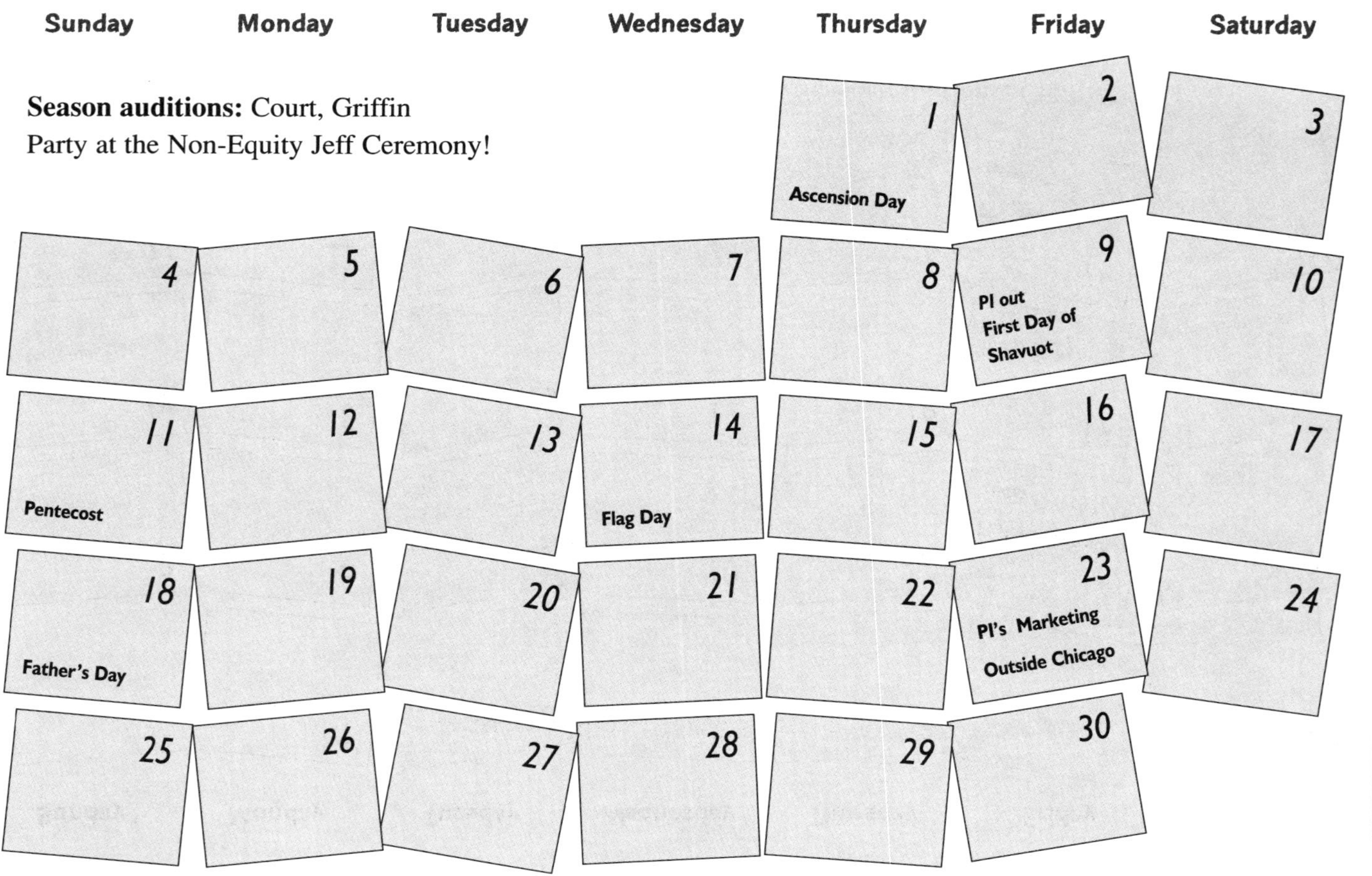
Sunday
Monday
Tuesday
Wednesday
Thursday
Friday
Saturday
Season auditions: Court, Griffin
Party at the Non-Equity Jeff Ceremony!
1
Ascension Day
2
3
4
5
6
7
8
9
PI out
First Day of
Shavuot
10
11
Pentecost
12
13
14
Flag Day
15
16
17
18
Father's Day
19
20
21
22
23
PI's Marketing
Outside Chicago
24
25
26
27
28
29
30

July 2000

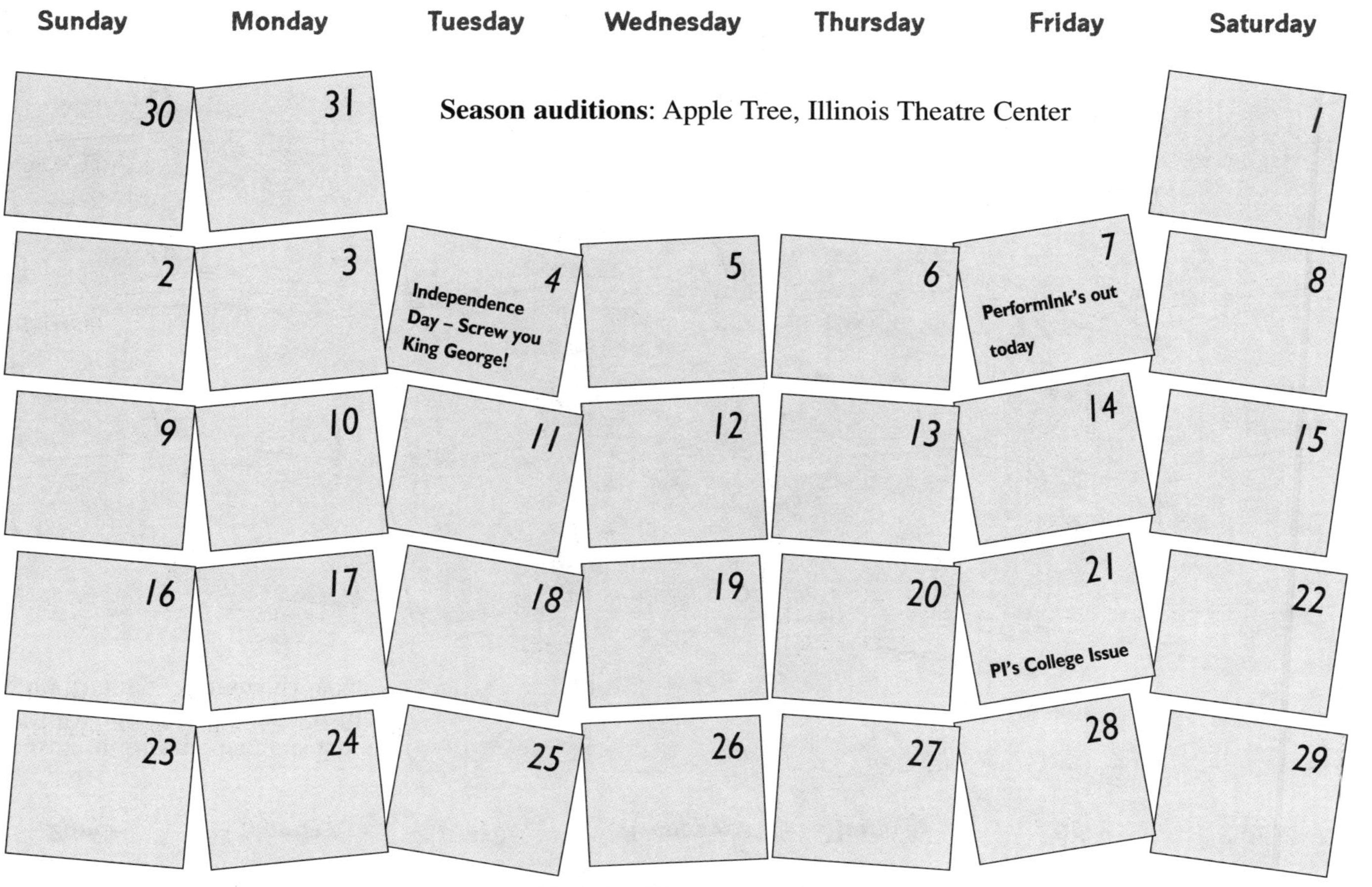

Sunday	Monday	Tuesday	Wednesday	Thursday	Friday	Saturday
30	31	**Season auditions**: Apple Tree, Illinois Theatre Center				1
2	3	4 Independence Day – Screw you King George!	5	6	7 PerformInk's out today	8
9	10	11	12	13	14	15
16	17	18	19	20	21 PI's College Issue	22
23	24	25	26	27	28	29

August 2000

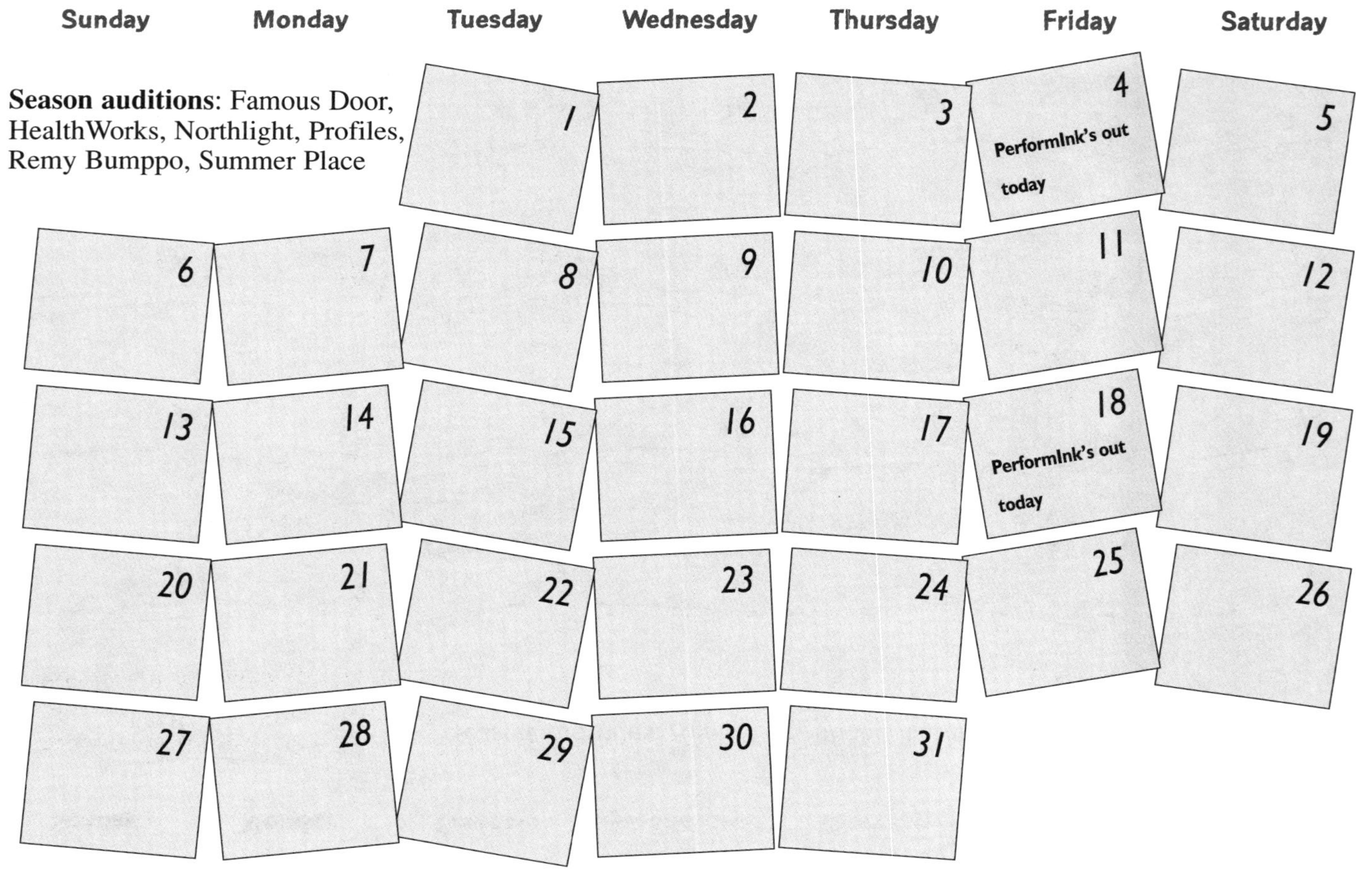
Sunday
Monday
Tuesday
Wednesday
Thursday
Friday
Saturday
Season auditions: Famous Door, HealthWorks, Northlight, Profiles, Remy Bumppo, Summer Place
1
2
3
4
PerformInk's out today
5
6
7
8
9
10
11
12
13
14
15
16
17
18
PerformInk's out today
19
20
21
22
23
24
25
26
27
28
29
30
31

September 2000

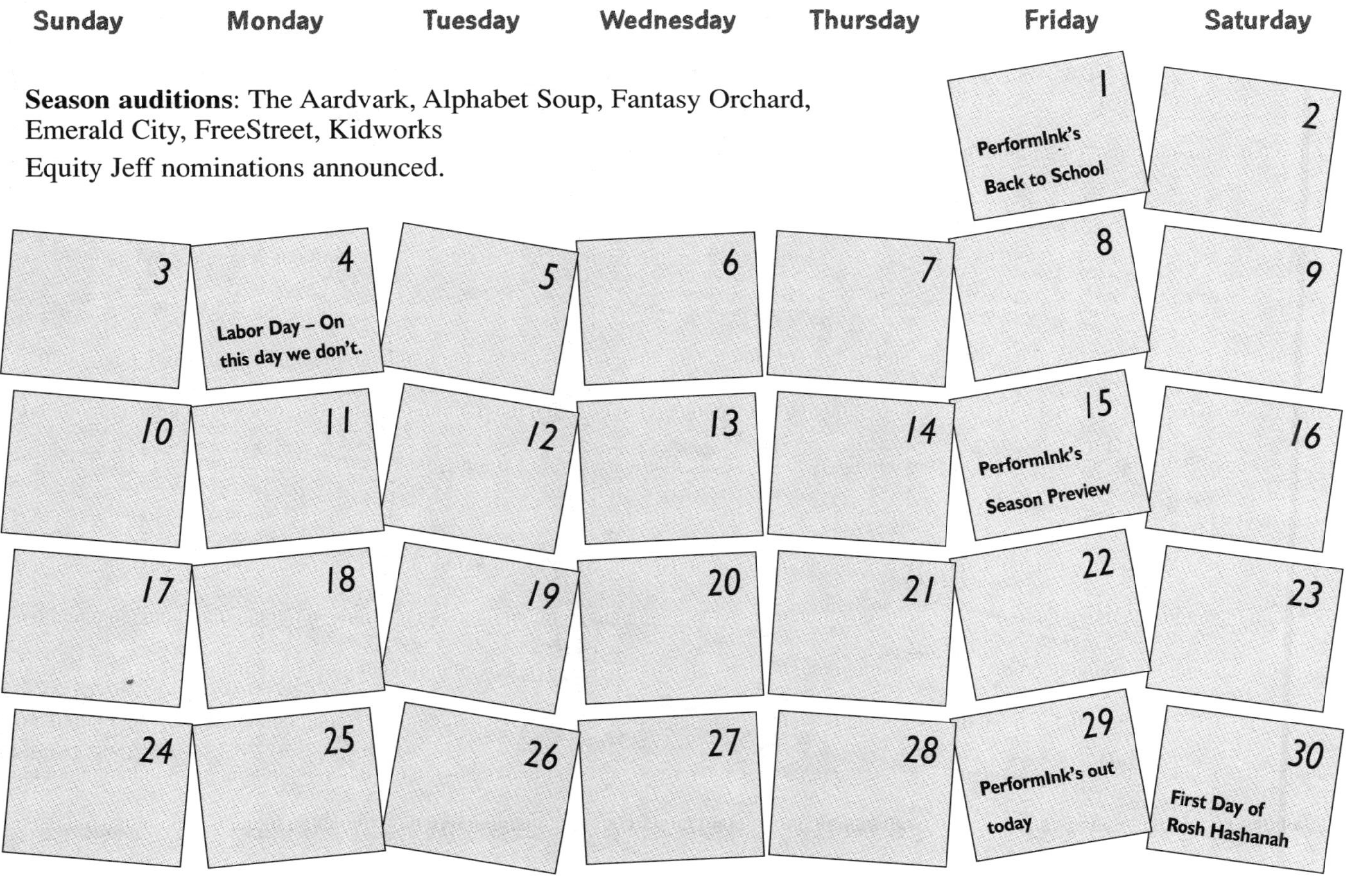

Sunday
Monday
Tuesday
Wednesday
Thursday
Friday
Saturday
Season auditions: The Aardvark, Alphabet Soup, Fantasy Orchard, Emerald City, FreeStreet, Kidworks
Equity Jeff nominations announced.
1
PerformInk's Back to School
2
3
4
Labor Day – On this day we don't.
5
6
7
8
9
10
11
12
13
14
15
PerformInk's Season Preview
16
17
18
19
20
21
22
23
24
25
26
27
28
29
PerformInk's out today
30
First Day of Rosh Hashanah

October 2000

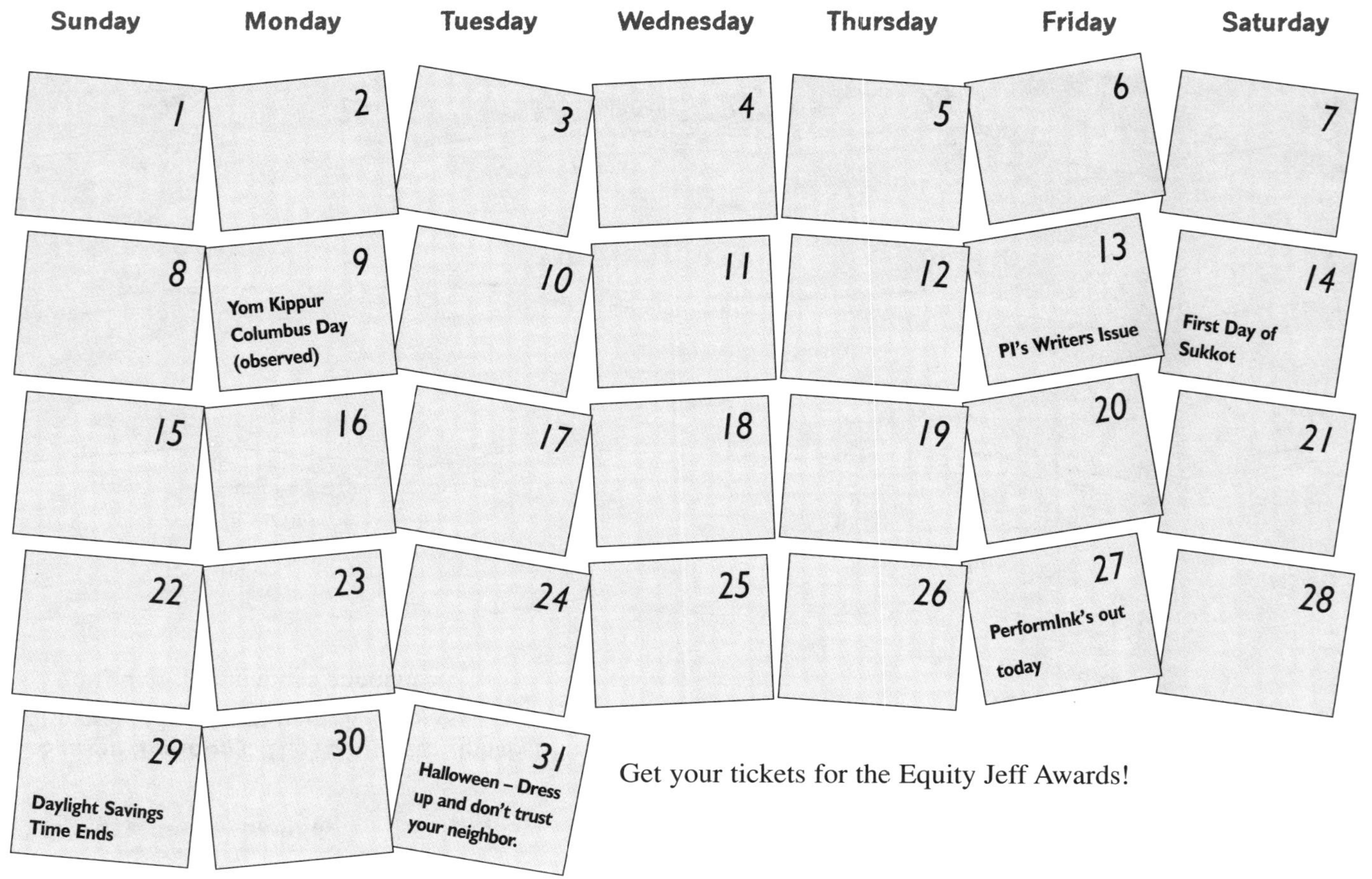

Sunday
Monday
Tuesday
Wednesday
Thursday
Friday
Saturday
1
2
3
4
5
6
7
8
9
Yom Kippur
Columbus Day
(observed)
10
11
12
13
PI's Writers Issue
14
First Day of
Sukkot
15
16
17
18
19
20
21
22
23
24
25
26
27
PerformInk's out
today
28
29
Daylight Savings
Time Ends
30
31
Halloween – Dress
up and don't trust
your neighbor.
Get your tickets for the Equity Jeff Awards!

November 2000

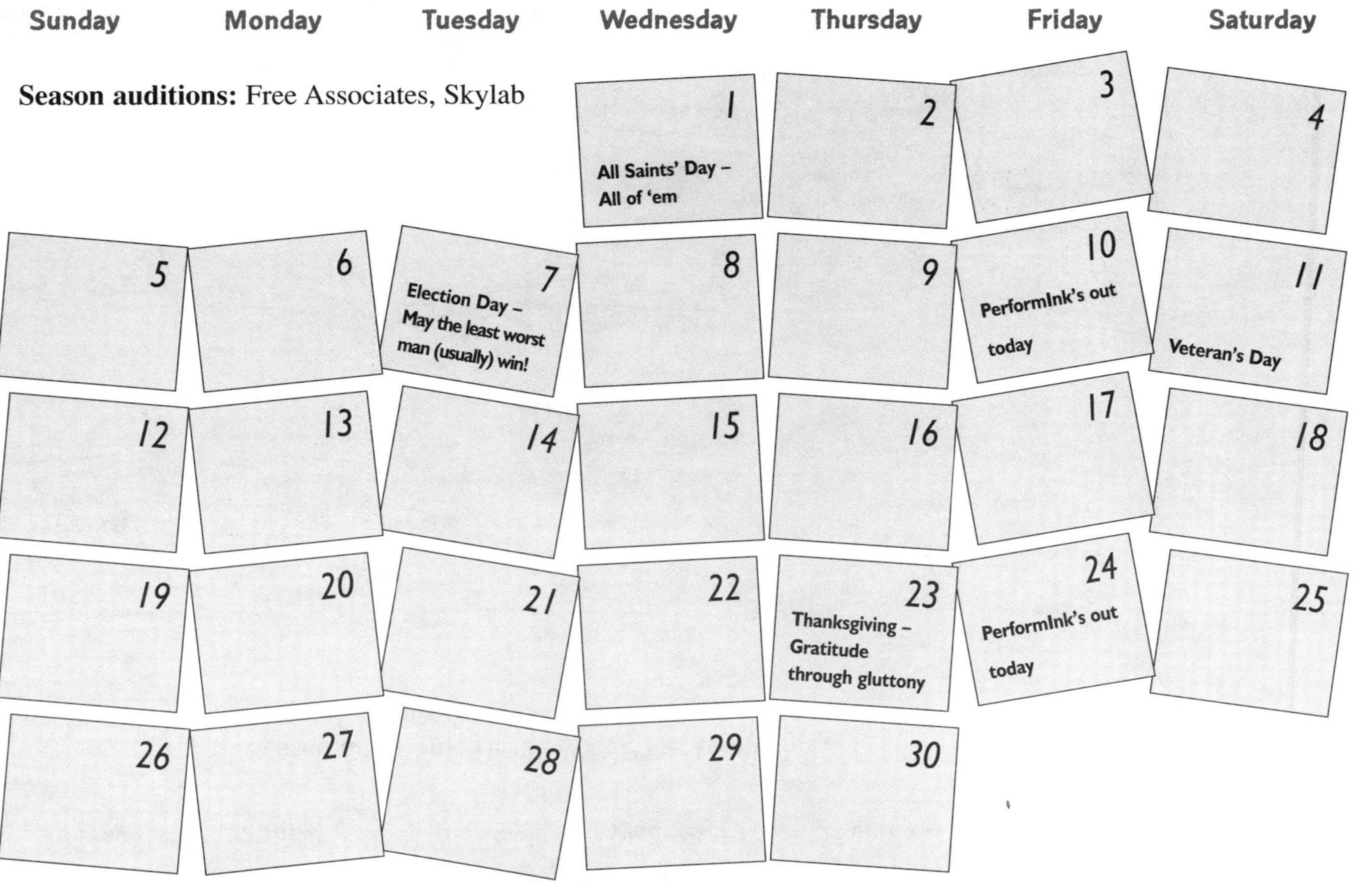

Sunday
Monday
Tuesday
Wednesday
Thursday
Friday
Saturday
Season auditions: Free Associates, Skylab
1
All Saints' Day – All of 'em
2
3
4
5
6
7
Election Day – May the least worst man (usually) win!
8
9
10
PerformInk's out today
11
Veteran's Day
12
13
14
15
16
17
18
19
20
21
22
23
Thanksgiving – Gratitude through gluttony
24
PerformInk's out today
25
26
27
28
29
30

December 2000

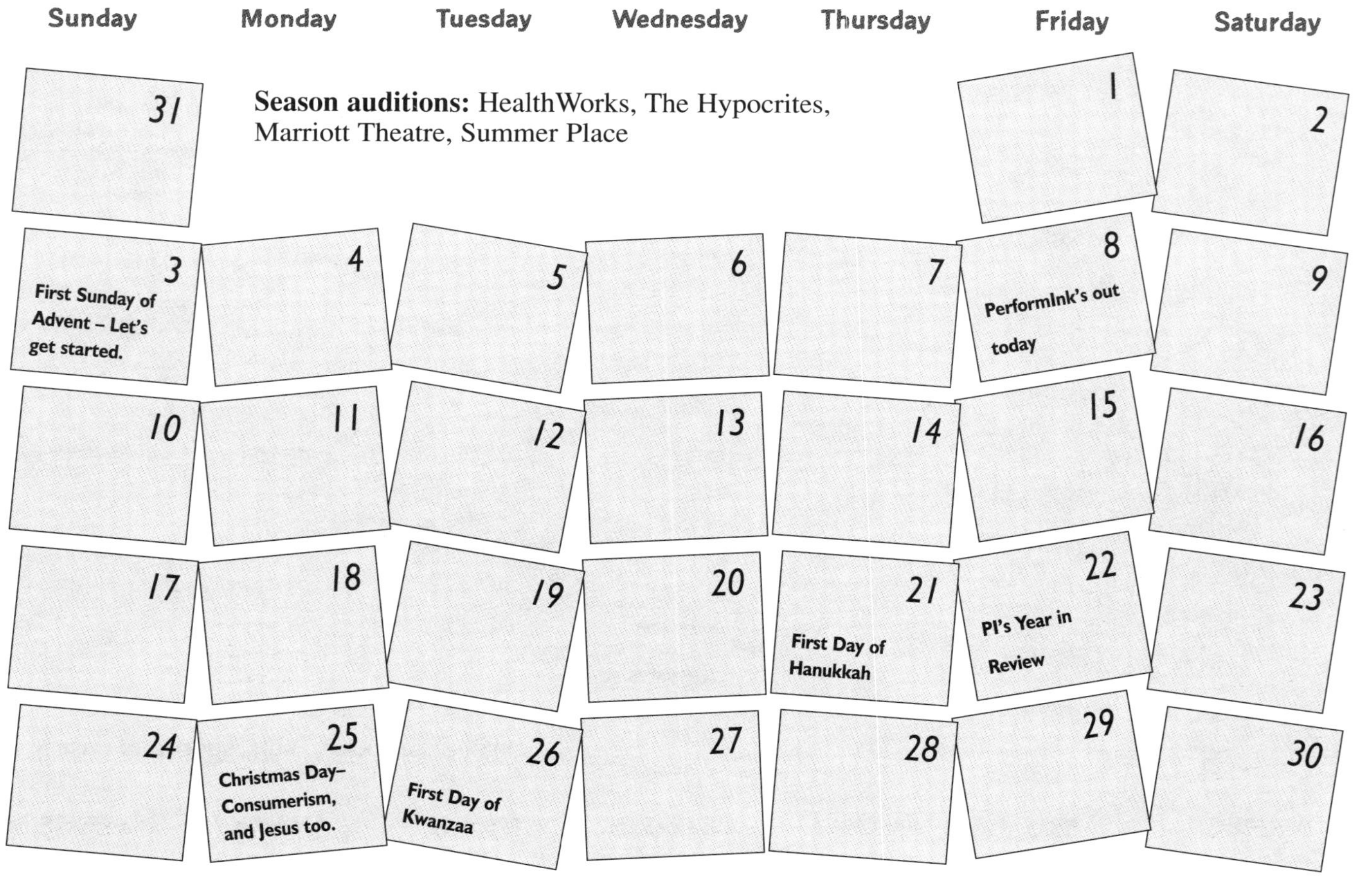

Sunday
Monday
Tuesday
Wednesday
Thursday
Friday
Saturday
31
Season auditions: HealthWorks, The Hypocrites, Marriott Theatre, Summer Place
1
2
3
First Sunday of Advent – Let's get started.
4
5
6
7
8
PerformInk's out today
9
10
11
12
13
14
15
16
17
18
19
20
21
First Day of Hanukkah
22
PI's Year in Review
23
24
25
Christmas Day– Consumerism, and Jesus too.
26
First Day of Kwanzaa
27
28
29
30

January 2001

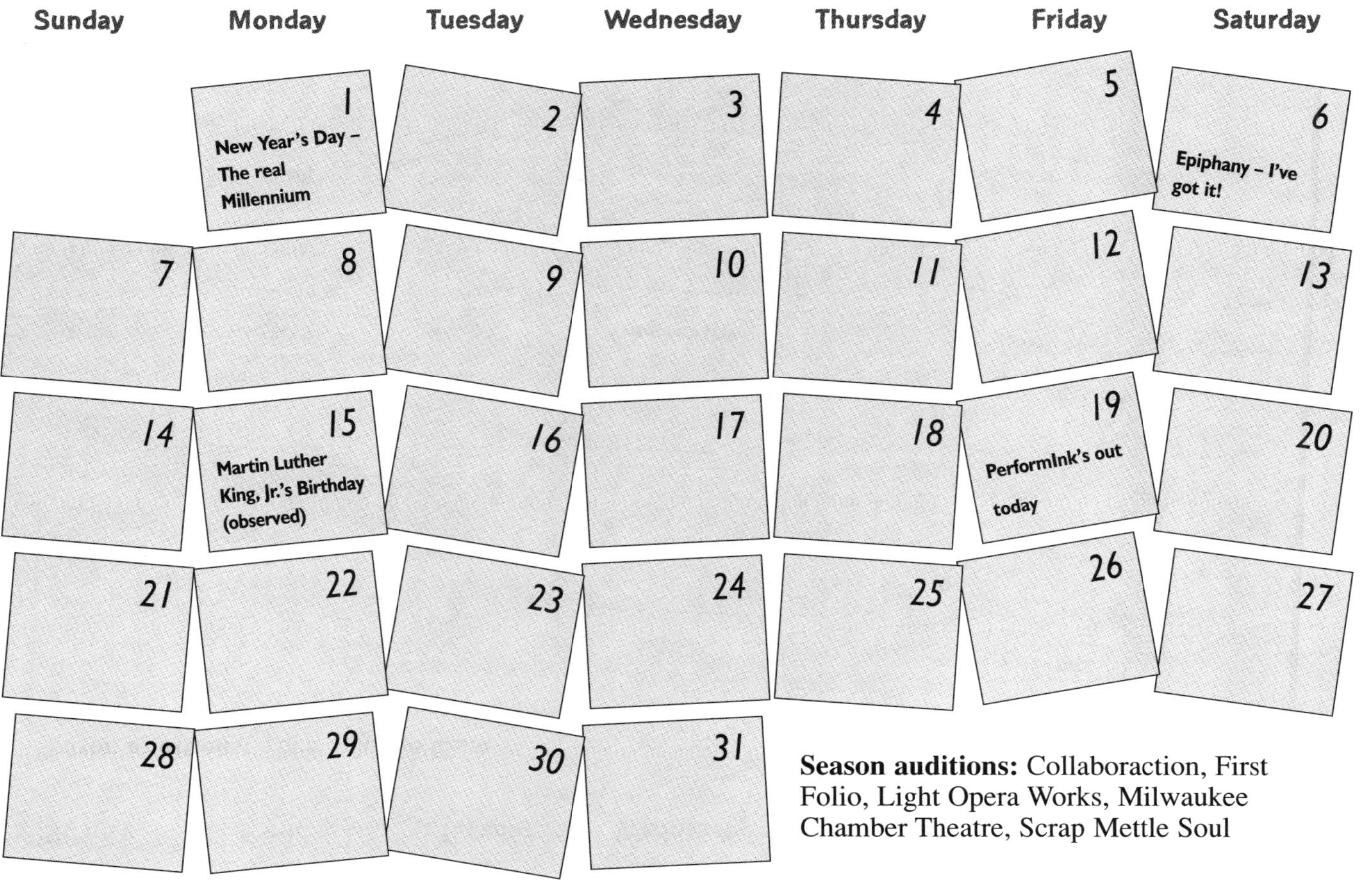

Sunday	Monday	Tuesday	Wednesday	Thursday	Friday	Saturday
	1 New Year's Day – The real Millennium	2	3	4	5	6 Epiphany – I've got it!
7	8	9	10	11	12	13
14	15 Martin Luther King, Jr.'s Birthday (observed)	16	17	18	19 PerformInk's out today	20
21	22	23	24	25	26	27
28	29	30	31			

Season auditions: Collaboraction, First Folio, Light Opera Works, Milwaukee Chamber Theatre, Scrap Mettle Soul

February 2001

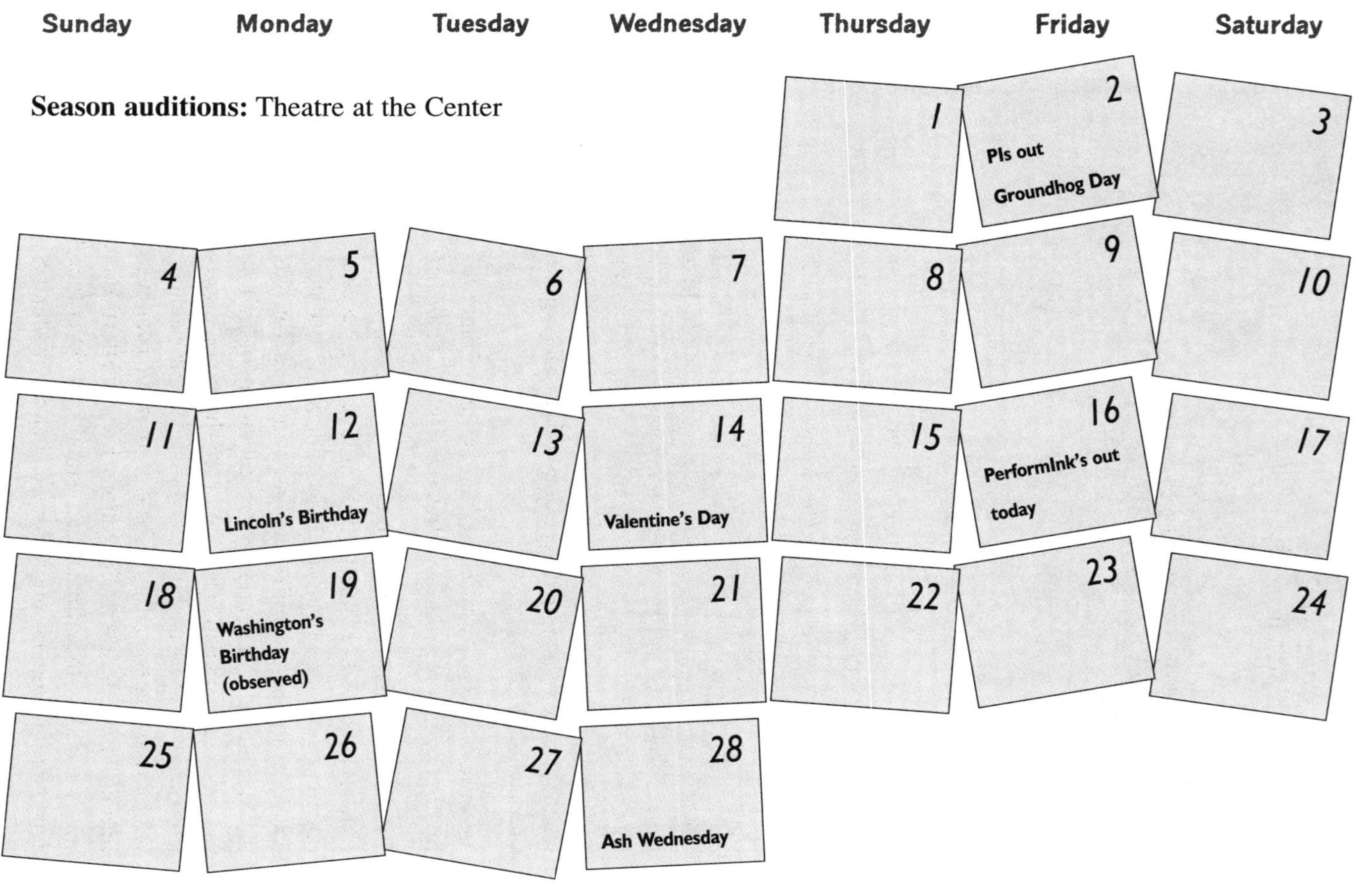

Sunday	Monday	Tuesday	Wednesday	Thursday	Friday	Saturday
Season auditions: Theatre at the Center				1	2 PIs out Groundhog Day	3
4	5	6	7	8	9	10
11	12 Lincoln's Birthday	13	14 Valentine's Day	15	16 PerformInk's out today	17
18	19 Washington's Birthday (observed)	20	21	22	23	24
25	26	27	28 Ash Wednesday			

Writer's Biographies

Who Dat?

Katie Ayoub is the editor of **PerformInk** Newspaper and an associate editor of **The Book: An Actor's Guide to Chicago,** Third Edition.

Robert Ayres is the Founding Director of Catbox Cabaret. He worked at the Massachusetts Cultural Council for four years before pursuing a Masters in Theatre at Northwestern University.

Tab Baker is a native Chicagoan and a graduate of Marquette University. Fifteen years of union membership have produced: Feature films for Columbia Pictures & United Artists; Television appearances on CBS, NBC, ABC & FOX; Voiceovers in national commercials & with Chicago Symphony Orchestra; and On Stage performances in 46 states and 5 different countries.

Jason R. Chin is the Director of the Training Center for the ImprovOlympic Theater and **PERFORMINK's** Comedy Bits columnist.

Julie Franz is the National Director of the Arts & Business Council of Chicago's The Arts Marketing Center. She is an accomplished market researcher and marketing strategist with nearly two decades of experience in both the for-profit and non-profit arena. She has consulted with the Museum of Contemporary Art on improving first-year member renewal rates and with The Goodman Theatre on attracting funding from small to mid-size businesses. She also researched parent's attitudes towards arts education for ArtSmart, an awareness program of the Illinois Alliance for Arts Education. For her efforts on ArtSmart, Julie was honored by the Alliance and won the David Offner Award from True North Communications for excellence in volunteerism in the arts and education.

Joan Gunzberg is the Executive Director of the Arts & Business Council of Chicago. A&BC provides a wide range of management assistance programs to non-profit arts groups, developing their organizational capacity and building links to volunteers, board members and the business community.

Michael Halberstam is the Artistic Director of the Writers' Theatre, where he has directed over fourteen productions and appeared in ten. He served on the Unifieds audition committee for the past five years and has chaired the committee for two of those years. As an actor he has worked with The Stratford Festival in Ontario, The Court Theatre, Wisdom Bridge, and the company formerly known as Shakespeare Repertory. He has also served as an adjunct professor of the Theatre School at DePaul (formerly the Goodman School of Drama).

Kevin Heckman has edited **The Book** for the last three years, and serves as listings editor for **PerformInk**. Additionally, he works as a director, actor, lighting designer and teacher. He's worked with a number of companies including Shakespeare Repertory, Apple Tree, Illinois Theatre Center and Bailiwick. Additionally, he's a company member with Stage Left and The Aardvark. Kevin attended Wesleyan University in Connecticut, where he received degrees in theatre and mathematics.

Carrie L. Kaufman is the publisher of **PerformInk** Newspaper and PerformInk Books.

Doug Long is a director, writer, teacher and actor. He has worked at many Chicago theatres, including Steppenwolf, New Tuners, Circle Theatre and Pegasus Players. He teaches performance classes at DePaul University and Victory Gardens Theatre. In addition to **PerformInk**, he has written and edited for several newspapers and magazines. He earned undergraduate degrees in journalism and theatre from Ball State University, and an MA and an MFA in Directing from Indiana University, where he taught several years before moving to the Chicago area.

Greg Mermel is a certified public accountant whose clients in the arts range from individual performers to major theatre companies and suppliers. He also sometimes produces theatre.

Notes:

Notes:

Notes:

Coupon

Notes:

Coupon

Notes:

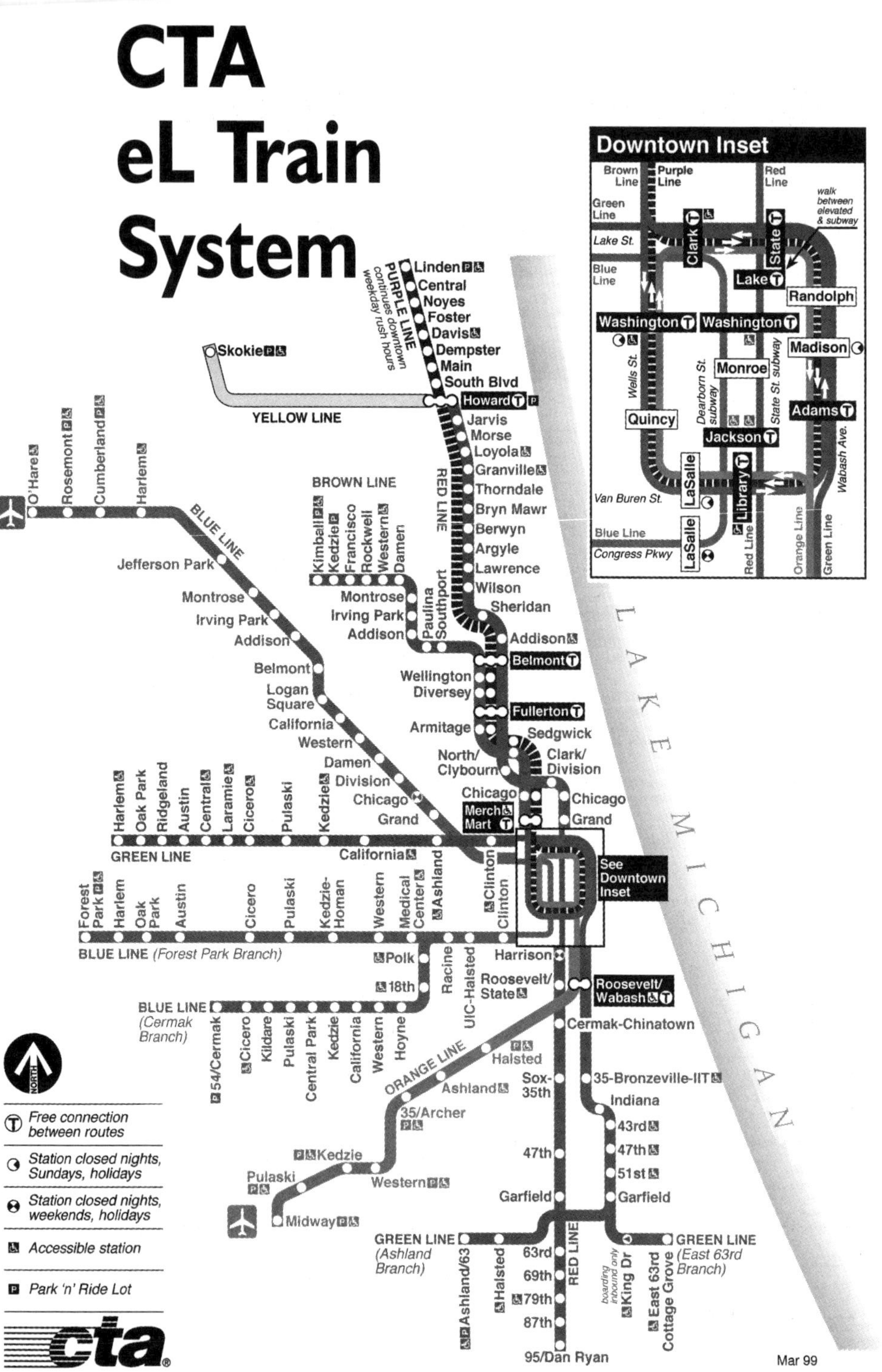

CTA
eL Train
System
Downtown Inset
Brown Line
Purple Line
Red Line
Green Line
walk between elevated & subway
Lake St.
Clark
State
Blue Line
Lake
Randolph
Washington
Washington
Madison
Wells St.
Dearborn St. subway
Monroe
State St. subway
Quincy
Adams
Jackson
Wabash Ave.
LaSalle
Library
Van Buren St.
Blue Line
Congress Pkwy
LaSalle
Red Line
Orange Line
Green Line
PURPLE LINE
continues downtown weekday rush hours
Linden
Central
Noyes
Foster
Davis
Dempster
Main
South Blvd
Skokie
YELLOW LINE
Howard
Jarvis
Morse
Loyola
Granville
Thorndale
Bryn Mawr
Berwyn
Argyle
Lawrence
Wilson
Sheridan
RED LINE
BROWN LINE
Kimball
Kedzie
Francisco
Rockwell
Western
Damen
Montrose
Irving Park
Addison
Paulina
Southport
Addison
Belmont
Wellington
Diversey
Fullerton
Armitage
Sedgwick
North/ Clybourn
Clark/ Division
Chicago
Chicago
Merch Mart
Grand
O'Hare
Rosemont
Cumberland
Harlem
BLUE LINE
Jefferson Park
Montrose
Irving Park
Addison
Belmont
Logan Square
California
Western
Damen
Division
Chicago
Grand
Harlem
Oak Park
Ridgeland
Austin
Central
Laramie
Cicero
Pulaski
Kedzie
GREEN LINE
California
Ashland
Clinton
See Downtown Inset
Forest Park
Harlem
Oak Park
Austin
Cicero
Pulaski
Kedzie-Homan
Western
Medical Center
Ashland
Clinton
BLUE LINE (Forest Park Branch)
Polk
18th
Racine
UIC-Halsted
Harrison
Roosevelt/ State
Roosevelt/ Wabash
BLUE LINE (Cermak Branch)
54/Cermak
Cicero
Kildare
Pulaski
Central Park
Kedzie
California
Western
Hoyne
Cermak-Chinatown
ORANGE LINE
Halsted
Ashland
Sox-35th
35-Bronzeville-IIT
Indiana
35/Archer
43rd
Kedzie
47th
47th
51st
Pulaski
Western
Garfield
Garfield
Midway
GREEN LINE (Ashland Branch)
GREEN LINE (East 63rd Branch)
Ashland/63
Halsted
63rd
69th
79th
87th
95/Dan Ryan
RED LINE
boarding inbound only
King Dr
East 63rd
Cottage Grove
LAKE MICHIGAN
NORTH
Free connection between routes
Station closed nights, Sundays, holidays
Station closed nights, weekends, holidays
Accessible station
Park 'n' Ride Lot
cta
Mar 99

Advertiser's Index